Super-Abundant Grace

Super-Abundant Grace

Reflections on Romans

Keith D. Stanglin

Foreword by Todd D. Still

CASCADE *Books* • Eugene, Oregon

SUPER-ABUNDANT GRACE
Reflections on Romans

Cascade Books
An Imprint of Wipf and Stock Publishers
199 W. 8th Ave., Suite 3
Eugene, OR 97401

www.wipfandstock.com

PAPERBACK ISBN: 978-1-7252-9475-2
HARDCOVER ISBN: 978-1-7252-9476-9
EBOOK ISBN: 978-1-7252-9477-6

Cataloguing-in-Publication data:

Names: Stanglin, Keith D., author. | Still, Todd D., foreword.

Title: Super-abundant grace : reflections on Romans / by Keith D. Stanglin; foreword by Todd D. Still

Description: Eugene, OR: Cascade Books, 2022 | Includes bibliographical references and index.

Identifiers: ISBN 978-1-7252-9475-2 (paperback) | ISBN 978-1-7252-9476-9 (hardcover) | ISBN 978-1-7252-9477-6 (ebook)

Subjects: LCSH: Bible. Romans—Criticism, interpretation, etc. | Grace (Theology)

Classification: BS2665.52 S73 2022 (print) | BS2665.52 (ebook)

06/10/22

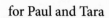

for Paul and Tara

Contents

Foreword

While some people seem to be obsessed with Paul's Letter to the Romans, this does not appear to be the case with Keith Stanglin, who acknowledges in his Preface to the present volume, "Romans is not my favorite book in the Bible." That said, Stanglin readily and gladly recognizes the importance and influence of Paul's most expansive extant letter as well as the ongoing interest in and intrigue with Romans among scholars and laypeople alike. Given as much, Stanglin seized the opportunity of a protracted preaching assignment to work and to walk through Romans section by section with a congregation. The result is the valuable volume that you now hold in your hands.

Although Stanglin's work is deeply appreciative of and fully informed by historical-critical commentaries, it is not a historical-critical commentary. Rather, in this book, Stanglin offers exegetical, theological, historical, homiletical, and pastoral reflections upon and insights into Romans in general and its message of God's super-abundant grace in particular. In seeking to describe the genre of *Super-Abundant Grace*, Stanglin likens it to Danish philosopher Søren Kierkegaard's "upbuilding discourses." Envisioned as a companion volume to scholarly commentaries on Romans, following each of his thirty-one meditations, Stanglin poses a number of probing questions for group discussion. Those who are rather familiar with the expansive secondary literature on Romans

will note similarities between Stanglin's *Super-Abundant Grace* and Ste-
phen Westerholm's *Understanding Paul: The Early Christian Worldview of
the Letter to the Romans*.

Whether one reads this book alone or as part of a Bible study or
reading group, one will delight in Stanglin's salient, relevant insights into
Paul's inexhaustible, magisterial letter to the Romans, which subsequent
generations of Christians have regarded to be "written for [their] instruction." To be sure, it is easy enough to lose the proverbial forest for the
trees in Paul's towering, demanding communication to Roman house
churches. Thus, Stanglin's accessible, thoughtful treatment is warmly
welcome as an excellent entrée into a biblical book that is often regarded
as too difficult, daunting, and demanding for rank-and-file folk. Furthermore, it succeeds in capturing and communicating the grace that grasped
the apostle and that animates his epistle to the Romans.

In a courtyard far away and long ago, Augustine heard a child chant-
ing, "Pick up, read!" This admonition led Augustine to consider Romans
13:13–14, which he applied personally. The transformation wrought in
Augustine's life is now the thing of lore and legend. All told, Stanglin's
volume can assist you in reading the transformative message of Romans
more perceptively; thus, you would do well to hear and to heed the re-
sounding and lingering call from a Milan garden to "Pick up, read!"

Todd D. Still
DeLancey Dean and Hinson Professor
Baylor University, Truett Seminary, Waco, Texas, USA
February 26, 2022

Preface

MY DECISION TO TAKE up writing on Paul's epistle to the Romans grew out of a prior decision several years ago to preach through Romans at a church where I served as an interim preaching minister. When I announced the sermon series, I was struck by how many people expressed to me their approval and excitement. The comments seemed more than mere convention; people (some people anyway) were genuinely happy at the thought of working through Romans. Romans is not my favorite book in the Bible. But the reaction confirmed my choice. Despite the fact that so much has been written on Romans, and despite its familiarity, there is more to say about Romans, or at least more for us to hear.

Although it is not a commentary—and by no means comprehensive—this book is exegetically based. At its most fundamental level, this exegetical goal is reflected in my close following of the Greek text and my translations of Romans used throughout the book; my renderings are sometimes brutally literal, if nothing else, to get the reader a little closer to the apostle Paul's idiom. More substantively, I am interested in the insights of historical-critical scholarship. For instance, I always strive to keep in mind what I take to be the immediate occasion of Romans, a church conflict apparently exacerbated by the Claudian edict of AD 49 and its presumptive termination in 54. I have attempted to keep this historical setting and the big picture of Paul's purpose ever before the reader.

In addition to modern critical insights, I am interested also in what can be learned from pre-modern biblical interpretation, with which I engage occasionally in the course of the work.

Upon the exegetical foundation—which is at times more or less visible but always present—stands the main edifice, which is homiletical, aimed at application. As such, this book may be best conceived as an expansion of those sections of bridge-building found in many commentaries after the technical comments (for example, the section labeled "Explanation" in the Word Biblical Commentary). In other words, on the basis of a careful reading of Romans, what does this mean for us? For the student of Romans who is interested in avenues of application to today's church, this book is also a supplement to a technical commentary.

As homiletical, the address is intentionally direct and perhaps "preachy" at times. The applications are personal and missional, aimed at the church and the individual believer. The reader may be relieved to know that I, the writer, am the primary audience, the first hearer. Like Romans, I aim to comfort the afflicted and afflict the comfortable. I would call the genre of this present volume "upbuilding discourses," to borrow a Kierkegaardian phrase. If just one reader finds in this book something upbuilding—through appropriate admonition and/or comfort—then my intentions and effort will be fulfilled.

I intend to convey what the biblical text means to convey. Admittedly, my text is guilty of sins of both commission and omission. I sometimes transcend the biblical message and incline toward making a modern exhortation that may not be present in the original human author's argument, a practice that is legitimated by the greatest preachers of the Christian tradition, including Paul himself. I also do not have the space to unpack every rhetorical point Paul seems to be making. But I at least seek to begin with some of the ancient arguments.

I was inspired early in my seminary training by reading Thomas Long's *Preaching and the Literary Forms of the Bible*, which argues that the sermon should reflect the rhetorical function of Scripture. Preachers should pay attention not only to what the biblical text says but also to how it says it. I learned from Long that what the Scripture does—what it says, what it accomplishes, how it makes the audience feel, what it inspires the audience to do, and so on—the sermon ought to do. Of course, it's all epistle here, no narrative. But if there is an ambiguity, a surprise, a particular emotion, bad news, or good news present in Paul's text, I have tried to communicate the same. Readers can decide whether these discourses achieve that lofty goal. If there is one theme that I (and Romans) keep returning to, it is God's super-abundant grace. This is what should be communicated, in all its facets.

With few exceptions, these discourses have mostly followed the modern section breaks provided in standard English translations such as the New International Version. I have chosen not to use tagged notes, which tend to interrupt the flow of the text in a book like this one. But I have provided brief endnotes that cite sources, point readers to further information, and sometimes provide more rationale for an exegetical or translation decision.

This volume can be used for personal study, but it is also intended for use in group and class settings. In order to facilitate discussions, questions have been provided at the conclusion of each section.

Although I have taught the Epistle to the Romans on multiple occasions in various settings, the immediate backdrop for this book is a series of sermons I preached over the course of a year at the Leander (Texas) Church of Christ. I am grateful to those fine people for their friendship and encouragement. I thank my family for allowing me to be gone for so many Sundays in a row, and particularly Amanda, who had the idea for this book. I also wish to thank Todd Still, who graciously provided the book's foreword, Eddie Sharp, who read part of this manuscript and offered helpful comments, and James Thompson, who read with a keen eye particularly with regard to exegetical matters. I am especially thankful to Woody Woodrow, who carefully read the entire book and whose comments improved both its style and content. Any mistakes that remain are my own. Finally, I thank Michael Thomson for his encouragement over the years and for giving this book a chance. All these people are evidence of God's grace in my life.

I dedicate this book to Paul and Tara on the joyous occasion of their wedding. "May the God of hope fill you with all joy and peace in believing" (Romans 15:13).

Keith Stanglin
Austin, Texas

1

A Life-Changing Letter

Romans 1:1–7

ONCE THERE WAS A young man who went searching for truth. He had been raised by a Christian mother and a non-Christian father. He knew a good bit about Christian teaching, but he never fully embraced it. He was an endlessly inquisitive and intellectually curious person—the smartest person that anyone knew—and he felt like Christianity did not provide satisfactory answers to his deep questions. He was never baptized as a youth and was never a full member of the church.

After he grew up, this young man pursued his own career in academia, became a professor of rhetoric, and continued his search for truth. He attached himself to different philosophies that he thought could make sense of his questions—questions about the origin of the universe, the nature and origin of evil alongside good, his own personal struggle with evil, the deep longings of the human heart, and questions about the existence and nature of God. In his honest search, though, he found no satisfaction outside of the church. The more he learned of other faiths and philosophies, the more the faith of his mother recommended itself. He came to realize that, at the age of 31, no longer a young man, he needed to take the plunge and give his life to Christ.

But one thing held him back: *Sin.* He knew that if he became a Christian, he would have to give up his ways, his lusts, and he worried that he loved those too much. He knew the right thing to do, but he could not bring himself to do it. And then one day, as he sat in the courtyard outside his apartment building in the Italian city of Milan, grieving over his plight and what he would do with his life, he heard the voice of a child singing from a nearby building. "Pick up, read! Pick up, read!" He was puzzled. The chant kept repeating, over and over. "Pick up, read!" What was this? He could not see the source of the sound. Nor could he think of any children's game or song that used this phrase. Maybe it was a sign, he thought.

So he went back inside his building and picked up the New Testament. He flipped it open and began reading the first thing he saw: "But let us behave properly as in the day, not in carousing and drunkenness, not in sexual promiscuity and sensuality, not in strife and jealousy. But put on the Lord Jesus Christ, and make no provision for the flesh in regard to its lusts." These words are found in Romans 13:13–14.

He read those words and felt they spoke to him. He was convinced. He was baptized. He left his teaching job, at the height of his career, and went straight into ministry. He remained in ministry for the rest of his life and never stopped searching for truth and seeking God's face. The year was 386, and the man's name was Augustine. He went on to become, after the apostle Paul, the most influential theologian in the history of the church—his influence still being felt today. His was a conversion sparked by reading the book of Romans.

Fast forward over 1,100 years to the German town of Wittenberg, where an Augustinian monk named Martin Luther felt oppressed by the church's requirements for penance. Scrupulous as he was, he confessed every sin he could think of, did all the works, said all the right prayers but simply could not shake the feeling that he couldn't do enough and that God was out to get him. After all, when he came to confess his sins, he could not remember every sin. And if he did remember them all and felt proud of his accomplishment, well, then he just sinned again! It was a desperate cycle. He saw God's righteousness as a justice that would only condemn him.

That is, until he read Romans 1:17 with fresh eyes: "For the righteousness of God is revealed in it [the gospel] from faith to faith, as it is written, 'The righteous one from faith will live.'" The righteousness from God, Luther concluded, is not God's righteousness *against* me, but his righteousness *for* me. God *declares* me righteous, even though I am not righteous on my own. When Luther translated the Bible into German, he wrote about this life-changing experience from 1519 in his preface to the book of Romans. Luther said that when he discovered God's righteousness for him, he felt that he was "altogether born again and had entered paradise itself through open gates." He went on to become the leading figure of reform in the Western Church during the sixteenth century, the effects of which we still feel today. And it was sparked by his reading of Romans.

Fast forward 200 more years to 1738, now in London. John Wesley, a failed missionary who had recently returned from the North American colony of Georgia, went unwillingly one evening to a prayer meeting and devotional. In this period of his life, he was seeking divine comfort and assurance of salvation. He heard the speaker reading, not exactly from the Bible, but from Luther's preface to the book of Romans, in which Luther describes his life-changing experience. Wesley, upon hearing this reading, felt that comfort—as he put it, he felt that his heart was "strangely warmed." Wesley went on to lead a movement of revival within the Church of England, the Methodist movement that still influences global Christianity today. Wesley's revival was sparked by someone else's reading of Romans.

I could multiply examples of people whose lives were shaped by the book of Romans, and who then went on to change the world. I don't mean to endorse all the beliefs or experiences of these great men, but one thing is for sure: if you let it, Paul's letter to the Romans can change your life.

Its importance throughout church history is evident. Not only has it changed the lives of both well-known and countless unknown individuals, but Romans is also the most commented-on biblical book in the history of the church. Since Luther and other early reformers, Protestants generally and consciously have used Romans as the "canon within the canon". That is, of all the inspired and authoritative books, it is at the center. It is considered the most important book because it answers the most important questions. As I have often heard it said, "If you get Romans, God will get you."

In the introduction to this letter (1:1–7), Paul identifies three, let's say, parties: Paul, God, and the Roman Christians. The first is Paul himself. Paul wants to say a little something about himself. He does this in all his letters, but it is particularly important that he introduce himself to the Roman church. Why is that? It's because he has never been to Rome. Unlike most of his other letters, he writes this letter to a church that he did not establish and that he has never visited. This is kind of like a blind date. How did Christianity come to Rome? We don't know for sure. One possibility is that the residents of Rome who visited Jerusalem on the day of Pentecost (Acts 2:10), after hearing and receiving the gospel, took the good news back home with them. Otherwise, given all the traffic that passed to and through the imperial capital, the Christian faith could have come to Rome in many ways. At any rate, Christianity in Rome predates Paul's letter, which he wrote around AD 55. Because this letter is basically the best ancient substitute for his personal presence, what he says about himself in these opening remarks is essential for the people who have never met him. What he chooses to say is revealing, as is what he chooses to omit. And there are only two things he says about himself here. If you blink, you might miss them.

First of all, he is a *slave of Christ Jesus*. He does not tell them how old he is or what his favorite color and foods are. He doesn't say whether he is a husband, a father, or a friend to anyone important. Not a student of a famous rabbi. Well, he is, but he doesn't say so here. He doesn't want to begin with those kinds of credentials. He is not a servant of the emperor or of some Roman proconsul, as you would see at the beginning of a letter from someone impressed by such associations. He is definitely not a slave of sin. He is first and foremost a slave of Christ.

Second, Paul mentions his vocation. He says that he is called as an *apostle*. That is, he has a special mission from Christ. His life has been changed. He has no worldly ambition for anything else. His ministry, including this ministry through writing, is what he lives and breathes. He will reveal more about himself throughout the letter, even in the very next section, but this is it for now. So, again, what he omits may be just as important as what he includes. Paul's identity should not be the focus. What he wants to focus on instead is the gospel of God, which takes up the bulk of this introduction.

This gospel is the good news of what God has done in Christ. And to proclaim this gospel, as Paul does here, is an act of defiance, for the God revealed in this gospel is very different from both the pagan and the philosophical understandings of God. Who is this God? We see that Paul assumes the Trinitarian nature of God, speaking of God the Father, his Son, and his Spirit. This is a God who is divine but also, for us, became flesh, born of a woman. His divinity was clearly demonstrated in his glorious resurrection from the dead. That is the good news. Salvation, rescue from sin and death, has come! Paul's mission, his task as an apostle, is to bring this good news to all the gentiles and for their lives to be changed.

And, finally, we see to whom this letter is addressed: the church in Rome. What do we know about the city of Rome? It is the capital, the largest city in the empire, the political and economic center of the Mediterranean world. Its population is probably just under one million, with a very high population density. Rome was a melting pot—many people came for financial or political reasons; others were imported as slaves. A great variety of religions were represented. In many ways, the city of Rome was not unlike large cities today.

And so far, we see the group of believers in Rome described in three ways. First of all, verse 6 implies that gentiles are numbered among this group of Christians. Later we will see that there are Jewish Christians there, too. But for now, gentiles seem to be the main group being addressed. Second, Paul calls these believers the "beloved of God." This point is especially important for people who lack a sense of identity or who are not exactly sure where they fit in. Roman society and government did not recognize Christians, and when they did, it was in order to persecute the Christians. It is important for these believers to know that they are loved by God. In other words, regardless of what these Christians think of themselves and each other, what others think of them, or even what Paul thinks of them, God loves them, and that matters more than anything else. Third, they are called *saints*. Just as Paul was called by God to be an apostle, the believers in Rome are called by God to be saints. The word translated as "saint" simply means "holy one." Saints are not just "the top one percent" of Christians; Paul uses it as a general term for disciples of Christ. Along with the family metaphor of "brothers" (which, of course, includes sisters), "saints" is the term that Paul uses most frequently to describe believers.

What does it imply, that Paul calls them saints or holy ones? What does Paul mean by using this word? Well, he's setting a very high standard for sure. If you are God's people, then you are by definition a holy people, or at least you should be. "Be holy as I am holy," says the Lord (Leviticus 19:2). They are holy because God is holy. What does it mean to talk about saints in Rome? It means the church is different. The gospel that the church proclaims, which Paul has just summarized, is unique. And that gospel and those beliefs affect the way they live. In the midst of this vast pagan community, the church is to think and live as a different people. Not separate or separated in the sense of secluded from the world, but different from it. To be holy is to be noticeably different, purified, dedicated to God and his will. They are called to be saints in a sinful world.

And Paul concludes these opening remarks with his typical greet-ing: "Grace and peace to you." Peace and especially grace are fundamen-tal themes that he will return to over the course of the letter. Paul's words of introduction really set the table for what is to come.

What a privilege it is to contemplate Paul's letter to the Romans! What we will find in this letter is that Paul has a message for the Roman Christians about how to think and how to live. How does God intend to use these words from the apostle to change their lives?

By God's providence, we get to listen in on this letter—like a fly on the wall. Although this letter was not written to us, it was written for us. So the question is the same for us. How does God intend to use these words from the apostle to change *our* lives? How will we be changed and formed by the study of Romans? Through this ancient letter, what is God calling today's church to be?

Romans can change you. Or, more precisely, *God* can use the book of Romans to change you. It can be a life-changing letter, but only if you seek it and allow it to be. In other words, it helps if you come looking for the change and are open to hearing a word from God. The three men I described went seeking to hear a word from God. If we are going to be transformed through the reading of Scripture and contemporary proclamation of this word, our study must be joined with a *desire* to be transformed by God. God will not force any change on us. He will bring it to us, but he will not coerce us. Let us approach with open hearts to hear what God is saying through his apostle and servant, Paul.

Discussion Questions

1. What assumptions and impressions about the book of Romans do you bring to this study?

2. Did you grow up thinking of the righteousness of God being against you or for you? Does the church you attend have a good news gospel or a bad news gospel?

3. In reading Romans as a life-changing letter, what are the implica-tions of being "beloved of God?"

4. What does it mean to see ourselves as "saints?"

5. What difference does it make to be "holy" in today's culture?

2

Not Ashamed

Romans 1:8–17

AT 8:07 A.M., LOCAL time, on Saturday, January 13, 2018, the Hawaii Emergency Management Agency sent out an alert to the whole state—media, residents' phones, and so on. Sirens went off around the state. The alert said, "BALLISTIC MISSILE THREAT INBOUND TO HAWAII. SEEK IMMEDIATE SHELTER. THIS IS NOT A DRILL." At the time, tensions were as high with North Korea as they had been in decades. The worst fears of Hawaiians appeared to be coming true.

But as we now know, there was no missile threat. An employee had hit the wrong button. Everyone wondered how such a thing could happen. I don't know if it was his first day on the job. Certainly, to err is human, but this was an unusually bad error. The worker who hit the wrong button, we were told, was quickly "reassigned." As astounding as the false alarm was, though, it is just as shocking that it took the Hawaii Emergency Management Agency thirty-eight minutes to send out a follow-up message saying that the alert was a false alarm. Clearly, the failure was multi-level.

Thirty-eight minutes! There are about 1.5 million people in Hawaii. I don't know if all of them knew about the alert, but I assume most did. What was life like during those thirty-eight minutes? Thirty-eight minutes may not sound like a long time, but I imagine it's pretty long when you think a nuclear warhead is headed your way. Many assumed that they would die. Hawaii has very few shelters, so people took cover wherever they could. According to witnesses, most people didn't really know where to go or what to do. They hunkered down in their bathtubs to pray. They distracted their young children. They called loved ones, even those back on the continent, for a last goodbye. Those thirty-eight minutes were characterized by panic, chaos, confusion, fear, sadness, and despair. According to many, it was the worst thirty-eight minutes of their lives. If there was any danger at all, it was no doubt in the way people reacted to the false information.

What if you had known the truth? What if, during those thirty-eight minutes, you knew the truth? What if you were sitting next to the person who pushed the wrong button? You saw what happened—you saw the whole thing—and you know the truth. You know that there is no threat and that everything will be all right.

If I were in the know, and I also knew that my family and friends didn't know the truth, I would want to tell them the good news that there is nothing to worry about. Otherwise, they would be at the mercy of the false information—deep in that state of panic, chaos, confusion, fear, and sadness. If I were in that position, I would feel *obliged* to call my family and friends and tell them the good news and urge them to call as many people as they can to spread that news far and wide. I wouldn't want to waste any time in delivering the good news.

Recall that, according to the first verse of Romans 1, Paul was in the know; he had some good news. And he had a calling to be a messenger, an apostle, a bearer of this gospel—the good tidings. The little that we learned about Paul himself in his opening statement will now be expanded in the following section, Romans 1:8–17. Paul's initial reluctance to say much about himself has now turned into a moment of self-disclosure. In this self-disclosure, he reveals his feelings and emotions about the Roman Christians. He is thankful for them (Romans 1:8), and he prays for them constantly (1:9–10). In the past, he has been prevented from coming to them (1:13), but he wants to finally come visit them and bless them spiritually in person (1:10–11) because he knows that they will be encouraged together through their mutual faith (1:12).

Later in the letter (Romans 15), we will learn that Paul has a long-term plan. As he writes this letter, Paul is in Corinth, in the middle of what is now called his third missionary journey. He is planning to go first to Jerusalem, in the east. So he will request prayers for his trip to Jerusalem and for the collection he is taking to them. Then he plans to go to Rome. This letter is, in some ways, Paul's self-introduction to the church—a message that will precede and prepare the way for his personal presence. Then he plans to go to Spain, in the west. So the letter is part of his early preparation for his Spanish mission to the far west via Rome, and he hopes that the Roman Christians will help him in that mission effort. But first he will help them and bless them by his message in this letter. The epistle to the Romans is, in part, a missions fund-raising letter.

So Paul explains his mission—his mission throughout the world (east and west), his mission in his letter-writing, and his eventual mission in Rome itself. As he said back in verse 5 and implies again in verse 13, his special calling is to the gentiles. What we need to realize about the Roman church is that, although it is a mix of Jews and gentiles, the majority are gentiles. It is to them that he is primarily writing, though he will occasionally address the Jews directly. He always knows that both groups are listening in on this letter that would have been disseminated and read orally to all the house churches in Rome.

Note the three ways that Paul now describes himself in relation to his mission. First, he is a *debtor* (1:14). Most translations say he is obliged or under obligation, which is about the same idea. But the word "debtor" to our ears really brings out that idea of *ought*—of owing something to someone else. Because of his divine calling to be an apostle to the gentiles, Paul is now in their debt; he owes them something. He is in debt to all gentiles, both to the Greeks (culturally "wise," as society thought of them) and to the non-Greeks or "barbarians" (inherently "foolish," as society thought of them).

Second, Paul declares himself *ready* or *eager* (1:15). He is more than ready to proclaim the good news. Knowing what he knows about the good news, Paul can't be anything but eager to share it. He will not sit on this information.

Which brings me back to the opening analogy. Like the Hawaiians for those few minutes, ours is a world, sadly, torn apart by a false knowledge. It hardly rises to the level of knowledge at all. It is, in its barest form, unreflective living based on uninformed assumptions. It is a philosophy—if it can be called that—whose only goal is individual choice and momentary pleasure. It is people, regardless of what they say they believe, who behave as if there is no God and there is nothing except the moment.

On the popular level—where, by definition, most people live—if the going philosophy is ever put into words, it is a philosophy that asserts that God is dead. Why?—"because science has proven it," a thing which no consistent scientist would ever assert. It is a world that claims there is no truth and no right and wrong, except what I believe or make for myself. Humanity is the only measure that counts. That system can't sustain peace, internally or externally. It is false information, like the false bomb threat. Yet the falsehood is widely believed, and no common or transcendent moral order is acknowledged. So we are at each other's throats, internationally and locally, corporately and individually—and scarcely able to engage in a rational and civil conversation anymore. Fear, anger, hate, and suffering reign at all levels, perhaps like never before. If you doubt it, just turn on the evening news. In a sense, our world is living in that mood of thirty-eight minutes, confused and wishing for a way out, not knowing when the existential end will come but believing that it is imminent, certain, and final, not knowing where to go or what to do.

We who witness a world driven to despair, chaos, confusion, fear, and sadness, all on account of false information, if we know the truth that delivers people from this situation, then we ought to reveal it. We "ought" to. That is, we owe it—simply by virtue of the privileged knowledge we possess—we owe it to everyone who does not yet know. We are a debtor to them. Not only that, but there is a sense of urgency in getting this news out. We are to be eager to spread the news. The news is that God *is*, that Christ has conquered and now reigns, and that the Spirit he has given fills us with his love! There is no need for despair, confusion, or fear. What the world thinks it knows is a false alarm.

Unlike the Hawaii case, however, the world is in real trouble—the despair and fear are real—but that danger comes as the result of rejecting Christ. That is, the false information creates another kind of danger—a real threat from which we need to be saved—and it is equally our obligation to warn of the real, impending catastrophe. In this sense, our obligation is similar to the six Nashville police officers who, on Christmas morning 2020, went door to door warning residents of an actual bomb whose detonation was imminent.

Like the hypothetical worker who knows the truth about the false alarm, like the six police officers who warned of the genuine threat, and like Paul, we too are obliged and eager to share the good news in a world that desperately needs it. If somehow the emergency management employee who knows the truth were walking around outside during the thirty-eight minutes, he wouldn't even need to say anything to anyone. His actions say it all. He probably would say something, but he wouldn't necessarily have to say anything to stand out. While people run for cover, trying to persuade him to do the same, he simply keeps walking with a smile on his face. And they ask him, why aren't you running and finding shelter? Because he is different and is not overwhelmed by confusion and fear, *they* approach *him*. Does your eagerness to share the gospel and your knowledge of this good news show in your actions? How can you show it? How can we show that we live above the fear and the hate?

Paul says one more thing about himself: "I am not ashamed of the good news" (1:16). To say that he is not ashamed could imply that someone might see the gospel as something shameful. How could good news be shameful or bring shame on someone? First, it might be helpful to know that ancient culture was much more concerned about honor and shame than we are today. Honor and shame may still be important today, but status in the modern world is more defined by economic factors, and after that, perhaps, education or which social agendas one supports. But in the ancient world, the categories of honor and shame, of reputation, surpassed all those. Honor was thought to be of utmost importance, and anything that could cause shame was to be avoided at all cost.

What could someone possibly find shameful about the good news, so that Paul would have to insist that he is not ashamed? Particularly in a gentile context, a couple of things come to mind. First, this particular good news was inseparably connected with the God and the Messiah of the Jews. To the gentile, the Jewishness of Paul's gospel is clear. In fact, Paul himself makes the priority of its Jewishness crystal clear in verse 16: the gospel is the power to save, "first for the Jew." The good news is directed first to Jews before gentiles, but this Jewishness was an offense to most gentiles. By the way, Paul here is laying a foundation that will be essential in his argument and purpose throughout the letter, which will go on to address Jew and gentile relations. The gentile Christians are listening to this.

The other potentially shameful thing is the connection of this good news to the cross. As Paul says in 1 Corinthians 1, the cross is foolishness to Greeks. "Cross" was a nasty word to dignified Romans; it is not something for polite conversation, and definitely not a place to look for a savior or for the ultimate truth. The real question here is, where does truth lie? Greeks seemed to be the intellectual leaders of the day. Where did Greeks look for truth? Greeks had sought truth in their wisdom, their *sophia*, their philosophy. But Paul suggests that ultimate, final truth resides in a crucified Jew. To Greeks, this is foolishness, not wisdom. It is shameful. From a sane Greco-Roman perspective, nothing is more foolish than the idea that the highest God could, much less would, become flesh and suffer. To the cultured despisers, such a thing is shameful to suggest.

Are believers today ever ashamed of the gospel? Are we ever ashamed to be identified as disciples of Christ? The world definitely considers it to be shameful. But it's not. It's an honor. If we feel ashamed, it could be that we don't know what this good news is really about, how good it really is, and how much the world needs it.

Paul is not ashamed. Why? Because the truth of the good news trumps the perceived shame to those who do not grasp it. Human wisdom and impressive powers are subordinate to the cross of Christ, that is, to self-sacrificial, redemptive love. The heart of the gospel is the good news that God's love is for all. The good news of Christ crucified and risen, of self-giving love, is the truth by which all other "truths" must be measured.

Paul goes on in verse 17 to speak of the righteousness of God revealed. "For the righteousness of God is revealed in it [the gospel] from faith to faith, as it is written, 'The righteous one from faith will live.'" Over five centuries ago, Martin Luther saw in this verse that the gates of paradise were opened up to him. To the believer, it is God's grace, "from faith to faith." That is, saving grace is given on the condition of faith, and greater trust is the result. The phrase "from faith to faith" is based on Paul's quotation from Habakkuk 2:4, which provides an outline for the next few chapters: "The righteous one from faith will live."

What was life like in Hawaii after the thirty-eight minutes were over? What came after the pandemonium, after the good news was announced, after people knew the truth that it was only a false alarm? Those who went out in public reported a calm and friendly attitude like they had never seen before. Aside from justified anger over the false alarm, there was also a sense of gratitude for life and its simple pleasures, a gratitude that swept over the whole population.

Chris Lee, a state representative from Oahu, was a witness to this surreal atmosphere. "It was like Christmas morning and everybody got a car—there was an amazing sense of camaraderie," he said. According to the story in *The Atlantic*, "He noticed myriad strangers greeting one another, for example, exchanging stories about their morning and offering each other their spot in line." And he said, "The little things that people worry about in day-to-day life and get frustrated with . . . completely evaporated." I would say, it was like a new life, a reprieve from an awful punishment. Life is a gift, a grace offered from above.

This is indeed what happens when people hear and believe the gospel, the good news. The good news is that what the world thinks it knows is wrong. This world in its fallenness is not our home, not our final stop. Nor is it meaningless. Life is not an accident. That is misinformation, false knowledge, fake news. It is a false alarm. The good news is that God has redeemed us in Christ and offered his gift of new life to all people. A reprieve from the deserved punishment. And, Paul tells us, that good news has the power to save, to deliver, to rescue. It saves from the dread and worry. It delivers from the anxiety in a world seemingly spinning out of control. It rescues from sin, guilt, and death.

On top of the good news itself is more good news. The further good news is that the good news is ours to proclaim. Like Paul, and like the hypothetical worker who knows the truth about the false alarm, we have the truth that can rescue a troubled world. What are we doing with it? Are we eager to share it? Let us never be ashamed to spread a message of truth, beauty, and love, and let us live in such a way that others see it. Let us walk down the streets of chaos and confusion with a big, calm smile on our face that reflects that truth, beauty, and love, the message of a God who created us for eternal fellowship with him.

Discussion Questions

1. What parallels do you see between the Hawaii during the (fake) missile threat and our world today?

2. What responsibility do those who believe the gospel have to those who do not know it? Does that sense of *ought* affect our lives and actions?

3. Do you ever feel ashamed of the gospel or of being a Christian? Why? In what circumstances?

3

The Economy of Sin

Romans 1:18–32

A FEW YEARS AGO, I said goodbye to an old friend. It was difficult, because for seventeen years straight we spent so much time together—
nearly every day. Her name was Corolla. Toyota Corolla. After a few days
of mourning, when it became apparent that I really did need another car
urgently, I had the bad fortune of shopping for a used car. One always
wants a bargain. When you exchange that much money for a product,
you want a good deal. In most cases, though, in a capitalist system, with
information readily available online, both parties can come to the bar-
gaining table informed, and both are probably getting a fair deal. No one's
getting a steal. I suppose it's rare when the product is right in front of
you that the exchange is going to be completely lopsided. But the bigger
the deal, the more risk that is involved, the greater the chance that the
exchange *could* be lop-sided.

On October 12, 1989, another exchange was made; a huge deal was
struck. It was a deal for the ages. As a native and resident of Dallas, this
trade would come to have a big impact on my teenage years. It was an
exchange between the Dallas Cowboys and the Minnesota Vikings. What
did the Cowboys get? Immediately, they received five players, six draft
choices, and a first-round draft choice in 1992. (In case you don't speak
NFL lingo, that's a lot of stuff.) So that's five current players and seven

good near-future players. What did the Vikings get? They got one player: the Dallas Cowboys' star running back, Herschel Walker. One player.

What was the impact of this trade on both teams? What results did the Vikings get with their trade? For the Vikings, Walker played two and a half more years, never ran for 1,000 yards again, and they won no playoff games. What results did the Cowboys get with their trade? They made other deals with other teams, eventually involving fifty-five different players, including getting the number one pick in 1991. From there, they built a whole team. They went from a record of 1–15 in 1989 (the year of the trade) to 13–3 and Super Bowl champions in 1992, in just three years. From that one trade, they built their team of the 1990s that won three Super Bowls.

That, my friends, was a lop-sided exchange. Or from the Vikings' perspective, it was a very bad trade. Of course, the Vikings didn't know. Walker could have been the one missing puzzle piece. But he wasn't. I'm oversimplifying, but in some ways it was a short-term outlook versus a long-term outlook. The Vikings wanted it now. The Cowboys decided to rebuild patiently, and success came more quickly than anyone would have predicted.

What exchanges have we as a culture made, have we as the human race made, have we as individuals made? What eternal things have we given up in order to satisfy the moment?

When we left off in the previous reflection, Paul had just spoken of the gospel, the good news. In Romans 1:17, he said that in the gospel the "righteousness of God is revealed." After reading that line, you would have good reason to think that Paul is now going to talk about what God's righteousness is, how it is revealed, and what it means when he says that "the righteous from faith will live." He will tell us all about that, but not yet. First, an aside, and it's a long aside.

Before he talks about the righteousness of God, Paul gives us a glimpse first of the other side. Before he explains how the righteousness of God is revealed, Paul explains why the *wrath* of God is revealed. Before he digs deeper into the good news, Paul tells about the bad news.

In Romans 1:18–32, we have the bad news. In some letters of Paul, you get the bad news and good news in quick succession. But in Romans, he settles into the bad news for a while. To consider one section of the letter at a time, as we are doing, means that we dwell for a bit in this bad news, too. To appreciate how good the good news really is, you have to appreciate how *bad* the bad news is. Think of my previous analogy, of the person spreading the good news that the missile threat was only a false alarm. If he went out and told people who didn't have a phone or hear the siren, who didn't know about the alert, then his good news wouldn't have seemed so good. But we're not talking about a false alert anymore. A bomb is about to explode. The sickness is real, whether we know it or not. And we have to hear the diagnosis before we can prescribe the medicine. Yes, before we hear about the righteousness of God, we are going to hear about the "unrighteousness of men" (Romans 1:18).

So let's look more closely at what Paul says about this human un-righteousness. What have people done with regard to God? They have suppressed the truth in unrighteousness (1:18). Did they know the truth? Yes! At some level, yes, they knew. But they suppressed the truth, re-pressed it, stifled it. They swept the truth under the rug.

What is this truth? It is a truth about God (1:19). "What may be known about God" is clear to them because God made it clear to them. Think for a moment about this question: How does one know about God? Knowledge of God comes in two ways: general revelation and special, or specific, revelation. General revelation yields natural knowledge about God. It's what we know by nature and innately. It's still given by God, but it's general because everyone has access to it. "The heavens declare the glory of God" (Psalm 19:1). But special revelation regards saving knowledge of God. It's specific because it comes only to specific people. General revelation shows the importance of and need for special revela-tion. Nature proclaims nature's God, the Creator; Scripture and especially the incarnate Son reveal who he is. Specific revelation reveals God's pur-poses, his redemption of creation.

Think of all the things one can know about God apart from Scrip-ture—what is generally revealed to all people of all times and places. Paul lists some of those things in verse 20. These invisible attributes of God are plainly visible in creation, so no one has an excuse not to know things about God. Some things we just can't not know. Enough content is built into creation—still discernible even in a fallen creation—to promote be-lief in God and instruct in morality. But, oh, how we suppress the truth and sweep it under the rug! It's not that we don't know these things; it's that we ignore them.

Verses 18–20 are already enough to give us a clue regarding who Paul is talking about in this whole section. Which group of people had no specific revelation from God? (We know which group *did* have specific revelation: the Jews.) Which group of people fits the description here and in the rest of this chapter—people who worshiped idols, harbored sinful desires, endorsed homosexuality, were full of sin? He never says "gentiles" in this passage, but he did several times earlier in chapter 1, and it's clear that he means gentiles now. Pagans, non-Jews. This section is about the gentiles' bankrupt spiritual heritage. It is a generalization, but the city of Rome would have more of this corruption and decadence than most cities.

Beginning in Romans 1:21, Paul proceeds to spell out the results of sweeping the truth under the rug. Spiritual confusion leads to intellectual confusion and moral confusion. Paul is going to lay out what I call a genealogy of sin. He speaks of these pagans in the third person, and so will I. It is as if he is answering the question, how did sin start among them? How did the gentiles get this bad? They *did* know God, Paul says, but they didn't thank him. It all begins with stubborn ingratitude. Their hearts were darkened. They professed to be wise, but they became fools. Suppressing the ultimate truth made it hard for them to see and understand any truth. Willful ignorance turns into involuntary ignorance.

What exactly did the willful ignorance, the sin, look like? It's as if the gentiles said, "It's time for a trade. Let's make a deal." Like the 1989 Minnesota Vikings, they wanted the next big thing. And here we see the economy of sin. It is a trade-off. Three exchanges are made.

Exchange 1: The glory of the immortal God is traded for images made to look like people, birds, four-footed animals, and reptiles (1:23). What sin is this? Idolatry. Here is the beginning of idolatry. From the true God to images of crocodiles! This is worse than the Herschel Walker trade! What was the impact of this trade? What was the result? How did God respond to their idolatry?

Well, this is a free market, with little regulation. People wanted their own way, so God allowed it. Three times Paul says, "God gave them over to . . ." It's part of the economy of sin. God is not causing them to sin or determining their actions. He is abandoning them to the consequences of their free choices. This, as Paul puts it, is his "wrath." He is not going to prevent them from sinning and thus remove their free will. He leaves them to their own devices. And so this may be one of the most terrifying phrases in the Bible: "God gave them over . . ."

First, God "gave them over" (1:24) to sexual impurity for the degrading of their bodies. That is, idolatry leads to immorality. Paul doesn't say exactly how idolatry leads to immorality. But I think he means this: once you deny the truth about God, you begin to deny the truth about the moral fabric of the universe. Once you reject the true nature of the good designer, it leads to rejecting the true moral design that he infused into the universe. They reject the order inherent in God's creation.

Exchange 2: The true God is traded for a false god, literally, "the lie" about God (1:25). More idolatry. Now we have a downward spiral that becomes harder and harder to resist. What was the result of this second trade?

For a second time, God "gave them over" (1:26) to shameful lusts. More idolatry leads to more immorality.

Exchange 3: Natural relations are traded for those against nature (1:26–27). Paul has in mind homosexual practice, an exchange that may have seemed commensurable, but in fact it was a bad trade. They received the "due penalty in themselves." Immorality is followed by its natural consequences. This is one of those moral truths that can be known apart from special revelation and Scripture. We should know there is design to the universe, including moral design. We ought to know there are natural consequences for breaking the moral law, natural consequences to sin. Bad consequences don't make a thing wrong, but they can be testimony that it is wrong.

Again they rejected knowledge of God, so for a third time, God "gave them over" (1:28) to a depraved mind to do what is improper.

The results of these exchanges are evident in the vice list of verses 29–31. What strikes you in this list of sins? "Disobedient to parents" always stands out to me. It is a sin that we normally overlook (or even embrace) but was punished with stoning in the Old Testament. Different descriptions probably stand out to different readers. These verses also exhibit heightened rhetoric, some of which is lost in translation. Note, for example, the word plays that are lost in translation. Paul says these people are full of "*phthonou phonou*," that is, *envy, murder* (1:29). They are "*asynetous asynthetous astorgous aneleemonas*," that is, *senseless, faithless, loveless, merciless* (1:31). In sum, they have made their big trade, they have made their exchanges, and they have come out bankrupt.

Like Paul, I have been speaking in the third person about the people of his day. But 1:18–32 is not a bad description of the world today. I know of no better commentary on our modern society than this passage.

Willful ignorance (1:19–23)? Think of atheists who deny the clear evidence of nature and reason.

Shameful lusts (1:24–25)? Our culture has a low, permissive view of sex—one of many factors that in turn enable the rampant sexual harassment that is roundly condemned by the same culture. Think also of how people dishonor their bodies, how people still worship humans and animals.

Homosexual practice (1:26–27)? Some say that Paul must be talking about rape or promiscuity, but no. Perhaps it is not about attraction, which is harder or perhaps impossible to control, but practice that goes against nature and is not directed at some level toward the possibility of procreation. The natural, God-given function of the reproductive system is, after all, reproduction.

Disregard of God's decrees (1:28–31)? Do people still have a depraved mind? Is there unrighteousness and untrustworthiness? Is there greed and disobedience to parents? Indeed, people are still inventing new ways of doing evil. It is a challenging word to the current culture of autonomous, limitless choice.

"Not only do they do these things but also they approve of those who practice them" (1:32). We move from excusing moral evil, then to condoning and doing it, and then to celebrating it. We suppress our deep knowledge of the true and good for so long that we effectively forget what is true and good. Sometimes it's hard to know when we've made the transition from trying to fool ourselves to being totally fooled, from intentional self-deceiving to being fully deceived.

One generation intentionally deceives itself and says—with a wink in its eye, while sweeping it under the rug—that it's permissible to practice homosexuality or to terminate unborn babies. Then the next generation simply accepts it—with no hint of irony, with clear eyes—and sincerely can't believe anyone would think these things are impermissible. And once the shift is complete, they think it's immoral to oppose homosexual practice or wrong to deny someone the "choice" to kill. In such situations, well into the downward spiral, it's hard to know where the blame lies anymore.

Forgiveness, abundant grace, is, of course, available for all these sins, but that will come later in the letter. The point right now is that the spiritual heritage of the gentiles is completely bankrupt. If not for the revelation of Jesus and his gospel, the gentiles in the Roman church would still be worshiping crocodiles. So Paul is telling those gentiles in Rome, look where you came from! "And such *were* some of you" (1 Corinthians 6:11). But that heritage is nothing to boast about.

If we trade away God's glory, his truth, and his intent for creation, then we know what we're going to get in return. It's not good. We're trading birthright for a bowl of soup (see Genesis 25:29–34). It satiates for a moment and then leaves you hungry for something more, wanting something better, only to despise the better thing. It may be tempting to say that all of this describes our secular society but not believers. We should ask ourselves, however, to what degree we are a part of that story or complicit in it. What have God's people been trading away? What good, divine, glorious, beautiful, natural things have we given up for the tacky, the distracting, the false, the unnatural, the evil? Why do we run from the things that we need the most? Let us not be those who suppress the truth, but instead allow the truth of God and the glory of his Son—his dying and his rising—to shine in and through us.

Discussion Questions

1. Have you ever made a really bad purchase or deal? What made it seem good at the time, and how did it turn out to be so bad?

2. What truths do we know by nature about God and about what is good?

3. How does Paul describe the pagan world's cycle of sin and ignorance? Does this ring true?

4. What do we learn about human culture and God's interactions with it?

5. What are our idolatries today, and what are the results of God giving us over to them?

6. What other sins listed in Romans 1 do we see in our society today? In our churches?

4

God's Righteous Judgment

Romans 2:1–29

ROMANS 1 ENDED BY talking about all those who "suppress the truth in unrighteousness" (Romans 1:18). They exchanged the glory of God for idols, truth for the lie, and natural relations for unnatural. They worshiped creatures rather than the Creator. They were God-haters who invent new ways of doing evil. So God gave them over to depraved minds and to the consequences of their immorality. Since they knew the truth, they are without excuse (1:20). I asked readers to consider chapter 1 as a commentary on our own society. As such, Paul provides a fairly accurate description of secular, post-Christian, late modern Western culture. Chapter 1 closes by speaking about those who practice such evil things and those who applaud them and give hearty approval to them.

But Paul goes on to acknowledge in Romans 2 that not everyone celebrates those evil deeds. No, there is a group of people that has registered its disapproval. Apparently, there are brave souls who *are* ready and willing to stand as witnesses against a culture that would be so godless. What does Paul have to say about these people—these principled protesters? Surely they are to be congratulated for pointing out evil when they see it. Not so fast! What he goes on to say in Romans 2 may be unexpected.

Notice that Paul shifts here from third person to second person. In chapter 1, it was they/them. "God gave *them* over." Now, it's *you*. Singular, in fact. Paul speaks directly to the individual, and now he's addressing

Christians in Rome—individuals who condemn and stand in judgment of that pagan behavior. Perhaps surprisingly, Paul does not congratulate the one who condemns the behavior that he mentioned in chapter 1. Instead, he condemns the condemners; he judges the judges. And he does so in the same terms that he used in chapter 1. In 1:20, he said that the pagans are "without excuse." They should have known better. Paul says the same thing about those judging the pagans: You, too, are "without excuse" (2:1). You should have known better.

As for these unofficial "judges" (let's call them), what have they done wrong? Why would Paul be rebuking them? After all, he's the one who just let the pagans have it. If condemning and judging is the issue, no one seems to do that more effectively than Paul in Romans 1. Shouldn't the Christians in Rome be proud of themselves for standing up against pagan immorality?

No, they should not. For those who might have felt a little smug satisfaction when Paul pointed his finger at the pagans, they now feel the pain of Paul's bony finger pointing straight into their own chest. Why? Why is Paul scolding them? It is because they practice the same things! When you condemn the pagans, he says, you condemn yourselves along with them, because you do the same things. And thus the pot calls the kettle black.

I said Paul's message about judgment would be unexpected and surprising, but maybe it's not surprising at all for those familiar with Jesus' teachings. The problem is like the one Jesus described so memorably in the Sermon on the Mount, in Matthew 7:1-5. In one of the more hilarious images in Scripture, Jesus says that harsh judgment is like a person trying to take a speck of dust out of someone else's eye, while the person himself has a log hanging out of his own eye. The incongruence is meant to be absurd.

Two solutions present themselves to the problem Jesus describes. First, there needs to be a little humility—the simple realization that there could be a log in one's own eye. Be self-aware enough to recognize that you are not perfect and haven't yet arrived. Second, the log shouldn't be there at all anyway. "Take the log out," Jesus says.

These are basically Paul's solutions here in Romans 2. He says that you shouldn't think lightly of God's kindness, forbearance, and patience (2:4). That involves recognizing your own imperfection and being moved to repentance. Furthermore, he says that you should be not just hearers of the law, but doers of it (2:13). In other words, take the log out of your eye. (I'll come back to these solutions in a bit.)

But, yes, people judge. Paul judges the people for judging. But there is only one judgment, he says, that makes a difference, and only one Judge who matters. Based on these verses, what are some things that God's judgment will be based on? I see at least four here.

First, and most importantly, God's judgment is based on the *truth*. "The judgment of God is according to truth" (2:2, but obscured in many English versions). This means that God *is* not, and cannot be, deceived. God's not unsure about who is guilty and for what exactly. He doesn't have to rely on other witnesses and wonder whether they are telling the truth. God's judgment is dispensed rightly, according to truth. The truth on the basis of which God judges is the point of departure for everything else that is said about God's judgment.

Second, verse 6 says that God "will render to each one according to his works." To those who seek the good, God will render *eternal life*. But there will be *anger* for those who pursue unrighteousness—the same anger or wrath that, back in 1:18, Paul said is revealed against unrighteousness. So that righteous anger is directed toward pagans, but it is also for anyone who practices evil or commits one sin. Verse 4 says that they cannot simply rely on God's mercy and patience and take advantage of it. If they try to do that, they are storing up anger (2:5) that will be revealed in righteous judgment.

Third, God's judgment will be based on equality—that is, without partiality. It is the same thing said of God in Acts 10 regarding salvation: All are welcome; God does not show favoritism. Just as he is impartial with salvation, here in verse 11, God does not show favoritism when it comes to judgment.

Are you rich and powerful? It doesn't matter. Are you part of God's covenant people with a special pedigree? It doesn't matter. Just as the gospel is for the Jew first and also for the Greek (1:16), so there will be trouble for every soul who works evil, for the Jew first and for the Greek. And there will be glory, honor, and peace for everyone who works the good, for the Jew first and also the Greek. God does not play favorites.

By the way, these verses (beginning with 2:11), indicate that there was an ethnic problem or tension of some sort in the church at Rome—a problem that is confirmed by other details that we will discuss later. The hints of the problem are here already.

In verse 12, we have the first mention of the "law" in Romans. Law is an important theme from here on in this letter. Paul will say different things about the law than in other letters (especially Galatians), mainly because of different situations being addressed, and it is sometimes difficult to know if he means the Law of Moses or law in general. But for now, he talks about those who are "apart from the law" or "without the law" and those who are "by" or "under the law."

What does Paul mean by these two categories? They refer to gentile and Jew, respectively. One of those groups (the Jews) had special revelation from God and had the law delivered right to their doorstep. They were "in law." The other group (pagans or gentiles) did not have that special revelation. They were "without law." Ultimately, it does not matter whether they heard the law in this special, specific way. God simply asks, did they practice the law? Did they do it?

Well, how could they possibly have obeyed the law if they didn't hear it? Verse 14 tells us, interestingly enough. Although they don't have the law and didn't specifically hear it, gentiles nevertheless may follow the law, Paul says, "by nature." It is reminiscent of what he said about the pagans back in chapter 1: They know the truth about nature and nature's God because God has revealed it to them. His invisible qualities are plainly visible. The design of the universe, including its moral design, is clear.

Of course, Paul also said that, by and large, they suppress that truth and sweep it under the rug. He seems pretty pessimistic about pagan culture without explicit knowledge of Christ. But he does say in chapter 1 that they have a deep conscience given to them by nature, and here in chapter 2 he explicitly says that the pagans have "the law written on their hearts." He seems to indicate that some of them indeed obey it. There is a great equalizing quality and impartiality to God's judgment, in which he takes a person's circumstances into account—for instance, how much of God's specific laws they have heard.

And that leads to a fourth characteristic of God's judgment. He will judge the *secrets* of people. Yes, external works will be taken into account, but so will internal thoughts, intentions, motives, affections, desires—all the things that no one really knows except you yourself . . . and God, who knows our secret things even better than we.

As for God's true and righteous judgment, people have occasionally asked me if this individual who behaves this way will go to hell, or if that group of people who believes such and such will be forever condemned. That's actually one of the easier theological questions to answer. The answer is always, "Eternal destiny is not mine to decide." (Thank God!) How could it be? That's Paul's point here. Only God knows the totality of someone's actions, their secret thoughts, and their circumstances. I can speculate; even better, I can help people find the truth. But only God judges in truth and in righteousness. For all these reasons, Paul seems to be saying, we need to slow down in our judgment, dial it down a few notches.

To be perfectly clear, it is not wrong to make judgments. When Jesus says "judge not," his very next words have to do with the severity of the judging (Matthew 7:1–2). In other words, we will be judged, he says, by the same standards we use, so watch out! Don't judge harshly or condemn.

And then, in Matthew 7:6, 15–20, Jesus talks quite a bit about the necessity of making judgments regarding other people. Paul obviously continues to make judgments. Calling out sin is not wrong. Paul does it. Jesus does it. But calling it out, without any humility or introspection, while we are complicit in it or actively engaged in the same wrongdoing? This is the problem. What then must we do?

We must check our own secrets—our motives, desires, thoughts, and intentions. We must evaluate our own actions—what we do, how we speak, how we spend our time, leisure, and money. Are we guilty of a sort of double speak? Are we complicit in the very evil that we decry? Thinking about all the vices mentioned in chapter 1, all those things that we along with Paul would readily condemn—how are we complicit in them?

Have we become the fools who fail to acknowledge God? Do we deceive? Do we lack understanding? While we condemn these things, do we somehow support or shrug our shoulders at, or are we positively entertained by, a culture that places other gods before the true God? Are we overtaken by greed and hatred? Do we in some way condone sexual perversion or even celebrate sexual misconduct?

Paul does not use the word "hypocrisy" in Romans 2, but that is the problem being addressed in the latter part of the chapter (beginning especially in 2:17). Hypocrites do not practice what they preach (Matthew 23:2–3). The word "hypocrite" comes from a Greek word that originally meant "play-actor." An ancient actor would put a mask over his face and act like he is someone that he is not. Also, the hypocrite is someone who thinks that he has arrived. But the worst and most *dangerous* hypocrisies are the unconscious hypocrisies, those we are not even aware of. Honest introspection is needed, and this is the kind of self-reflection to which Paul calls us.

What, then, is the right way to confront sin? And what is the way of courageous love and godly boldness? In our culture, at this moment in history, what is the strategy? It definitely can't be saying or doing nothing. That much is clear. We must say or do something. But what?

In short, I would recommend the two strategies implied by Jesus and Paul. First, Jesus says, we need to "remove the log." Notice that he does not say, "Don't ever call out sin, because you'll always have this log in your eye." That's the most common practical lesson people take from Matthew 7: "Since you have a log in your eye, you can't call out sin." That's the wrong lesson! Look again at what Jesus says: A log in the eye is not meant to be a permanent status. He says get rid of the log—your own sin—so that you can help others. Pay attention first to your own condition before worrying about someone else. The purpose is to see more clearly to confront sin.

If you think what Paul said back in Romans 1 was tough on outsiders, just think about this: What should *we* do to remove the log in our eye? Do we even have enough self-awareness to spot the log? How can we escape Paul's observation that if you practice the same things you condemn, then you condemn yourself? If the church in our day is going to have a voice about right and wrong, the most important thing we must do is get our own house in order first.

And then, second, with the help of God's Spirit, even when the log is removed as well as it can be, or we are in the process of removing it, we approach the question of sin with humility, for we are just as reliant on God's forgiveness as anyone else. At this point in the book of Romans, to suggest solutions is, in some ways, to run ahead of him. Paul is still in the diagnosis stage here. The prescription will involve transformation based on the grace and the love that God has lavished on us in Christ!

So, in light of this specific diagnosis, and in light of the solution that we will come to later in this letter, how then should we live? The most courageous action we can take is not only to *speak* against evil, but also to act in a loving way that is consistent with our beliefs and speech. I'm not recommending confrontations. But if you know people who need to hear the truth, then your relationship with them should inform how you communicate that truth to them.

Probably the best thing the church can do right now is model human flourishing. We must be genuine people in genuine relationships, modelling solid family love and solid Christian love—the many coming together as one because we have been united in Christ and are one in him. If we can do this, by the power of the Holy Spirit, then we successfully confront the sin not simply by condemning it, but by showing a better way, a truly alternative lifestyle, with Christ at its heart and center.

Discussion Questions

1. Even as Christians condemn the sins that Paul mentions in Romans 1, how have our own actions undermined our words?

2. What hypocrisies do you think Paul would identify in us and our churches today?

3. Is the church today too *quick* to judge harshly or too *reluctant* to judge rightly?

4. How does Paul's warning against hasty condemnation speak to our culture's judgment of past generations?

5. Have you seen positive examples of someone speaking the "truth in love," without compromising either true morals or genuine love?

6. Have you ever confronted someone about their sin, or have you ever been confronted about yours? How did that go?

5

The Great Advantage

Romans 3:1-8

SEVERAL YEARS AGO, I made the mistake of watching the movie *The Amazing Spider-Man* that came out in 2012 (Sony). People tell me that this installment was closer than previous movies to the comic book. If true, then so much the worse for the comic book. I much prefer the version from 2002 with Tobey Maguire. He plays the nerd so well. It takes one to know one—maybe that's why I like it! In the older movie, there are many notable moments, but the most memorable line comes in the car, when Uncle Ben is dropping off Peter. Ben says, "With great power comes great responsibility." As it would happen, those would be his last words to Peter, and they were words that he came to understand as the story progressed.

As we begin to reflect on Romans 3:1-8, my immediate thought is that this is the first difficult section to understand in Romans. In chapters 1-2, there may be a difficult phrase or word here and there, but overall, it has been pretty easy to understand what Paul is getting at. With this passage, however, I understand the words, but I'm not sure I get the point. Let me read that again, a little more slowly. Let me turn off the TV and actually try to pay attention here. I read through again, and it still doesn't really help. This is the first passage like that in Romans, but—and I hate to break this to you—it won't be the last. So we have to ask, what is the train of thought?

First, we have to back up just a bit to the end of the last chapter. On a side note, you shouldn't pay too much attention to chapter and verse number divisions, except for reference; and take the editorial headings with a grain of salt. When Paul's secretary, Tertius (Romans 16:22), wrote this letter down, the manuscript had none of those things—no verse numbers, no chapters. For that matter, it had no punctuation or quotation marks either. There weren't even spaces between the words. The point is that, when chapter 3 starts, even if it has a new heading, Paul is not talking about something completely different. Thus, and this goes for the entirety of the letter, it's always good to keep the immediate context and the big picture in mind.

Note what Paul said right before this passage: "For the Jew is not one outwardly, nor is circumcision outward in the flesh; but the Jew is one inwardly, and circumcision is of the heart, in Spirit, not letter" (2:28–29). What does this say about God's people? What makes a person a Jew—that is, Israel, part of God's people—is an inner reality, the Holy Spirit. Not the literal or outward keeping of the circumcision law, but the spiritual or inward circumcision of the heart. Of course, there are ethnic Jews. Paul also talks about them in this letter, so the language can be a bit confusing. But his point here is that if one is going to use the word "Jew" as equivalent to God's people, then ethnicity and literal keeping of circumcision are not the decisive factors. Thus, gentile Christians are, in this spiritual sense of the word, Jews.

What do you suppose the Jewish Christians listening to this are thinking? Well, we don't have to wonder, because Paul, a Jewish Christian himself, tells us. What we have in the opening verses of chapter 3 is what is technically called "diatribe." I don't mean that in the way we commonly use the word diatribe today, which is something like a complaining speech or a rant. A diatribe in the Greek-speaking world was a common rhetorical and educational technique to help someone get the point across. It is used to anticipate and raise objections, but in the voice of an imaginary opponent or objector. So it is like a dialogue. If you don't know that it's going on, or when it's going on, this also could be confusing.

You can easily spot the diatribe technique in a couple ways. First, taking on the voice of the objector, Paul asks questions and draws certain inferences—usually incorrect inferences. The objector says, "So, based on what you just said, Paul, are you implying this conclusion?" And, again, often it's, "Are you implying this terrible conclusion?"

The second characteristic marker is Paul's real answer to the erroneous conclusion of the imaginary objector. He answers often with *me genoito*. This Greek phrase the King James translators usually rendered as

"God forbid," even though there is no word for the deity in the original language. A more literal rendering is "May it not be!" A little more colloquial translation would be, "Of course not!" Or, and this is as vulgar as I'll get here: "No siree, Bob!" (Its first of several appearances in Romans is in 3:4.)

Now, let's see how this plays out in chapter 3 and if it helps us understand what's going on. Since Paul just said at the end of chapter 2 that being a Jew, a member of God's people, is not a matter of ancestry or physical circumcision, the objector asks in verse 1, "Then what advantage has the Jew?" That is to say, is there anything good about being an ethnic Jew? It seems like a fair question. After all, the objectors have read their Old Testament. They thought there was an advantage to being a Jew, a descendant of Abraham.

Paul agrees. It is advantageous to be a Jew (3:2). There is benefit or value in circumcision (as he also said back in 2:25). Even though they failed to observe the law, they were in an advantageous position because they had the law—they were the recipients of God's word. When Paul talked about the pagan gentiles in chapter 1, he said that they knew God from the creation around them. In chapter 2, he said that these same pagans were "without law," but that they had the law written on their heart and on their conscience.

Pagans had real knowledge of God, but it was very rudimentary. It was not saving knowledge of God's will. The Jewish people, though, had all that and more. They had the words of God—delivered through a mediator, yes, but delivered right to their doorstep. So they knew God's will in a way that the pagans never were privy to! Of course, this put them at an advantage.

But as Uncle Ben would say, with great power comes great responsibility. Or as Paul seems to imply here, with great privilege or *advantage* comes great responsibility. The Jews were entrusted, he says, with *God's words*. If you are entrusted with something, then you have a responsibility.

There's always something, as they say, lost in translation. Here is one of those places. In verses 2 and 3, we have four words that all come from the same root word in Greek. I'll try to clarify by translating with variations of "trust." Romans 3:2: "They were entrusted with the sayings of God." Romans 3:3: "If some did not trust, does their lack of trust nullify the trustworthiness of God?"

In other words, what if they didn't trust God? What if they didn't live up to their responsibility? Is God faithful? Will their "lack of trust nullify God's trustworthiness"? And here's where Paul gives us the *me genoito*, the "Of course not," the "No siree, Bob!"

If there is any question about the truth and righteousness of either God or humans, then God is true every time (3:4). "Is God being unfair to us Jews?" No, Paul says. "*You* broke the trust!"

The point here is that, when something good is contrasted with something bad, it makes the good stand out a bit more, at least to our fallen understanding. The force of the contrast is true in other areas of life. Fifty degrees Fahrenheit seems really cold and miserable, at least in Texas. That is, until it has been below freezing for six days in a row. Then when it hits fifty degrees again, it seems very pleasant.

As a professor, I see and teach, or try to teach, students of varying levels of eagerness and ability. I have some students who are very bright, inquisitive, intellectually curious, prompt, conscientious about assignments. I have had other students who are not so bright, who are lazy, tardy or absent, and if present, it is only bodily but not mentally. Of the two types, I have no trouble knowing which I prefer—the former type is good and I am always grateful for those students. But when I have one or more of the other type, the contrast is just more stark, and the joy of having eager students is all the more evident.

Paul makes a similar point in 1 Corinthians 11:19. He says that not only are there divisions in the Corinthian church, but there *must be* divisions. Why? Because when the factions are clear, when they have all staked their claim, it also becomes clearer who is in the right.

That's something like what Paul is saying here. God is true. It is humans who are false. It's not that God is actually *more* true or *more* glorious when humans are false. Our lack of trust does not actually make God more trustworthy. But it is the case that human falsehood becomes even more evident in the bright light of God's truth and faithfulness to his covenant. If we take God and humankind and ask, "Who is righteous and who is sinful?" the answer is obvious.

Imagine a mother saying to her young son, "Do not touch the stove. If you do, it will burn you." Imagine the child is old enough to know what that means. She asks him if he heard and understands, and he says, "Yes, I won't touch it." But, when mother steps away for a moment, he touches the stove anyway. He gets burned. He suffers the consequences. The mother's word of warning was already true before the disobedience. There did not have to be disobedience for the word of warning to become true. But with the disobedience and its consequences, the truth of her warning is clearer to the child than it was before. The child cannot blame his mother. She didn't leave him on his own with no warning or supervision at all. She trusted the child to heed her trustworthy warning for his own good. The child, however, broke the trust.

In sum, the Jews had an advantage, but it came with responsibility, and they, for the most part, broke the trust. God is still faithful to himself and to his promises, despite his people's lack of faithfulness. In fact, their lack of faith simply makes God's faithfulness more obvious. Not that God needs anyone to sin, any more than the child needs to touch the stove to make mother's warning true. Some people claim that, for there to be goodness, there must be evil. That claim is quite wrong. Good is good on its own without evil. God is the highest good, and the presence of evil doesn't make God's goodness any better. Given our limited perspective, mired in a world of evil, his constant, unchanging goodness just becomes more evident.

So if you grew up knowing God's words, you have an advantage over the average person raised in a secular household. Who is the average secular person? (The following description is a generalization, but there is truth in it.)

With no consistent or deep moral instruction, and no concept of spiritual reality or anything more real than physical atoms, and nothing more important than individual choice and pleasure, most people are chasing after lesser gods of one form or another. It is no wonder that levels of dissatisfaction with work and life are on the rise, as are depression and loneliness. Frustration, discontent, and restlessness—the constant movement from one relationship to another and from one pursuit to another—typify our times. We probably cannot expect much more from people whose greatest spiritual exertion is surfing the internet.

If you were taught something different than these secular pursuits, then you have an advantage. If you were taught that true satisfaction comes from devotion to the ultimate reality that transcends all creation, and if you were taught that our restless hearts will find rest only in the true God and that genuine freedom is found in seeking God's face, then you have an advantage. If people who loved you modeled for you the Christian faith and way of life (even if imperfectly), then you have an advantage. For this advantage we can and should be truly grateful. We didn't earn it. We didn't deserve, of all people, to be born into a family or meet a friend who taught us these things.

But with the advantage, with the privilege, comes great responsibility. If we disobey, it's not God's fault. If we choose instead to chase after other gods, if we choose to pursue selfish interests and fallen desires that are shaped more by our culture than by the moral law, then we are to blame. God remains faithful to his covenant. That covenant says that there will be consequences—consequences for disobedience and unbelief. And there are. When we see those consequences, we see the truth of God's moral law. In some ways, if people disobey God's law, they don't break God's law or moral design as much as it breaks them.

Although Paul hasn't gone there quite yet, I don't mind getting ahead a little bit and saying: Part of that covenant of grace is forgiveness, healing, and restoration for the truly penitent. When the child gets burned, does the mother put her hands on her hips and say, "See there! I told you so!" and then go right back to her cooking? No. Well, she still may say, "I told you so," but she immediately runs his fingers under cold water and rubs balm on the wound. She has compassion, and she heals. By the dying and rising of Christ, and by the power of his life-giving Spirit, abundant grace and healing are available to all, for the Father of mercies loves all people and wants all creation to flourish. By the work of the sanctifying Spirit working in us, we know the best way to flourish.

Discussion Questions

1. What do you normally do when you encounter a biblical passage whose train of thought or point is difficult to grasp?

2. Do people question God's faithfulness or trustworthiness today? How?

3. Why are we reluctant to explain suffering as a lack of our faithfulness or trust?

6

All Are under Sin

Romans 3:9–20

LIKE IT OR NOT, history has been punctuated with periods of increased government involvement in different aspects of American life. Again, like it or not—and there are plenty of people on either side of the preference question—federal, state, and even many local governments in the United States have enlarged their influence and power over the citizenry. The trend has mostly been gradual, but there have also been a few moments that mark more noticeable and even drastic changes.

The U.S. government's overall response to the coronavirus in 2020 was one of those drastic moments. When local and state governments forbade people from peacefully assembling for worship—a right enshrined in the Constitution's Bill of Rights—it marked a rare level of interference. Justified or not, it had never been tried on this scale in the United States in our lifetimes. But nearly everyone complied; it seemed there was little choice.

This kind of interference by the state in religious matters, unprecedented in the United States, is of course not unusual throughout history and in many regions of the world today. Such interference was a given in the world of the apostle Paul, and understanding this state of political and religious affairs will be key to grasping his letter addressed to the Christian residents of Rome.

We will return to that context in a moment. For now, we are moving on in Romans 3 to verses 9–20, a section that ends this long aside that began back in 1:18. The entire aside's main point is summed up very well in 3:9: "All are under sin." It is a point that Paul has been driving home since chapter 1. But why? Why is he talking so much about their *sin*? Is there a background point that he's trying to make and build on?

Part of understanding the point of this letter is to recognize the historical context in which it was written. At the beginning of this study of Romans, we briefly introduced the apostle Paul, his circumstances, and his reasons for writing. I did not say anything about the circumstances of the church in Rome. I was waiting for the opportune time, and I think now is as good a time as any.

What is the church's situation? In some letters and with some churches, it's fairly easy to see. It's probably easiest to detect in 1 Corinthians, because in that letter Paul comes right out and says, "You have problems with divisions and sexual immorality. You have questions about food sacrificed to idols and about worship. Here are my solutions to those and other specific concerns."

The one letter of Paul that most often gets treated as if it had *no* occasion is Romans. What is the problem Paul is addressing? He does not say. Did Paul even have detailed information about the Roman church? Many readers think not. Remember, he did not establish and had not yet visited the church in Rome. Thus, many interpreters ignore the possibility of there being a specific issue that Paul knows about and intends to address. Some read it merely as a general summary of Paul's theology.

This approach is natural because Paul never explicitly states the problem that he intends to address. Paul never says, "Here is the concern you have, and here is the solution." But the addressees knew what the problem was. The whole letter is the resolution to the problem. As readers who want to understand this letter, we do well to look in the solution for what the problem is. Once you know the problem, it puts the whole letter into context.

If you're an astute reader and you've paid careful attention so far, then you've noticed that Paul keeps bringing up Jews and gentiles. That fact alone tells us that there is something to it. Reading ahead, we can see that Jew-gentile issues are implicit in chapters 9–11 and chapters 14–15. We know from other letters of Paul and other New Testament documents that Jew-gentile tension was prevalent in the first-century church. This tension reflected not only the religious convictions of strict Jews, but also the social convictions of both Jews and gentiles. That is to say, in general, in first-century society, Jews didn't like non-Jews—and the feeling was mutual. But is Romans just a general exhortation to get along, or was there more going on? Was there more than just the usual animosity between these two groups, something that made this familiar tension even worse in the Roman church?

Indeed, there was. And the problem is related to government overreach. It was the year AD 49. The emperor was Claudius, and there was a disturbance among the Jews in the city of Rome. Roman history tells us that the disturbance was over someone named *Chrestus*. Suetonius reports, "Since the Jews made disturbances constantly by the instigation of Chrestus, he [Claudius] expelled them from Rome." Exchange one letter of Chrestus, and you have the Latin *Christus*, or *Christ*. The Jews in the city of Rome made disturbances about Christ! In other words, non-Christian Jews and Christian Jews were arguing in the synagogues about Christ, something we know took place throughout the whole Roman Empire. These controversies somehow spilled out beyond the synagogue walls and came to the attention of the Roman government and of the emperor himself.

The emperor Claudius was a traditionalist when it came to Roman religion. He did not much appreciate foreign religions such as Judaism; much less did he tolerate their family disputes. So, as Suetonius reports, Claudius expelled the Jews from Rome—not all of the 40,000 to 50,000 Jews in the city of Rome, but the leaders involved in the disturbances or debates. These were the ones expelled. Neither Suetonius's account nor Claudius's edict make any distinction between Jews who *are* Christians and Jews who reject Jesus. Just get all those synagogue leaders and church leaders out of here! So Claudius expelled the Jews from Rome.

We can see the impact on the church in Rome by following the story of Aquila and Priscilla, the most famous Jewish Christians in that community. We meet them first in Acts 18:2. Yes, this story about Claudius expelling the Jews from Rome ought to sound familiar, for it is corroborated in the book of Acts. It is through their expulsion in 49 that Paul met Aquila and Priscilla in Corinth, where they spent their exile. Aquila and Priscilla are among the Jewish Christians who were expelled, and so they represent this larger population of Jews who had to leave. It was through their exile that Paul met many of the Jewish believers banished from the imperial capital.

Return now to the church in Rome. In a church of Jews *and* gentiles, consider which group held the leadership. As in most first-generation churches, the leaders were mostly Jewish Christians. Jews had a background knowledge of God. They already knew the Scriptures. They had the divinely revealed moral law. All they did was add to their existing faith the worship of Jesus Christ. For gentiles, however, fresh out of paganism, the learning curve was very steep. In contrast to their gentile brothers who had just come out of paganism and idolatry, Jews were the natural leaders of the early church. Therefore, the church in Rome, which up to this point has been composed of mostly gentiles and some Jews who were the leaders, has been completely transformed by this forced expulsion, almost overnight, into a majority gentile church.

So now, those gentile Christians who had been the followers in the church are suddenly thrust into leadership. It is now their church in Rome. And there is no doubt that, as the church changed from a mainly Jewish to a majority gentile leadership, the church looked a little different. Leadership styles might have changed. Worship styles might have changed. Attitudes toward the Jewish law and how to apply it might have changed. Attitudes toward pagan culture and how to accommodate it might have changed. The Roman church is now a conglomeration of largely gentile house churches.

Well, for five years anyway. In October of the year 54, Claudius died (probably poisoned), and Nero became emperor. Claudius's imperial edict died with him; the decree that had expelled Jews from Rome was lifted. Jews could return to the city of Rome, including both non-Christian Jews and Christian Jews. Many did return, including Jewish Christians, to their beloved church in Rome.

Again we can follow the story of Aquila and Priscilla. They were among the exiles who made their way back to Rome and the Roman church. They are the first Christians to be greeted by Paul at the end of this letter (16:3). When Paul writes this epistle in AD 55, his audience includes Jewish Christians, like Aquila and Priscilla, who have recently returned to the Roman church. But the dynamics had changed in those five years.

Now, you know how, if you're not careful, a time of transition in a church can be a little tense. But imagine: How would things go if, by some government overreach, all the elders and ministers were forced to leave? Other Christians in the church have stepped in during this time and have done a good job leading. They've called and hired other ministers. Then, five years later, without warning, the old elders and ministers are allowed to return? And they're back just as quickly as they left? There would be tension. Even in the best of circumstances and relationships, there would still be some tension.

Now imagine that all those who left and have now returned are of another race or ethnic background than those who remained—a background that the culture tells us we should be in competition or conflict with. The added ethnic element would simply increase the natural tension within the group.

That's what happened in the Roman church—the dividing line reflects the volatile, first-century ethnic tension of gentile versus Jew. This specific circumstance of exile and return did not create this ethnic conflict, but it did exacerbate the friction and helps us understand a letter that seems predominantly general in its tone. This awkward tension is exactly what is going on in Romans, which was written about a year after the Jews returned. The gentiles, who are now in charge, are flexing their muscles against the Jewish Christians, now a minority in the church and with little or no influence.

So the Roman church to which Paul writes is a mixed demographic, but mainly a gentile church. The letter to the Romans is addressed primarily to gentile Christians, but it is also for Jewish Christians to overhear and to be addressed sometimes directly. Awareness of what is going on enhances our knowledge and application of Romans. Consider the following example.

Upon the return of the Jewish Christians to Rome, one way that the tension in the church has become clear is in the boasting that apparently occurs. How do we know that there was boasting going on in the church? For one thing, Paul tells them repeatedly throughout the letter to stop boasting. Later in this chapter (3:27), he says that boasting ought to be excluded. Both groups are doing it over against the other.

Imagine for a moment: How might a Jewish Christian boast over gentiles? "Yep, God gave those pagans over to a depraved mind. But we are God's chosen people. We are the favorites. He spoke to us and gave us the law" (as they say in 2:17). What is Paul's message to these Jewish Christians? "You who boast in the law, do you dishonor God through the transgression of the law? (2:23). Physical circumcision does not make you a Jew, part of God's people (2:28–29). God's judgment will be based not on favoritism, but on fairness. What makes a person part of the people of God is not some outward reality, but an inward reality—the Holy Spirit. Stop boasting."

How might a gentile Christian boast over Jews? "The Jews have had their chance, and they have mostly rejected the Messiah. So God has rejected them. *We* are God's chosen people now. We don't need the Jews. Forget about the law." What is Paul's message to these gentile Christians? "The gospel is the power to save, for the Jew first" (see 1:16). "You gentiles, who just came from worshiping reptiles, have a bankrupt spiritual heritage and bring comparatively little or nothing to the table" (see 1:18–32). The Jews, Paul says, have a great advantage (3:1–2). And the law is not excluded (3:31). "The gospel comes with a strict ethical code that you need to learn from the Jews." Later in the letter, Paul will say, "You gentiles are dependent on the Jews. Do not despise them and your connection to them. God has not entirely or permanently rejected them. Stop boasting."

And that brings us back to 3:9–20. Verse 9 summarizes the purpose of chapters 1–3. What is that point again? Paul's message to both Jews and gentiles is that all, Jews and gentiles alike, are "under sin." How does Paul prove the point? He rattles off a chain of quotations from the Old Testament whose uniting thread is that, without Christ, *all* are under sin.

This is typical of Paul throughout Romans. He makes a point and then shows the evidence in Scripture. (By the way, his method reveals the importance of supporting theological claims with Scripture.) The final quotation (3:18), from Psalm 36:1, effectively summarizes the reason behind all the sins listed in the preceding verses: "There is no fear of God before their eyes."

Jews would naturally think that these verses (3:10–18) are a good description of gentiles. And they are, but Paul doesn't let the Jews off the hook either. These verses are mostly talking about the Jews (3:19), but there is also a universal application: All have sinned. No one will be justified by works of the law (3:20). What if we had to be justified by works of the law on our own, without grace? What would be the result? Obviously, there would be no salvation and certainly no assurance of salvation. As verse 20 implies, the law was a great diagnostician but a poor physician; it could not heal the maladies that it diagnosed. That point will lead to the cure in the next section.

What Paul has done here is what Christians should always seek to do in a bad situation—make something good out of it. Yes, even in situations of government overreach. The government expelled these Jewish Christians from the church in Rome and now they have returned. This situation exacerbated the tension. And Paul is working to de-fuse and de-escalate the tension.

We live in a world that loves to escalate the tension, to light the powder train, and then to stick around to record the explosions, figuratively and literally. A twenty-four-hour news cycle demands that there be tension, conflict, and controversy to report and exploit. Where there might have been a little tension before, the world now assures us that there is full-blown hatred, "them's fightin' words," and the only proper reaction is, well, to fight.

When the news and media keep telling us that there is tension and hatred between the rich and the poor, that there is tension and hatred between political parties, that there is tension and hatred between young and old, that there is tension and hatred between different races, that there is tension and hatred between women and men, then we will start to believe it. Talking constantly about tension and hatred goes a long way toward creating tension and hatred. We are being trained by our culture to see every relationship in terms of power, and usually as an abuse of power.

I'm not suggesting that we ignore real injustice where it exists. But let us not be tricked into our culture's game of demonizing "the other," whoever that other may be. Let us not go out of our way to take offense where none was intended. The very fact that they keep telling us we're at odds with each other contributes to our being at odds with each other. If they keep telling me that the other means me harm, then I will come to believe it and see it where I never saw it before. We may start to view our neighbors in the world with suspicion and withhold from them God's love. Worse—could it happen?—we may start to view our own brothers and sisters in Christ with suspicion, mistrust, and animosity.

It's time to push back against the overreach and bad influence. It's past time to turn off the media and the talking heads who thrive on driving a wedge between different groups in order to satisfy the god of media consumption. The world, though it talks about unity, plays the endlessly divisive game of identity politics—the idea that your identity is based on your income, your political party, your age, your race, your sex or gender, your sexual preferences, and so on. Those things may play important factors or lend a distinct perspective. But make no mistake: paying ultimate attention to any of those things will never unite God's people. Our identity—the church's identity—is in Christ alone.

According to Paul, in fact, three things unite us. One: apart from Christ, *all* are under sin. We are united in our need. So there is no room for boasting. This is Paul's point in this passage and in most of chapters

1–3. Remember that the central theme of Romans is God revealing his righteousness to humanity. It is not about the Jews' righteousness. It's sure not about the gentiles' righteousness. It's not about your righteousness, and it's not about mine. It's all about God. We have no cause for boasting. I've often heard it said, "All are equal at the foot of the cross." To be more specific, all people are equally in need of God's abundant grace. All of us—Jews and gentiles, black and white, male and female, rich and poor, Republican and Democrat—we are all under sin. For Paul, that fact begins to open the door to mutual respect in a church where it was lacking.

There are two more things that unite us—points still to come in Romans. Two: We are all redeemed by *grace*. Again, there is no room for boasting. This will be Paul's point in the next section. And three: We are one with each other because we are *one in Christ*, in whom there is neither Jew nor Greek, slave nor free, male nor female (Galatians 3:28). We are members of each other because we are, first and foremost, members of Christ's body.

Paul could not allow the effects of the Claudian exile to divide the church in Rome. So he reminded the church of its common status under sin and need *apart* from Christ. He will go on to remind them of their common status of redemption *in* Christ. Just as Paul refused to play the game of divisiveness, God's people today also would do well not to allow the divisive politics of our time to filter into our minds and creep into our hearts, and cause us to forget the most important aspect of who we are. We are children of God; we belong to Christ; we are indwelt by the Spirit.

Discussion Questions

1. Is today's church hesitant to talk about "sin?" If so, why?

2. How does the story of the Claudian exile help explain the dynamic in the Roman church?

3. Does any of the boasting in the Roman church sound familiar? How do Christians still boast?

4. How can we rectify the common human inclination to see other people's sins so clearly but not our own?

5. How does Paul prove his point about the universality of sin? Is there a lesson for us in his method?

7

Made Right by Grace

Romans 3:21–31

As an occasional viewer of the evening news, I've noticed that a great deal of it is filled with reports about individuals or groups of people who think they have been wronged. Have you ever been wronged? Of course you have! To ask the question is to answer it. As long as there is human interaction—even if that interaction comes to be mediated entirely through machines—there will be injustice. So, of course, everyone has been wronged. But when I ask about when you have been wronged, what comes to your mind?

Most of the time it's probably the daily, piddly things—you get cut off in traffic or someone cuts in line while merging. Sometimes it's more serious. Though you are more qualified and have more experience, maybe you were passed up for the job or the promotion. Maybe you were slandered behind your back by someone who assumes but doesn't know anything about your situation and what really happened. Maybe you were cheated out of the security deposit that was rightfully yours. Maybe the car accident really was the other person's fault, but the police didn't see it that way. Maybe the physicians, instead of healing, were negligent, and seem to have done harm to or even killed your loved one.

To live in this world is, at times, to be a victim of wrongdoing. How do we respond in those situations? Especially when we know who the culprit is? We want to make things right. We still want the promotion after all. We want our money back from this person. Or we want to sue that physician for malpractice. We want what is rightfully ours. But we do not get it. Why? In most of these cases, we don't get what is rightfully ours because we can't. We have no recourse. It's not that we refuse to pursue justice because there's some relationship there worth salvaging; it's just that we don't have the resources we need. We won't get that job or promotion. Or we don't have an attorney on our payroll. We won't get our loved one back. How do we make the wrong right?

So far in Romans we've heard quite a bit about unrighteousness or injustice. As we get into this next section (Romans 3:21–31), we are reminded of the theme of these early chapters: the righteousness or justice of God. Remember the theme stated in Romans 1:17: "The righteousness of God is revealed." As if picking up from 1:17, without missing a beat, Paul returns to the theme of God's righteousness in 3:21. I would not recommend it, but you could skip from 1:17 to 3:21 without really noticing you missed anything. The righteousness of God (1:17; 3:21), attested by the law and prophets, has been made manifest, made evident to everyone. So, do you see what Paul has done? While he was talking about the righteousness of God, he basically interrupted himself, from 1:18 to 3:20, to talk about the unrighteousness of humanity. This was the long aside. Finally, he returns to the righteousness of God. And he is finally going to say how the righteousness of God has been made manifest.

But before Paul tells us about God's righteousness, let's just pause for a moment to ask: What should we expect here? Given what he has laid out in this long aside, what do we think God's righteousness should look like? Keep in mind that this word righteousness can also be translated as "justice." (Anytime you see justice, righteousness, justified, made right—these all come from the same root word in Greek. But the different translations may have a slightly different connotation.) What if I said, what should we expect God's *justice* to look like? Does anything come to mind?

Paul has made it clear, up to this point, that God is the one who has been wronged. God created all people for loving relationship and fellowship with him. He revealed himself clearly to gentiles through the created order. He revealed himself even more clearly to the Jews through the law. But all, both Jews and gentiles, are under sin. With regard to God and humans, God is true and every person false (3:4). "All have sinned and fall short of God's glory" (3:23).

How, then, is the wrong to be made right? What is God's justice going to do with all this human sin? This is the issue set up in 1:17: the

righteousness or justice of God. This righteousness or justice of God we
might expect to be punishment for the guilty. Rightful, *just* punishment.
If justice is defined as "everyone getting what they deserve," then justice
means sinners receiving death, for, as Paul says later in Romans 6:23, "the
wages of sin is death." In light of Paul's negative but realistic picture in
chapters 1–3 of human rebellion, pride, hypocrisy, depravity, and disobedience, we could expect harsh but fair retribution. In other words, given
what we've seen, it could be bad.

And so we read on to see what it means to have the righteousness
of God revealed to us. And what we find is that the righteousness of God
has been made clear through the "faith(fulness) of Jesus" (literally, 3:22,
26). Jesus' faithfulness toward God and his faithfulness to us form the
foundation of our faith in him. It is both the "faith of" and "faith in" Jesus.
We can trust him because of his trust in the Father and his fidelity to us.

Instead of a retributive justice, which God has every right to, God's
justice or righteousness is not merely to punish sinners but to make them
right through faith. Righteousness, Paul says, is for all who believe (3:22).
Just as all have sinned (3:23), the same "all" are justified freely (3:24).
Paul's use of "all" here emphasizes that this justification by grace is for
both Jews and gentiles, for the "other."

Now, there is a large concentration of what I call "churchy" words
here in these verses—words that we don't often use in everyday life. It's
important to take a moment to explain them, because most of these
words in their original Greek were not specifically religious words. Even
if we occasionally use this word in everyday life, *justified* is one of those
words we tend to think of as a "church" word. But it simply means to
be *made right* or *upright*. As already mentioned, anytime you see words
like justify or righteous, they all come from the same Greek root. To be
justified means, as a dear old preacher I knew used to say, "just as if I'd
never sinned"; being justified means the guilt is removed. When we are
justified, we are forgiven, acquitted, declared guiltless, and made right.

We "are made right freely by his grace" (3:24). *Grace.* There's another one of those "church" words that's not originally a religious word.
It simply means a free gift, undeserved or unmerited favor. Grace means
getting the good thing that you don't deserve. It is related to *mercy*, which
we might describe somewhat arbitrarily as not getting the bad thing
that you do deserve. They are really two sides of the same coin. Grace
and mercy come through redemption (3:24). *Redemption* is yet another
religious-sounding word. It simply means buying back, release, acquittal,

liberation. Perhaps more properly, redemption is the price paid for setting someone free.

In verse 25, we do come to a more specifically religious word: *atonement*. Some translations say that God set forth Christ as a "sacrifice of atonement," but the word sacrifice is not present in the Greek. The word translated as "sacrifice of atonement" is the same word that, in the Old Testament, means the place of atonement or reconciliation. It is the word for the mercy seat, the cover over the ark of the covenant. It is the very presence of God for the purpose of redemption, mercy, and forgiveness. Paul says Christ is that for all people—the very presence of God, the embodiment of grace, for our redemption, buying us back from the death penalty that we so richly deserve. So how does God make the wrong right? The answer, in some ways, is very simple: Christ. Christ brings atonement, redemption, reconciliation.

Verses 25 and 26 both say that this was the demonstration or showing of God's righteousness. Now, here, one must pay attention. In verses 21 and 22 the old NIV says "righteousness," but in verses 25 and 26 it says "justice." In all four instances, it is the exact same word in Greek. It can be translated as righteousness or justice, but to translate it differently in verses 21 and 22 than in 25 and 26 is misleading, and there is no reason for it here. God's *righteousness* that comes through faith is the same as God's *justice* in atonement. You could lose the very point that Paul has been working toward, the culmination of the case in these first three chapters. How is God's righteousness revealed (1:17)? It is this: God demonstrates or reveals his righteousness in Christ (3:25). God is the one who is right, and the one who makes us right by faith (3:26).

I don't know what the old NIV intended by translating it as justice in verses 25–26. Maybe the translators want to bring the idea of retributive justice or punishment or wrath into this. But it is not that the wrath of God was satisfied. It's not that the Father actively inflicts punishment on the innocent for the guilty. And it's definitely not, as some people worry, child abuse—the Father crucifying his Son to satisfy his own anger. That's not there. Again, this is the point: Through the gospel, God's justice becomes his mercy. God is right and makes us right by the grace of withholding the penalty. God's righteousness is his grace. If we understand justice as getting what we deserve, then through the gift of Jesus Christ, God's justice becomes grace (getting a good thing we don't deserve) and his righteousness becomes mercy (not getting a bad thing we do deserve).

Again, who in this story does wrong, and who has been wronged? Paul is very clear about it. God has been wronged. We are the culprit. We are to blame. It is not God who has to reconcile himself to us. It is we who are reconciled to God in Christ. In this story, it is God who loves infinitely; it is we who have turned away. Unlike us, it is not that God doesn't have the resources to mete out retributive justice. If it were us, we would be tempted to pursue that justice and get it if we could. Well, God could. God has unlimited resources. He has recourse.

Rather, for the sake of the relationship, God simply allows himself to be wronged. It is not that the Father punishes an unwilling Son. It is that God, in the Son, simply chooses to be wronged, by the worst that humans have to offer, for the sake of relationship and reconciliation. God makes the wrong right by forgetting about the wrong. It is not to suggest that the wrong is insignificant; human sin is weighty and hurtful. Such forgiveness is very costly for the forgiver. God shows his righteousness or justice by saying, "I've been wronged. But I still love you and forgive you. Press on toward the goal." There may be more to the atonement than God simply forgiving and allowing himself to be wronged. It should not be reduced to this analogy. But it is not less than or exclusive of this understanding.

Such atonement is not uncommon in everyday life. This kind of justice or righteousness we know best in a family setting. The best parents show their children love in every way that they know how. Suppose they bend over backwards to do for their children what they need most. Did you know, by the way, that it costs, on average in this country, over $200,000 to raise a child from birth through graduation from high school? (As my kids can testify, I'm aiming for getting under that total.) That's a lot of money. And then there is all the immeasurable and unquantifiable love and sacrifice.

But let's suppose that, for all these good things the parents do, the children fail to show gratitude. Let's say that they even display a bad attitude or disobey and lie every now and then. What do you as a parent do? Do you start charging them money? Do you charge them a fee for each wrong done? Do you try to get back at them for what they've done? Of course not! In fact, if you did any of those things in the name of justice, we would be inclined to call it unjust. The same goes for children when the parents make mistakes, as well as for our spouses when they have wronged us. Can you imagine the father of the prodigal son, after forgiving him and clothing him in a robe and giving him ring, then presenting him with a bill? I suppose some parents might try that. But not our heavenly Father.

Justice looks different when a relationship is at stake. When we are wronged by those we love, we simply allow ourselves to be wronged, for the sake of the relationship. I'm not saying that there's no limit or never any punishment or that we should let our own family members run right over us. But if there is punishment or penalty, it is for the sake of the relationship. Remember, as Paul says, that God is right and the one who makes us right (3:26). His grace and even his punishment are there to set right. It is not for retribution or vengeance against the penitent, but for rehabilitation, restoration, reform, amendment of life, to make the wrongdoer a more just or righteous person in the future. God justifies or makes us right by grace in order to make us holy.

That leads to verses 27–31, which one should remember to read in light of the situation going on in the Roman church. Boasting is excluded, for salvation is by grace, not by religious or ethnic heritage. Paul's language indicates that there is definitely a Jew/gentile problem or conflict going on in Rome. "Is the law nullified?" he asks. *Me genoito*; "No siree, Bob!" (3:31). If Paul had wanted to say that the law is nullified, this would have been the perfect opportunity. Instead, Paul says that we establish, or uphold, the law. He's not throwing out the Old Testament, but the Old Testament supports him. The law, he says, is a necessary step, but not sufficient by itself. The law brings knowledge of sin, but not justification. Paul is not against the moral law, as some accused him of (3:8). As we will see later in the letter, faith produces a spirit of service that the law never brought successfully. Faith brings new motivation to keep the same laws.

So what have we seen, as we close out these first three chapters of Romans and set the stage for what follows in the rest of the letter? We've seen that relative human goodness won't cut it. We can't say, "Well, I'm mostly good, and that's good enough." All have sinned, and "all our righteous acts are like filthy rags" (Isaiah 64:6). We have to see ourselves in this story and really experience the depth of the misery of the human situation without Christ so that we can then appreciate the height of the joy of life in Christ.

After all the bad news of Romans 1–3, the good news is finally proclaimed. The good news is good indeed. No one is good enough (on their own) to be saved, and no one is bad enough not to be saved (with Christ). God will be righteous. God will be just. God will demonstrate his righteousness. But it is not a justice that finally condemns us. God's justice is his mercy; God's righteousness is his grace through Jesus Christ our Savior. And it is available to all, an important point that Paul stresses in his attempt to help unite a multi-ethnic church.

What is the exhortation for us? If we really understand salvation by grace, then there is no place for boasting, and there should be no feeling of superiority. God has done his part in salvation, which is to say, every-thing! He has made us right by a gift, abundant grace in Christ. What is our part? Gratitude. We simply accept the gift. Faith is the condition of acceptance, manifested in repentance for the wrong and in baptism as a rejection of that wrongdoing. It is saying yes to God's love. Even in the conditions of acceptance, God is the worker, through his grace, drawing all of us into his heart.

Discussion Questions

1. Describe a time when you were wronged and justice was never done.

2. How could that wrong have been made right?

3. How can the wrongs and rights in our lives help us understand Christ's forgiveness and atonement on our behalf?

4. What is the significance of being justified by grace versus justified by the law?

5. If the law is not nullified, then what role is left for it?

8

Made Right through Faith

Romans 4:1–25

WHAT DO YOU THINK about this statement: God saves his people in such a way that "they do not contribute at all to salvation"? Does that sound right or wrong to you? Or, what do you think of when you hear the phrase, "faith only"?

Sola fide, by faith alone, was one of the central themes of the Protestant Reformation. The reformers were countering a late medieval theology of penance that implied that one's salvation was dependent in some way on performing the right rituals. Their intended point is that we are not saved by works. Some folks have heard that and thought, "But we are saved by works, or we at least contribute something to our salvation." The basis of this thinking is reflected well in James 2, where the writer clearly says that we are justified by faith and works and not by faith alone (James 2:14–26).

What does Paul have to say about this? In Romans 4, we come to the next part of the outline suggested back in Romans 1:17, which is a quotation of Habakkuk 2:4 (using Paul's word order): "The righteous *from faith* will live." Paul has already talked about righteousness or justification. God has made us right by his abundant grace. Now it is time to talk about the means to righteousness. Justification by faith. The point was brought up at the end of Romans 3, when he mentioned that we are justified, or made right, by grace. He also mentioned faith in 3:22, 25, and 26. So "faith" is a kind of hook word that he introduced in chapter 1, hinted at since then, but now returns to for deeper discussion. And that brings us to chapter 4.

Paul elaborates on the salvation that God brings to all by grace, and faith is the key in Romans 4. Who is the poster child for faith? Abraham. Who could be a better example than Abraham, the one whom God chose and called out of pagan Ur, the one to whom God promised land and a great nation and that his seed would be a universal blessing? How was Abraham justified, or made right, with God?

On the basis of Romans 4:2, we see that boasting in the church is still a concern. Abraham could have reason to boast if he had been saved by works. But since he wasn't, he doesn't. And this is a reminder to those groups in the church who would boast. Abraham had no reason to boast because he was not saved by his works. Instead, what does Genesis 15:6 say? Paul quotes it. "Abraham believed." Abraham heard the call and the covenant promises, and he believed.

It's time for another linguistic aside. The words translated as *faith* and *believe* are simply the noun and verb of the same term in Greek—*pistis/pisteuo*. Faith is the noun; believe is the verb. They look like completely different words in English, but they are the same and mean the same thing. When it says in English translation that "Abraham believed," it is the same as saying, "Abraham had faith." When it says anything about faith, it is the same as belief. But the Greek word means so much more than belief, which I'll get to in a moment.

It was Abraham's belief, his faith, that was credited to him as righteousness (4:3, quoting Genesis 15:6). Now, as you read Romans 4:2 and 4:4–6, Paul never says Abraham was justified by faith alone, but that is definitely the gist of what he is saying. He was justified by faith "apart from works" (4:6). What else is faith apart from works? Faith apart from works is what is meant by faith alone. So we need to begin by acknowledging that Paul says as much as Abraham was made righteous by faith alone. As it says in verses 23–24, this holds true not only for Abraham, but also for all people.

Now, how can this claim be reconciled with James 2, which goes to great lengths to say that we are saved by faith and works, not by faith only? I don't want to get too bogged down here, but, for one thing, there is a different emphasis for a different audience that may need to hear another side of the same truth.

But, more important, Paul and James use *faith* in two different ways. When James says it takes more than just faith, the faith that he describes is certainly a very bare thing. It is mere assent, belief *that* . . . such and such. The faith that James describes is something so minimal that even the demons have it. The demons believe that God is one, he says, and they shudder (James 2:19). If by faith alone we mean mere assent to a proposition, then, as James asserts, that faith alone will save no one. Paul would agree.

But Paul does not use the word faith in that way. For Paul, as for most of the New Testament, faith (*pistis*) is a much richer concept than intellectual assent. At the basic level, it *is* assent; it is belief that something is true. But it is much more. It is also the word for "faithfulness" or "fidelity." Faithfulness and fidelity are relational terms. They are not just states of mind; they are terms that imply relationship and even action.

If someone is faithful to his wife, then that's not just a feeling or an intellectual belief. The inward reality unfolds into actions—refraining from certain actions, and engaging in other actions. If you are faithful, there are some things you won't do, and other things that you will do, that you must do. Actions—or works, if you like—are natural consequences of fidelity and faithfulness. In the case of this passage in Romans, it is faithfulness to the covenant, fidelity to the God of the covenant.

For Paul, faith means faithfulness, trust, commitment, submission of life for obedience. Faith is obedient trust. It is joyful trust in Christ joined with obedience. Faith means trust in Jesus for salvation, not in works of merit, which is to say, not in oneself. It is to acknowledge that fallen humans cannot save themselves.

Just as James and Paul use the word *faith* in different ways, they also use the word *works* in different ways. For James, the works that save us are the good deeds that flow naturally from saving faith. It is helping the poor and hungry, the widows and orphans in distress (James 1:27; 2:15–16). Works of faith are part of being made right. The NIV in James even translates the word *works* as *deeds*—an apparent attempt to highlight the distinction and to mitigate the confusion. By contrast, for Paul, the works that don't justify us are the Jewish identity markers, such as circumcision and dietary restrictions. Works of the law—works that later Christians would associate with the so-called "ceremonial law," works by which we try to merit or earn salvation and become part of God's covenant people—won't cut it.

In Ephesians 2:8–10, Paul does a very good job of harmonizing James and Paul. We are saved *by* grace *through* faith *for* good works. (It's all in the prepositions.) Understood correctly, one can say that we are saved by all of these things. *Grace* is the ultimate ground or foundation of our salvation. The righteousness *by* which one is justified is not one's own. In this sense, we are definitely not saved by works. It all begins with God. The whole rescue operation is the gift of God. *Faith* is the instrument, the means *through* which we are justified. It is how we appropriate that rescue that has been offered to us. It is the life-saver thrown to us and our merely holding on for dear life—still a gift. Faith is our part, but it is enabled by the Holy Spirit.

What about good *works*? We are saved not *by* good works, but *to do* good works. It is the purpose *for* which we are justified, and good works are the evidence of the salvation. As Jesus says, a good tree produces good fruit. Good fruit does not cause the tree to be good and healthy; it is the evidence of its good health. Good works are not the basis of salvation, but the natural result of covenant fidelity, a life of faith and faithfulness. Such acts are evidence of our covenant relationship with God. But if good works are absent, this is a bad sign. So it is not about doing "as little as possible." It is about sanctification, the process of becoming more holy, more like Christ.

So, back to the original question: "Do we contribute anything to our salvation?" No. If by contribute we mean we do a little bit to make it happen, or hatch the plan, or deserve a little credit, then . . . no. If by contribute we mean simply accepting the gift, willingly saying yes to God's yes, opening the door to the Christ who knocks (Revelation 3:20), then . . . yes, I suppose we contribute. But I would rather say, with the great Christian tradition, *cooperate*. We cooperate with God's prior work on our behalf.

Romans 4:9–12 reminds readers that Abraham was justified by faith before and after circumcision, but the focus is on the "before." Physical circumcision (Genesis 17) came fourteen years after the covenant, fourteen years after Abraham's justification by faith, mentioned explicitly in Genesis 15:6. The circumcision played no causal role in his being made right. So Paul uses Abraham's example to prove that circumcision is not a prerequisite for justification. As such, not only is Abraham the physical progenitor of the circumcised, but he is also a spiritual father to uncircumcised gentiles, to "all" those who follow in his steps of faith. He is "the father of us all," Jews and gentiles alike (Romans 4:16)—an important point that Paul continues to emphasize for the Roman church to hear.

And here is where another important element of faith (*pistis*) comes in. Not only can this word *pistis* be translated as *faithfulness* or *fidelity*, but it also includes the element that we call *trust*. The word trust adds another layer to this idea. In a faithful relationship, there is trust. In a relationship, we trust even when we lack some relevant data, even when we are short of a guarantee. Trust is about something we don't have in front of us, based on knowledge we do have.

I don't know what my teenage children are doing 24/7. But, because I know them, I trust them (within reason). I don't know everywhere my wife has been and who she has seen without me. I don't track her; I trust her. Likewise, Abraham trusted God. When he heard the call in Ur and decided to follow God, what guarantee did Abraham have of this promised land? When he was one hundred years old, about twenty-five years after hearing that he would have a son, what hard evidence did he have that this would ever be fulfilled? Not much. But he trusted.

It is important to be clear about what Abraham trusted or *whom* he trusted. Abraham placed his trust not in any person—an unreliable or fickle human—not in any thing, and not in a clever philosophy. The same is true for us all, Abraham's offspring. We, like Abraham, trust the "God who brings the dead to life and calls non-being as being" (4:17). This is where the trust comes in. But it is not a groundless trust. It is trust in a powerful God, the God who creates out of nothing and brings life out of death.

Note 4:18–21. Abraham, "in hope against hope"—now there's a fascinating phrase—could believe that God is both willing and able to do the impossible. And it was impossible. This is the "against hope" part. Abraham "considered his body already dead . . . and the deadness of Sarah's womb" (4:19). In one sense, they had two good reasons *not* to believe God's promise. First, Abraham's body was "already dead." Second, Sarah's womb was dead. The concreteness of death is evidence, so to speak, against hope. Yet there remained hope, hope in the midst of a situation that was set against hope. Abraham believed that "what God promised he is also able to do" (4:21).

Hope against hope. We know Abraham's "against hope." "I don't see any land for me. I don't see any children for me. My own body is dead. My wife's womb is dead." Now, whence the hope that fights this "against hope" and believes? Where does that hope come from that Abraham possesses? It comes from the "God who brings the dead to life and calls what does not exist into existence" (4:17).

I wonder if we take salvation for granted. If we are inclined to do so, that's what Romans 1–3 was all about. We are mortal. On the scale of being, from non-existent things to the God who always exists, we are at the non-existent side of things, just lifted out of that nothingness and brought into existence by God's creating power. We are disobedient, sinful, guilty. We haven't done enough—and we can't do enough—to earn God's infinite love. It's impossible. It's simply a gift, and we simply receive it.

Without God, it's all quite impossible. And Paul connects salvation, all people being made right, to this pervasive theme of God making the impossible not just possible, but actual. God brings non-being into being. God turns death into life. In hope against hope, God does the impossible: He justifies all who are impious, those who don't deserve it.

How? Jesus Christ, who was "handed over for our trespasses and raised for our justification" (4:25). It is Jesus' death and resurrection, made possible by the God who brings life out of death.

What is your impossible? What is your "against hope"? For Abraham, he saw no land, he saw no children, he saw only decay and death. For Jesus, what was his "against hope"? He saw unfaithful, weak disciples. He faced a cup of anguish, humiliation, and suffering. He cried out, apparently abandoned by God in death. But it is in weakness that God's power is most evident. It is in death and in nothingness that God works his wonders. It was over the chaotic waters of the primordial deep that God's life-giving Spirit hovered to bring order and life. Or, as Paul says elsewhere, "When I am weak, then I am strong" (2 Corinthians 12:10).

So what is your "against hope"? What is your impossible? What do you see around you? Is it constant sin, guilt, the impossibility of conquering it, and so the impossibility of forgiveness? Loneliness, depression, regret? Is it disappointing, difficult relationships that are not going the way you wanted? Illness, decay, and death? And there will be decay and death. Whatever it is that ties your stomach in a knot and presses on your heart and mind and keeps you up at night. You know what stands against hope.

But now, what is your *hope* against hope? It is the same for us as for Abraham and as for our Lord Jesus: Our hope is in the eternal God. So we believe, we trust—and with good reason—that God will make those things right, that the lamb and the lion will rest together and the wrongdoer and the one wronged will be reconciled, and that being will be brought out of nothingness, and death itself will forever die.

So all are justified by faith, that is, by trust and fidelity to the God who brings non-being into being, who makes the dead alive, and who raised the Lord Jesus from the grave. The word calls us to hope against hope, because the one in whom we hope is faithful, and he will do it.

Discussion Questions

1. Why do you think Paul makes Abraham the poster child for faith?

2. "We contribute nothing to our salvation." Would you qualify that statement? If so, how?

3. What part should works play in our salvation?

4. In what ways is Jesus the ultimate model of faith and hope?

5. What is your "against hope," and how does Romans 4 speak to your situation?

9

The Foundation of Hope

Romans 5:1–11

HUMANS SHARE A COMMON plight. It doesn't matter who you are, where you live, how much money you make, or what color you are. All of us are limited. We all have problems. We all have sin. We are all mortal and must face death. What's more, we have no control over these things; we are bound by this situation. It is inescapable. This situation of utter dependence is common to us all, and it leads us to one of the greatest concepts in the entire Bible—hope.

Many wonderful themes are introduced in this next large section of Romans, chapters 5–8. Now that Paul has described righteousness and faith, he begins to shift to the topic of how to live for God (cf. Romans 1:17). As we have in previous sections, we would do well to see this section also through the lens of the Jewish-gentile conflict. To some Jewish Christians, Paul was proclaiming a too-easy gospel, with the result that gentiles were multiplying in the church, but not many Jews were trusting Jesus as their Messiah. Paul nevertheless sticks to his method of detoxifying pagans who come to Christ: it's not about shoving the law down their throats; it has to do with "freedom," a recurring word in chapters 6–8. Living for God also requires the Holy Spirit, given to help Christians keep God's ethical requirements (Romans 5:5; 8:4).

More specifically, in the first few verses of chapter 5, Paul focuses on the results of faith. By faith, he says, God's people appropriate God's grace and have assurance (5:2). Standing in grace does not mean a life without suffering. Sufferings remain, but grace gives us the stamina to endure suffering, which in turn produces character and hope (5:3–5). In many ways, these first five verses anticipate themes that will be especially prominent in chapter 8.

Of the many important topics that could be pursued in Romans 5:1–11, this discourse will focus on hope as a foundation for Christian living. *Hope* is a hook word that was introduced in the last section when Paul spoke of hope against hope (4:18). In light of our common plight, Paul calls on Christians to respond to our situation in hope.

What is hope? Hope is looking forward to something, with a reason for confidence in its fulfillment, confidence in the future. "Reason for confidence" is important here. Hope is a present state of mind or heart that is oriented toward the future, based on something firm. Hope is certainly not merely a religious or Christian word. The word can be heard outside of church buildings. The word seems to be more prominent around the holidays, especially at Christmas. We also hear about hope during political campaigns—at least, we used to. Politicians like to talk about hope. In the past, American citizens have been asked to "embrace the politics of hope" and told that "hope is on the way." Which raises the questions: Hope *in* what? Hope *for* what? Where do we *find* hope? When secularists talk about hope, it is not always clear what they mean, because the basis of their hope is not clear.

I remember that candidate Barack Obama inspired many voters with his language of hope. Hope was one of the key words of his first presidential campaign. He even spoke of the "audacity of hope." We like hope. I would much rather hear about hope than doom, which seems to be a more pervasive theme in recent years. But when a politician like Obama says "hope," does he mean what the apostle Paul meant by "hope?" I have a feeling that when politicians say hope, they mean more jobs and less war, more security and less fear. It is not quite the kind of hope that Paul was talking about. Paul means hope in the God who brings non-being into being (4:17).

Christian hope must mean more than what pop culture and the politicians mean by hope. Our hope is not in President Biden, any more than our hope was in President Trump. So what is the basis of our hope? Is there something worthy enough to be the source and object of our hope? Is there something that we can live for and die for?

When we think about hope, we can think about three types of people. A person can have three possible relations to hope, based on *where* that hope is placed. And these result in three corresponding conditions.

1) The first person has no hope. This person places hope in nothing. A hopeless person is without God (Ephesians 2:11–12), one who lives for nothing. He wakes up in the morning, and does not know why. This is also known as the condition of despair. Despair is a sickness of the spirit, a disease of the soul or self—the most dangerous illness known to humanity. Its symptom: not wanting to be who you are, a true soul or self. This does not happen overnight. It's not that the desperate never *had* hope, but that they lost it somewhere along the way, perhaps in the process of suffering (Romans 5:3).

To lose one's way is not like losing a leg or arm. It is not that noticeable. It happens *gradually* and quietly. Sometimes the person doesn't even know it's happening. A person in despair does not want to accept that he lives his life before God. So despair itself is sin. He lives his life as if there is no God. This person loses all consciousness of the fact that he himself is a beloved child in the Father's presence. He thinks that he is independent, but he is really the most dependent. He fancies himself to be ruler of his own self, but on closer examination, he is like a king without a country.

A person in despair is, by definition, desperate, but often doesn't know *what* he's desperate for. He knows there's a hole in his heart, but he doesn't know how to fill it. So a person in the state of despair—when taken to its logical conclusion—sometimes wants to end his life. He has no hope of anything on the other side of the suffering (5:3). The hopeless person simply goes on living for nothing. He respects no one, and no one respects him. He is, for all practical purposes, dead. He walks and talks, and lives and works, but he is dead. The disease has been diagnosed, and the patient refuses the medicine.

2) Second is the person who has misplaced hope. Unlike the hopeless individual who lives for nothing, this person lives for something. He wakes up in the morning with a purpose. He places his hope in something. But the problem is that this person places his hope in a false something. He bases his hope on something that can never be an adequate basis. It is to "glory" in the wrong thing (5:3). And to put one's hope in a false something has the same result as putting one's hope in nothing.

I call this condition *presumption*. As much as despair, presumption is a sickness of the spirit. But what makes it worse is that many people who have this condition don't know it. It is presumption because they presume to have a solid hope, and don't realize theirs is a false hope, a false sense of security that often leads to carelessness. It is almost an arrogant presumption that hopes in an illusion, a future that will never be fulfilled. This is like the talent contest wanna-be who makes no preparation, never bothered to take lessons, never got a second opinion, but is as confident as anyone else and thinks she's the greatest singer. But what is their purpose? What do they place their hope in?

Some people spend all their time pursuing money and stuff. That's their *goal*, their hope, as if it will somehow secure their future. Sometimes they will not admit this, but their greed cannot be hidden. Some place their hope in sex or drugs or the state—all false gods. A person who thinks blowing himself and others up will get him a front row seat in heaven has a misplaced hope. More often, there is the hope in adventure or endless entertainment, to distract from the reality of humanity's common plight. Do you know people like this? Others place their hope in friends, even family, whereas others place hope in themselves. Their goal is to be an independent or successful individual. Of course, friends and family can be good; self-confidence is good. Some of these things can be good in their proper place. But none of them can be an adequate source of our hope. None can really make the future palatable.

I'm afraid that many people who call themselves Christians really have a misplaced hope. Some people who go to church every Sunday, who live good and honest lives, do not have much of a foundation for their hope. They place their future in the hands of medical science. Or their future has everything to do with their career, money, houses, cars, and things, with entertainment and busyness as distractions from reality. Yet, they still consider themselves to be God's children. They avoid at all cost the suffering that can produce character (5:4). Following James, we would rightly call these people "double-minded" (James 1:8; 4:8). Their hearts try to hope in two things—God and anything else. The double-minded person wants two things that are mutually exclusive.

Does the pursuit of things satisfy? Can a person ever have enough things? Money cannot keep a lonely person company; it won't comfort you on your deathbed. What about friends and family? Even the best friends in the world can let you down; we let ourselves down. God said through the prophet Jeremiah, "Cursed is the one who trusts in man, who depends on flesh for his strength and whose heart turns away from the Lord. He will be like a bush in the wastelands; he will not see prosperity when it comes. He will dwell in the parched places of the desert, in a salt land where no one lives" (Jeremiah 17:5–6).

Pretty soon, after it all comes crashing down, the presumptuous person sees that his hope was misplaced; then, he sees that his true state is not much different from the one who has no real hope. Presumption is just despair without knowing it; the disease is the same, but the diagnosis has not been heard or believed.

3) Third and finally, there is the person who has true hope. The difference is that his hope is founded or based on a solid foundation. Our common, human sense of hope only finds true fulfillment when it is placed in the promises of God. Any other hope falls short, and is sure to be dashed to pieces eventually. We do not hope for the riches of fame or fortune that may never be ours anyway, but for the riches of Christ's glorious inheritance (Ephesians 1:18). The Christian is single-minded, with a pure heart. The gospel that we proclaim is the only basis of Christian hope—that, while we were still sinners, Jesus Christ died for us and rose again for our salvation (Romans 5:8).

This gives us a hope that is not a *blind* wish for something impossible, but a confidence based on the certainty of God's love, the assurance of his promise—which is not to be confused with the uncertain promise of an indifferent father or a power-hungry politician. We hope in the God who brings creation out of nothing, being out of non-being (4:17), light out of darkness, life out of death, and hope out of despair!

Today's world tends to lead people to despair. But the good news of the gospel is that anyone with the condition of despair is offered the cure. The good news is that you need not live without hope. The one suffering from despair, once he identifies the problem, need not refuse the medicine. Jesus, the great physician, is the one who gives us good hope (2 Thessalonians 2:16).

And what is the condition of the person who *has* hope? Cured—like a person released from the hospital's ICU and sent home with a clean bill of health. By believing in Jesus and being united with him in baptism, we begin to live a life of hope. What about the "audacity of hope?" If our hope is in a politician, we might as well call it what it is: the folly of hope. But *true* hope is here, and it is ours through a relationship with God in fellowship with Christ.

As Jeremiah said, "Cursed is the man who trusts in man." He goes on to say, "But blessed is the man who trusts in the Lord, and his trust is the Lord. He will be like a tree planted by the water that sends out its roots by the stream. It does not fear when heat comes; its leaves are always green. It has no worries in a year of drought and never fails to bear fruit" (Jeremiah 17:7–8).

Life tells us *no*. Despair, suffering, sin, guilt, punishment, and finally, death, all tell us no. But hope in God tells us *yes*. Hope enables a person to live life with joy. As Paul says, "We boast in hope of the glory of God." Patient endurance in suffering finally produces hope. "And hope does not disappoint" (Romans 5:3–5). Paul says suffering can produce hope, and this is something to take joy in. That is why he exclaims in Romans 12:12, "Be joyful in hope!"

Hope enables us to say "Yes" to all the "No's" of life. It doesn't matter where you are in life. If you're the richest person on earth, but you're depressed with no hope, or trusting in your money, then you are like the walking dead. But even if you are the poorest man on earth, suffering, living in a ghetto or a cell, if you have true hope in Christ, then you are truly alive. We must challenge conventional wisdom and say with confidence, that the poorest Christian living in the slums or on the streets is worlds better off than Jeff Bezos. Paul says that in this hope we are saved (Romans 8:24).

And what is the ground of that hope, according to Romans 5? It is the love for the ungodly that God has revealed in Christ (5:6). One will hardly die for a just person, though for a very good person one might dare to die (5:7). But while we were sinners and rebels against God, Christ died for us (5:8, 10). If he showed such love to sinners, then "how much more"—a comparison type of argument that Paul enjoys—"how much more," now that Christ has reconciled us, will we certainly be saved (5:9–10)! Christian hope is a firm hope in the one who, out of his infinite love, creates, reconciles, and saves.

What is the ground of your hope? Is it a saving hope based on a *solid* foundation, or is your future based on sinking sand? As long as there is a now, a present, something can be done about your future. As long as there is a now, the cure is available for the one suffering from despair. You are never beyond the reach of hope. God invites you to take hold of his promises—the promise of forgiveness for the believer and healing for the one who hopes in him.

Discussion Questions

1. What does ultimate "hope" mean to non-Christians or atheists?

2. What is the source and object of Christian hope?

3. What things besides God are we Christians tempted to place our hope in?

10

Super-Abundant Grace

Romans 5:12–21

SOME PEOPLE, FOR WHATEVER reason, seem to invite dysfunction and court chaos. They are not truly living unless there is a disaster at hand, a new tragedy or trial to face. Do you know someone like that? It reminds me of the meme at despair.com: "Dysfunction: The only consistent feature of all of your dissatisfying relationships is you." Maybe you're that person?!

And this is more than simply bad things happening to people. Bad things happen to everyone. Anybody can have a car wreck. But after six or eight car wrecks in a short period of time, we may start to wonder about this driver. At least the insurance company takes notice. Some people have addictions that ruin their lives. Or there are people who have not just one failed relationship but, over and over again, have failed relationships and keep driving people away.

Have you ever noticed how dysfunction tends to spread? Wherever we see it, and call it what we like—dysfunction, disorder, chaos, sin—it rarely remains the exclusive property of just one person. Often, sadly, the dysfunction spreads like leaven in the family and it becomes generational. The dysfunctional individuals can't keep it to themselves. The tendency toward broken relationships is handed down to their children, who have seen the dysfunction modeled so well. And so we breed cycles of dysfunction, of violence, of instability, of addiction, and of poverty that spread to the next generation. The bad habits seem to snowball, gather momentum downhill, and then become an avalanche of snow-balls. Nothing, it seems, can stop the powerful trend, the spread of the leaven, the snowball effect of sin.

In truth, this is not just the story of an isolated individual or a black sheep that you may know. This is the story of the whole human family, and it is therefore our story. Dysfunction and sin, part of our human family history, seem to reign in the world and in our own lives. Paul recounts for us, in Romans 5:12–21, the story of how and where the dysfunction and sin began.

This passage can be perplexing—perhaps the most difficult since the opening verses of Romans 3. With chapter 5, a new section of this letter has begun. In Romans 1:17, Paul said that "the righteous from faith will live." He talked first about the unrighteousness of humans and the righteousness of God. Then, in chapter 4, he talked about being made right by faithfulness. Now Paul gets a little more into the "living" part. It's not that there has been nothing about the life of discipleship before this, but the question comes to us in a more poignant way.

Now that we have been justified, or "set right," now that we see what faithfulness and trust looked like in Abraham's life, where do we go from here? And, particularly, what about the lingering, pesky problem of sin? Here at the end of chapter 5, Paul begins to answer the question about where sin came from and what is being done about it. In other words, what did that state of sin look like, and how did Christ reverse it?

So Paul takes us back to the beginning: Adam. In 5:14, Paul calls Adam a "type" or pattern of the one to come. We now call this interpretive technique "typology"—when persons or events from the Old Testament foreshadow a future person or event. A "type" is a model or pattern, a prototype. What is Adam a type of? In Jewish literature outside the New Testament, he is either exalted and respected as the father of the human race (Genesis 2), or he is disparaged and blamed as the first sinner, the father of sin (Genesis 3). (I remember when I was a kid that a family friend had a baby boy they named Adam. The older sister, a small child herself, protested this name and said, "But Adam sinned." Apparently the parents were thinking of the former Adam, the Adam of Genesis 2; but the little girl was thinking of the Genesis 3 Adam.)

Paul focuses on the Genesis 3 Adam, the prototypical sinner through whom came sin and death. In this sense, as the first sinner, Adam is the type or prototype of every man, every human being. In Adam's sin, we see our own loss of innocence, our own guilt, our own desire to be our own god because *we* know so much better!

It is unfortunate that this passage in Romans 5 became the favorite proof-text of those who teach the doctrine of "original sin" as inherited guilt. By the way, here, as for so many other things in Western Christian tradition, Augustine is the primary influence. Around the turn of the fifth century, he read this passage to be saying that all people sinned in Adam.

In its strongest form, original sin means that not only the penalty or consequences of Adam's sin are passed on to the human race, but also the *guilt* of that first sin. In other words, all people are guilty of that first sin. We may refer to this very strong notion of original sin as "original guilt," which I mostly use here interchangeably.

Of course, if sin and guilt imply personal responsibility—and they do—then the idea of "inherited guilt" is quite incoherent. Thus, one might well ask, if we didn't all sin in Adam and inherit his guilt, what does Paul mean when he writes, "Through the disobedience of the one man the many were made sinners" (5:19)?

Consider this very literal translation of 5:12: "Because of this just as through one man sin entered into the world and through sin death, so also death came to all men, because all sinned." Verse 12 is simply saying that sin came into the world through Adam, and death was the result; death has spread to all. Why? Because all sinned. Paul is stating what he later calls "the law of sin and death" (Romans 8:2), which, in its simplest terms, is, "If you sin, you die." This is what God said would happen in Genesis 3, that death, on that day, would be the consequence of eating the forbidden fruit. In what way did Adam die when he sinned? Did he die that day, as he was warned (Genesis 2:17)? If he did, it was probably in this way: he was separated from God; there was a *spiritual* death. Paul is saying that the law of sin and death began with Adam and has spread to all who sin, which is to say, to everyone. Sin is the cause, death the result.

A careful reading reveals that Paul never says anything that entails original sin or any category beyond guilt for actual, personal sins. He really says nothing much here about the nature of the ruin or how it is appropriated. It definitely never says that guilt is being passed on without choice.

Paul never says how we become sinners. It could just as well be through nurture and imitation of others. (I think there is probably more to it than nurture and imitation, but the text does not necessitate anything more.) Let me attempt a stark analogy, an analogy that assumes erroneously that drinking any alcohol leads to alcoholism. Compare the following statement with Romans 5:12 (quoted above): "Our grandfather brought alcohol into this family, and alcoholism through that; alcoholism spread to us all, because we all drank the alcohol." And this is analogous with 5:18: "Through Grandfather's introduction of alcohol to the whole family, the whole family has become alcoholics." It's just an example. In the analogy, no one was born an actual alcoholic, born with the habit of the bar and the hidden bottles. It is just saying that alcoholism came in as a result of growing up around alcohol and alcoholics and, by choice, imbibing it ourselves. Ultimately, it happened to us all because Grandfather introduced it.

Likewise, Paul does not explain the mechanism by which people become sinners. We are left to assume that we become sinners the same way it happens throughout the rest of the Bible, namely, by individual choice. We are not born *guilty* for Adam's sin. By definition, sin is something we are held responsible for. If we had no choice and didn't commit it, then we cannot be held responsible for it. You can't be guilty for something you didn't do.

So he's not teaching a doctrine of original guilt. But what *is* he saying here?

We need to have a balanced view of fallenness or brokenness and its effects on the human race. The truth is somewhere between the two extremes of original guilt, on the one hand, and no effects of the fall, on the other.

In a fallen world, which is not the way God intended creation, everything leads to death. Thus, just as ill effects do befall the children of alcoholics, physical disease and death touch all, even the innocent infants and children among us. But physical death is not the only effect. Most anti-Calvinists (for lack of a better term) are prepared to acknowledge that we inherit physical disease and death from Adam. But is there more? When I asked above how or in what way did Adam "die," we acknowledge spiritual death. Thus, there are spiritual consequences of being born into a fallen world.

Look around at the world, at the church, and inside ourselves. We walk in Adam, according to the flesh. Every part of human nature has been negatively affected. Our physical bodies have been negatively affected—indeed, they are born to die. But also our mind and heart and soul are negatively affected—that is to say, our intellect, our will, and our affections. Every part of us is affected. Whatever combination of things makes a human person, it has all been negatively affected.

Consider, for instance, that as affected and fallen, we can look at the created world and contemplate being, consciousness, and beauty, and yet have the gall to ask, is there a God? Our intellect has been darkened. We can know exactly the right thing to do in a circumstance, and know that the wrong thing will bring us harm and brokenness in the long run, and still we do the wrong. Our will has been twisted. We can see fellow human beings in need and fail to love them as image-bearers of God. Our affections have been corrupted.

The human race may not live with the *guilt*, but we do all live with the many *consequences* of the first sin. What does it mean to suffer the ongoing penalty of what someone *else* before you did, that you yourself didn't do? How is it fair?

I'll attempt an answer by continuing the analogy of alcohol. The baby carried by a drinking mother and born into a family of alcoholics is not born like other babies. For this child, there will be a tendency toward alcoholism, by nurture, yes, but also by nature, a nature that has been corrupted. It is more than mere imitation. The baby does not begin with a clean slate. The baby is born with fetal alcohol syndrome, and thus suffers some ill effects, exhibiting a tendency toward alcoholism, though not held responsible or punished for the inherited effects or mere tendency. The ill effects and inclination themselves are the penalty or consequences inherited. The baby is not predestined to become an alcoholic as an adult. She will have a choice.

All people are born like the baby with fetal alcohol syndrome. We are born suffering the effects caused by the alcoholics before us, and we ourselves are inclined to the addiction. We suffer the consequences, the corruption, of our predecessors. The consequences of fallenness or brokenness are allowed by God to teach us dependence on God. For those of us who want to be our own gods, depending on God is something that we need to be trained in, this side of Eden.

So we are not born sinful and guilty, but we are born fallen and broken. By no means are we predestined to sin, but it doesn't take long for that fallenness to shape us. It doesn't take long for the inclination and the temptation to take hold and overpower us—for the dysfunction and disorder to spread in our lives and in our communities, like a snowball effect.

Death reigned, even over those who did not transgress the law (5:13–14). We are not born like Adam was created. We are not born with original righteousness. Adam was made in the image and likeness of God. The likeness has been lost. To the degree that the image of God is "natural" to us, we are already and always graced with knowledge of God and his will. Sin does not efface the knowledge of the good. But we tend to suppress that knowledge (Romans 1). We, on our own, cannot turn to God and pick ourselves up by our bootstraps. We must rely on Christ's work and the power of the Spirit to have that righteousness restored, the image of God renewed, to grow again into the likeness of God and be what we were created to be, the new man, Christ, members of Christ's body.

And that must bring the text back to Paul's main point, which should be our main point. If we focus on sin and its effects here in chapter 5, then we have obscured the main idea.

By the time we get to Romans 5, the main topic is no longer sin or the fallen state. Chapters 5–8 are about the change that has happened in Christ. Paul does this by introducing Adam as the prototype of Christ. But he is a prototype not in similarity, but in contrast. Life in Christ, being led by the Spirit, is set in contrast with life in Adam, walking according to the flesh.

For Paul, it began in 1 Corinthians 15:21–22 (probably written before Romans), where Paul first notices this contrast. Christ, raised from the dead, has become the firstfruits of the general resurrection. All will be made alive in Christ. He is undoing what Adam did. Death came through Adam, but life came through Christ. So when Paul says in Romans 5:14 that "Adam is a type (or a pattern) of the coming one," it's a typology not of similarities and comparisons, but of differences and contrasts. Christ is the counterpoint to Adam. Adam introduced death into the world, but Christ introduced new life, resurrection life.

Consider again Romans 5:15–17, the series of contrasts between humanity in Adam and humanity in Christ—that is, the contrasting effects of Adam's actions and of Christ's actions. The free gift is not like the transgression (5:15). Dissimilarity dominates these verses. What is the dissimilarity? It is simply in the effects—death versus grace and life, sinners versus the righteous.

Note the dissimilarities in the typology: By the transgression of the one (Adam), *many* died (5:15). "Much more"—Paul loves this phrase, which he already used back in 5:9–10—how "much more" by the grace of the one (Jesus), *many* received grace. The dissimilarity is not in the number affected, but in the effect itself.

In 5:16 Paul observes another dissimilarity: One transgression brings judgment and results in condemnation. Many transgressions bring the free gift and result in justification. That's amazing! Do you see it? We would expect many transgressions to bring something bad. But no! Many transgressions bring grace! It is so counter-intuitive. One sin brought disaster, but many sins have resulted in good things!

In 5:17, by the transgression of the one (Adam), death reigned. "Much more," those who receive grace will reign in life through the one Jesus. (It is almost the same statement as in verse 15.)

To summarize this fairly complex typology of dissimilarity, there is a contrast between, on the one hand, the transgression, disobedience, and its results (death, judgment, condemnation) in Adam and, on the other hand, the righteous deed, obedience, and its results (grace, free gift, justification, righteousness) in Christ. In addition to these dissimilarities, part of the contrast has to do with the extent or degree of the results of Christ's work—"much more." That is, not only are the results of the two men's actions as different as condemnation is from justification, but Christ's results somehow "outdo" Adam's results. The many transgressions come rolling down the hill like a snowball—like an avalanche of snowballs—and Christ's free grace counters the whole thing, like a blast of heat instantly neutralizing it and melting the whole thing away.

In 5:18, Paul writes, "Through one transgression condemnation came to *all*." If we stop there and focus on how transgression came to all, we miss the point. We have to read on. The contrast is meant to magnify Christ. It's the second part that we're meant to remember. "Through one act of righteousness justification came to *all*."

In 5:19, Paul continues: Through one man's (Adam's) disobedience, *many* were made sinners. Through one's (Jesus Christ's) obedience, *many* will be made righteous.

And the contrast is summed up well in 5:20. "Where sin increased, grace super-abounded" *(hypereperisseusen)*. This is one of my favorite New Testament words: Paul takes the verb for "abound," and he adds the prefix "super" to it. Again, the grace outdoes the sin. And this is Paul's point. The whole message of this chapter is the overwhelming power of grace to vanquish sin and death.

Paul's point in Romans 5 is not the power of sin but the power of grace. We know it's his point because of the conclusion he's afraid his hearers will draw when they hear that sin results in grace. Grace is so "much more" effective, enough that the interlocutor at the beginning of chapter 6 doesn't say, "If sin is that deep and death that powerful, then how will we ever be saved?" Instead, grace is so impressive in absorbing everything that sin throws at it, and pouring more grace on it, that the interlocutor asks, "If grace always increases, shall we sin so that grace may abound?" (cf. 6:1). In other words, "If sin causes grace to super-abound, then . . . ?" He'll come back in chapter 6 and answer that apparent logic. For now, however, we should confess that, to the degree that we focus our attention in chapter 5 on sin and its terrible effects, we obscure the main point, namely, that grace triumphs over sin. The fallen state has changed in Christ.

The sin of Adam is the story of us all. His fall is the prototype of our own loss of innocence. But the story of sin and its effects is not the focus of Romans 5. That's fake news. The real headline in Romans 5 is the super-abundant grace of God. Wherever sin is present, God's super-abundant grace is there to set things right. The message of Romans 5 is that the righteousness of Christ is the rightful story of us all—the story that supersedes Adam's, the story that makes all that is wrong right. What Adam did, Christ has undone. What Adam did to us all, Christ, the new prototype for humanity, has undone for us all. While we were yet unlovable sinners, Christ loved us anyway, died for us (5:8), and granted to us, by grace, his resurrection life.

Sin is part of the human family history. But it won't be the last word in the human story. It doesn't have to be the last word in your story. Maybe you've inherited some dysfunction; maybe you've inherited some sinful habits. You've seen it, and now you've practiced it. If you're that person—and it is, at some point, each of us—racked by guilt, by troubles and trials, failed relationships, or, if at some point in the recent past, you've thought, "I just can't go on," or "I don't see how God can love me." As Paul reminds us, wherever sin and chaos are present, grace and life are not just abundant, but over-abundant, super-abundant. God's grace is greater than all our sin, more than enough to set us right, through the death and resurrection of Jesus Christ.

Discussion Questions

1. Have you seen dysfunction in a family get passed down to the next generations?

2. How is Adam, as portrayed in Genesis 2–3, a representative of all humanity?

3. What are some effects of fallenness or original sin? Do you think guilt is one of those inherited effects?

4. If guilt is not inherited, then how are the many/all made sinners?

5. How does Paul present Christ as the new representative of all humanity?

11

Dead to Sin, Alive to God

Romans 6:1–14

IF THERE'S ONE THING that Paul has emphasized thus far in the letter to the Romans, it is that we are saved by grace through faith. As we saw in chapter 4, Paul doesn't quite say we're saved by faith alone, but he does say we are saved by faith apart from works, which is to say, well, through "faith alone." Then, as we saw more recently in Romans 5, even though the taint of sin is long, powerful, and pervasive in the human race, the grace of Christ is more powerful, counteracting and outdoing sin and its effects. Paul explains in Romans 5:16, "Many transgressions brought justification," and in 5:20, "Wherever sin increased, grace was super-abundant." Or to paraphrase Paul, the more sin there was, the more grace and forgiveness came along and obliterated it.

But when it is put that way—and that is precisely the way Paul put it—one might see where this could go. If more sin results in more grace, and if nothing is better than grace, then it sounds like we need more sin. It sounds logical. And so it's time for Paul, and for us, to pause in his letter, to take a break from the flow of the argument, and to address this issue in Romans 6:1–14.

So what about it? Shall we sin more in order to get more grace? What could be better than more grace? It's interesting the lengths we will go to in order to rationalize our wrongdoing, especially in contrast with the wrongdoing of others—a point worth pondering throughout this meditation. In this case, it looks like an attempt at rationalizing. There may be some logic, but it is faulty logic. So Paul responds, "No siree, Bob!" (Romans 6:2). As we've seen earlier in the letter (Romans 3), Paul's imaginary dialogue partner has drawn a false conclusion that some may actually be thinking, and he refutes it. More sin equals more grace? No siree, Bob! But why? Why is this not the transaction that should characterize the Christian life—more sin, more grace? What reason does Paul give? We are dead to sin. Think about that, and let it sink in. Dead to sin.

What does it mean to be dead to something? I think it's pretty self-explanatory, but I'm going to suggest an analogy, in order to drive the point home. Have you ever heard the expression, "You're dead to me"? I hope you haven't heard it said to you, but perhaps you have heard the phrase. What does the expression mean? It means that there is a breach in a human relationship that is so drastic and final, there will no longer be any contact. No connection, no thought for the other person. The "dead" person will be ignored and given absolutely no regard, as if dead. It is a total shunning, a complete ban.

It is, of course, a terrible situation in a human relationship, but the point is clear. If someone says, "You're dead to me," that doesn't mean that they're now going to call or text just once a day instead of twice a day. Being dead to someone doesn't mean that these people will exchange a secret smile as they pass by one another. It means there is no communication, no reaching out, no smiles exchanged.

So what does Paul mean that believers have died to sin? To carry on the analogy, if we've died to sin, that doesn't mean that we sin only once a day instead of twice. It doesn't mean that we give sin a secret wink and acknowledgment. If we've died to sin, Paul asks, how can we live in it any longer? Paul doesn't say, our relationship with sin has gotten a little awkward, or it has grown a little cold, or we should be a little more standoffish with sin now; we're growing apart; we should date someone else. No.

Christ died to sin once for all, and the life he lives, he lives to God (6:10). Likewise, we are dead to sin (6:11). If we're actually *dead* to sin, then there is no communication with it, no contact, no thinking about it, no regard for it. What else could Paul mean by "dead to sin?" We may protest and say, "Yeah, but . . . we all still sin." Yes, we know that objection very well, and depending on how quickly we raise that objection, then I wonder if we are not allowing this hard but very clear word to have its voice and sink in. I wonder if it says more about us than it says about Paul's teaching. We know what it means. Before we re-interpret it, let's hear it. Let's not spit it out before we've had a chance to chew on it for a while. "Dead to sin."

What is Paul's ground for saying that we've died to sin? He says, "Don't you know? You should. It's baptism" (see 6:3–4). Baptism—the initiation rite that he simply assumes all the Roman Christians have experienced—is the embodiment of the death, burial, and resurrection of Jesus. In baptism, all three of these things take place. It is the moment of death to sin, it is the last rite for the dead, and it is the beginning of resurrection life. As surely as physical death marks a definite transition to a new state, a moment in which we come to recognize our total dependence on God, baptism likewise marks the transition between death to sin and a new life of total dependence on God. In baptism, we have died to sin and been raised to a new life.

Another objection may be presented, and though Paul does not directly address it here, it might occur to the reader: If we're saved in baptism, doesn't that contradict being saved by faith apart from works, a point Paul just highlighted in chapter 4? No siree, Bob. They only contradict if baptism is a human work of the law. Those are the works that Paul excludes from justification. But baptism is not a work. It is a reflection of faith and the reception of grace, the moment of covenant commitment. In fact, of the many things we are called to do in response to grace—for example, believe and confess (Romans 10:9–10), repent and be baptized (Acts 2:38)—it is the only verb put in the passive voice. It's the only thing we don't do at all; it's done to us. We are baptized by someone else. In my experience, repenting takes a lot more effort than being baptized!

Being dunked in water is the most passive thing a person can do. Notice kids horsing around at the swimming pool. They will quite readily go under water on their own. But if they are trying to dunk each other, they generally resist it with all their might. Being plunged under water is a very humbling thing to submit to. You cannot breathe. It is a way to kill someone, and that's the point here: A death takes place. No, the only human working is the one doing the baptizing. Otherwise, if baptism is a work at all, it is entirely the work of God, as Paul tells us in Colossians 2:12. Baptism is the operation of God on our hearts. Humans and water do nothing; God's Holy Spirit is the one working in the moment. And it is baptism, Paul says, that is the visible sign of our death to sin.

So what are we to make of ongoing sin in the life of a person who is supposedly dead to sin? It is incongruent, to put it mildly. It is an inconsistency. A dead person doing things that he should not be doing. It reminds me of the crude premise of the old movie, *Weekend at Bernie's*. I've not seen the movie, but I know the main storyline. In this alleged comedy, a man had died, but his friends wanted everyone to think he was still alive, so they put sunglasses on his face, propped him up, and made it look like he was still alive and well. Paul doesn't quite go there, but he is saying that there are some things dead people don't do. If you're dead to sin, you shouldn't *live* in sin any longer. Some things just shouldn't be. At some point, the incongruity will be exposed.

The person who is dead to sin, but still sins, may be more like a zombie. The old, sinful self was put to death, but it still rears its ugly, stinking head. Again, it's just not right. It needs to be put down for good.

As a putting to death, baptism is an act of rebellion. We tend to miss this aspect. At baptism, we look at the one path that leads to despair and death, we size it up, and we positively turn away from that direction toward another direction, another path, another way—the way of life. It is rebellion against the world. It is to cast aside all the glory and glitz and glamor that the world offers. Baptism is the act of renouncing all the world's honors and comforts and idols. It is to put them to death, or properly, it is to be dead to them. We have to die to sinful passions, or else, ironically, they will kill us. It's much better to be dead *to* sin than dead *in* sin.

Dead to the world, dead to the "voices that call me." What are those voices that we're now dead to? What are those sins and temptations that we have died to? Lust? You're dead to that. Greed? You're dead to that. Indifference to the needs of others? You're dead to that. Overeating and overdrinking? You're dead to that. Sloth, envy, anger, seeking status, failing to love? You're dead to all of it. These things that you were once alive to, you, by virtue of your baptism, are now dead to. How can you live any longer in them (6:2)?

There is another movie that I also have not seen called *Dead Man Walking*. "Dead man walking" is what prison guards say as they accompany a death row inmate to the execution chamber. If you have been united with Christ's death in baptism, then, when it comes to sin, Paul says, you are a dead woman, a dead man, walking. But we are not walking to our death. We are walking away from it; we are on the other side of the execution. The old person has died to sin. The new person is dead to sin, a dead man raised to walk "in newness of life" (Romans 6:4). We have been united with Christ's resurrection. We have been raised for something so much better than sin—raised to freedom and life.

And if believers have died and been raised in Christ, then death no longer has mastery (6:9). When you're dead, you've got nothing to lose. This is why Christians for nearly 2,000 years have been able to stare down their persecutors and say, "You're threatening me with death? I've already died." It's like Lazarus after being raised from the dead. Do you think he was afraid of the Jewish opponents who wanted to kill him again? I suspect he was not. And, on a more mundane and daily level, there is no sacrifice too costly for us, no burden too hard for us to bear. The world's values and its accolades and trophies mean nothing to the one who has died to them. The old has passed away; behold, all things have become new (2 Corinthians 5:17)! The change wrought by the grace of Christ in baptism is as different as death is from life.

As long as we are in this life, which is a testing, separation from sin is rarely as final as death. Perfection does not happen in a day; we remain imperfect. For all our imperfections, Scripture assures us that there is grace, that there is the infinite love of God, always reaching out and ready to embrace and, if necessary, ready to punish in order to redeem us. Yes, we acknowledge the imperfection and the nagging presence of sin. We don't love God enough, and we don't love each other enough. *Of course* we're not perfect.

But haven't we acknowledged that enough? Paul doesn't seem to think we need to keep talking about our imperfection. Acknowledging the ongoing temptation and the fall into sin does not mean we should stop talking about the true goal. Dead to sin, and alive to God in Christ. This is what Christ calls us to—perfection in him, and we must not be ashamed of that. As Ephesians 2:8–10 says, we are saved by grace through faith for good works. It is time for the good works, for sin to end its reign. We must not be ashamed to expect progress in our understanding and practice of the faith. We must not be ashamed to say to each other and to ourselves, "We have died to sin; how can we live in it any longer?" We can't. And Paul's point in Romans 6 is, "By grace, you are in Christ; now act like it." Paul's not trying to make us feel bad. He intends to motivate us, to challenge us. He is putting before our eyes the goal that we have already accepted. How will we respond?

Perhaps you have never been joined with the dying and rising of Christ in baptism. Christ calls you to be born of the water and the Spirit in baptism (John 3:5). His grace is more than abundant. If you haven't been acting like or thinking like someone who has died to sin and been raised to life in Christ, if you haven't been acting like or thinking like someone who has been united with Christ in his death and resurrection, then what are you waiting for? In the name of Jesus, and through the power of the Holy Spirit, bury that old, dead, sinful person, and be raised to walk in newness of life.

Discussion Questions

1. Have you ever been tempted by the logic, "More sin equals more grace"?

2. If grace is always available, why should we not keep on sinning?

3. Are you "dead to sin?" If not, what would look different if you were?

4. How does baptism symbolize or re-present a death?

5. What sins have you died to that used to tempt you but no longer do (or tempt less)?

6. What can we do about the sins that still tempt us?

12

License to Live

Romans 6:15–23

IN THE FIRST PART of Romans 6, Paul focused on being dead to sin and alive to God in Christ. In the latter part of this chapter, he focuses more on the metaphor he introduced in verses 6 and 7—namely, instead of being slaves to sin, believers are slaves to righteousness and to God. But he's still answering the same question, which is, stated succinctly: What does being "saved by grace" mean for the Christian life? So we continue to ask and answer that question, here with reference to Paul's dominant metaphor of slavery.

One of the core themes of the Christian faith is the reality of grace. If you've ever had the experience of trying to sum up your faith—maybe to teach a child or to tell a seeking unbeliever—you can't go very long without talking about grace. Think about the elevator presentation or the airplane passenger presentation of your faith, the two-minute version (that's a long elevator or short airplane ride). Whatever things you would include in the two-minute version, if you get it right, then those are probably the core beliefs. And no summary of the faith would be complete without grace.

Some things are clear about this important concept of grace. As we all know, "We are saved by grace" (Ephesians 2:8). Some statement like that is likely to make it into your summary version. But beyond that brief summary, I wonder if there aren't some *misconceptions* about grace—what grace is and what it means for the Christian life. As we meditate here on grace, let's think about what grace is and what grace is not.

First of all, the word *grace* simply means gift. It is a wrapped present. But what does grace mean in its biblical context? Paul calls this grace "indescribable" (2 Corinthians 9:15), but I'll try to describe it anyway. I always heard that grace is unmerited favor, a point we made in a previous reflection. In other words, from the recipient's perspective, it is an undeserved gift, getting a benefit that we don't earn. That is a good initial description. But think about it also from the perspective of the giver, in this case, God. Grace is an un-owed gift, an unnecessary, extravagant donation. From God, it is an expression of freely-given, divine love, a gift that we cannot give to ourselves. As the nineteenth-century writer George MacDonald put it, "There is no claim on God that springs from us: all is from him."

In this sense, grace should not be narrowly conceived; if *all* is from God, then grace concerns much more than salvation. Grace is any gift from God. Creation out of nothing is God's first act of grace, and the forming of humanity out of the dust is a gift. Our very existence, as well as our continued thriving, is a result of grace. "We live and we move and we are" by grace (Acts 17:28). Surely the greatest gift of all is God becoming man, taking on human nature, in order to purify it and lift it up into fellowship with the divine, so that human nature can partake of the divine nature (2 Peter 1:4). Everything God does in eternity (past, present, and future), and everything God does in our lives to bring us into that divine fellowship of Father, Son, and Spirit—that is, everything he does to accomplish our salvation—is grace. It is the summation of his goodness to humanity.

And now, what grace is *not*. Grace is not selective, in the sense that God wants only a few people to be saved. On the contrary, God wants all people to be saved and to come to knowledge of the truth (1 Timothy 2:4). Grace is available to all and able to save all.

Furthermore, grace is not irresistible. It's not that God chooses, and then we have no say in the matter. God's grace enables us to love; it perfects our nature, but it does not override our freedom.

Now, when we think about the grace of salvation, here are some misconceptions that may be a little more common among us, and were also common in the first century, because they are directly addressed in the New Testament.

First misconception: "We do 50 percent of the work and God makes up the rest"—or 90 percent, or 1 percent (I suppose it depends on how good a person is). I suspect that, when it is said that some denominations have neglected the doctrine of grace, this may be what they mean: promoting the idea that we *work* for our salvation. But no. God initiates and completes salvation. It is not without our acceptance, our response; call it conditions of acceptance. Faith is the condition, expressed in repentance and baptism. But it's not that we are doing a percentage of the work. God does all the work. Again, Ephesians 2:8–10 is instructive: We are saved by grace through faith *for* good works. As Paul says, Abraham was not saved by his works, nor was David (Romans 4:1–8), and neither are we.

To be clear, accepting salvation through faith is not earning it. We do not earn it or even attempt to earn it, in which case it wouldn't be a gift anymore (Romans 4:4). Think more generally about conditions of acceptance. Let's say someone comes and gives you a check for $10,000. Not because you worked for that person, and not because that person was trying to buy some favor from you. He just knew that you could use the money.

To fully receive that check, to get any use out of it at all, you must endorse the check and take it to the bank. Otherwise, the offer of the check does not benefit at all. But, having endorsed it and taken it to the bank, having deposited the money in your account, would you say, "Well, they did their part in giving that money, but I did my part in acquiring it; I worked for it; I contributed, oh, about 10 percent to the process . . ."? Or would you say, "My free choice to accept the money made all the difference; I could have that money or not have it as I choose"? Would we say all that? Tone is not easily communicated in writing. But no, we would never say those things! It's *all* due to the donor. In fact, we could add to the analogy that the donor provided you with the car to drive to the bank and probably opened the bank account for you.

Christ is the ultimate almsgiver who comes to us first, and before we even want it, offers himself to us. As Revelation 3:20 says, it is Christ who stands at the door and knocks. We can let him in. But we didn't go out and seek him; we didn't bring him to our door and cause him to seek us. Our letting him in doesn't change the fact that our response is just that: a response to the grace that comes before us. So, no, it's not that we carried ourselves thus far, and God took us the rest of the way. When we were unlovable, God loved us. We can't stand on our own, so God picks us up and carries us.

And now, for what I suspect is today's most egregious misunderstanding of grace. It is a misconception that also was prevalent in the first century. It goes something like this: "Since believers do nothing to earn salvation, then grace means that being good and doing good works finally do not matter. Once saved, always saved." Paul was worried about the influence of something like this in the Roman church. "If we sin more, then we get more grace. What's better than more grace?" (see Romans 6:1).

It sounds logical, but that is not how grace works. It reminds me of a scene in the Star Wars movie, *The Force Awakens*, where the old veteran Han Solo asks the newcomer Finn how he plans to infiltrate and disable the shields at the enemy base, and Finn says, "I don't know . . . We'll figure it out. We'll use the force." Han immediately sets him straight, "That's not how the force works!" I can imagine Paul saying, "That's not how grace works!" In 6:2, he sets the Roman Christians straight: "By no means! No siree, Bob!" You've died to sin, how can you live in it any longer? As we have seen, baptism is the symbol of, and the moment of, death and resurrection. Dead to sin, and alive for God.

The epistle of Jude also claims that it was an ongoing problem in the church. He warns against those who would turn "the grace of our God into licentiousness" (Jude 4). The NIV effectively conveys the gist when it says that these people have turned the grace of God into a "license for immorality." What is a license for *immorality*? A license is a permit, a permit to do something. License implies freedom.

In recent years, my family has heard quite a bit about the license. We have three teenagers who all turned sixteen within a span of four years. Turning sixteen meant one thing, and only one thing, to them. They were of legal driving age. After successful completion of the driving test, they were able to drive without an adult in the car. These have been exciting times, for which I appreciate the reader's prayers. License means permission, liberty. Rules and restrictions are for the immature; freedom is for the mature. But license can be misused, leading to unwanted slavery.

There is a license to drive. A license to fish and hunt. Restaurants have to get a license if they want to sell alcohol. Agent 007 has a "license to kill." *Grace* is a license, but a license for what?

For some, according to Jude and Paul, grace is a license for immorality. Do you know what this means? This would be a misuse of the freedom that grace provides. But you can see, easily enough, how this could happen. As Paul and Jude both feared, the fact of God's eternal love causes some people to take advantage of his mercy and forgiveness.

From this perspective, sin is bad, but it's not really *that* bad; it's not of eternal consequence. Why? Because I can ask for forgiveness later. Does this sound familiar? We may not say it, but do we assume it and act out of that assumption?

But is this the way we treat each other? I hope not. If we offend our spouse, and they forgive us, would we immediately think, well, it's no big deal then! Carry on with my ways, and get forgiveness again later! Only the immature think this way. If it would be insulting to treat a loved one this way, how much more the Almighty God? When God is the one offering forgiveness, is this way of thinking not a misuse of grace, an attempted abuse of God's love? God's people must realize that although license implies freedom, license for immorality means, paradoxically, a license to bondage, under the control of sin and sinful desire. And that's what Paul is pointing out in Romans 6. We sometimes act like it is impossible to fall away from grace, which becomes a pretext for becoming a slave to sin. Freedom without limits becomes slavery—slavery to sin.

Yes, only the immature think that way, and too often our response to grace is impoverished, childish. It is like *some* teenagers who taste for the first time the freedom of adult-free driving. A driver's license is not meant to be a permit for intentionally reckless driving. The primary purpose of driving is to get the driver from point A to B safely and efficiently, and secondarily to enjoy the journey. But reckless driving, perhaps temporarily enjoyable to the teenager behind the wheel, is potentially and almost certainly counter-productive to those two goals. Sooner or later, that kind of driving will result in a wreck, which then prevents one from getting to point B, and also generally ends up being less enjoyable. Freedom without limits becomes slavery. The license entails great responsibility. But slavery to righteousness, as Paul reminds his readers throughout Romans 6, results in *true* freedom. To be a slave to righteousness is to live freely and abundantly.

So we need to learn the lesson of grace. We need to listen to what grace is teaching us. Yes, not only does grace save us, it instructs us. The point is very clear in Titus 2:11–14. Grace doesn't just save us, but it also "teaches" us, trains us to say "no" to ungodliness. Will we heed the lesson? God calls us to participate, to cooperate in this great project of restoring creation back to himself. Grace meets us where we are, but it doesn't leave us there. Through grace, God purifies us and makes us eager to do good. Grace carries us, yes, but not to make us lazy; grace picks us up and teaches us how to walk. Grace frees us to be the kind of people we were made to be. Grace instructs us how to live righteously. When I say grace, I mean God; "God" is the agent.

Grace *ought* to inspire its recipients to work harder. A former colleague of mine was teaching a university course on the book of Romans. The students did not do very well on the first two exams, and they were hoping for some extra credit, so he thought he would attempt an object lesson (since grace was a prominent topic in their class). He announced to the class that everyone would get a 100 percent on the upcoming third exam, regardless of their actual performance. He would still mark their tests for them, but, as a gift, he would record a 100 for everyone. It sounds good. When he announced this, he read to them 1 Corinthians 15:10, where Paul says, "But by the grace of God I am what I am, and his grace to me was not empty. But I labored more than all of them—yet not I, but the grace of God that was with me." God's grace was "not empty," not without effect. Grace spurred Paul to work harder. He had become a slave of righteousness.

As the apostle Paul worked harder, so the professor wanted the *students* to be motivated to continue to learn, study, and work as hard or even harder than before for the third exam. How would they respond to the grace? Well, test day came, and a few students did better, but the class average was virtually the same as on the first two tests—which was not great. It's not clear that they were inspired to "labor more." It's not clear that they learned the lesson that grace teaches. There are many differences, but in some ways this scenario is analogous to our reception of grace. We know that we are forgiven and saved, and we know that we will get a 100. So how will we respond?

Let not God's grace be without effect. Grace is a "license," but for what? Grace is not a license for immorality that leads to bondage and death. Grace is freedom, a license for *morality*. Grace is a license to live— to truly live. It is a license to love. A license to love our neighbor as our very self. It is a license to care, the freedom to forgive, a permit for peace and patience. Grace is a license to enjoy God's good creation to its fullest, to enjoy one's family and friends, to enjoy one's marriage or singleness, to enjoy one's work and virtuous leisure—yes, to enjoy one's very existence. Grace is a license to rejoice, even in the midst of suffering and heartache, knowing that God will kill death, end loneliness, and right what is wrong. Grace grants us the right to approach the throne of God boldly. Grace is a license to grow eternally in our knowledge of God, endlessly extending our reach towards him, as he invites us and draws us into higher heights.

Grace is the invitation and the assistance to grow toward perfection. The freedom to be more like God, and to see others and all of creation through his eyes—all of this is the purpose of grace. A license to live as "slaves to righteousness"—for this is what it means to live freely and abundantly—in this life and in the next.

I've heard it said that it's hard to be saved by grace. It is. Maybe it *shouldn't* be, but it is. We react with one of two extremes. Either we don't want to be carried, or we never want to walk. On the one extreme, we think we can do it on our own, and we think we've got it all together. "I've got this. I may need some grace in the beginning, but not as much as those people over there. Isn't God, and everyone else here, lucky to have me?" Then we experience the fall that follows after pride; we realize we have not done enough, and then we despair, deprived of the grace that we thought we didn't need.

On the other extreme, we think we can never make any progress, and so we have given up trying. "After all, we're saved by God's grace, not our goodness, so what's the point in striving?" But our reception of forgiveness requires contrition and a change of heart and mind. Either way, if we focus on whether we've done enough or haven't, if we focus on how good we are or how bad we are—guess what?—either way, we're focusing on the wrong thing. We're focusing on ourselves, when the focus should be on Christ. As Romans 6:21 says, we should focus on being slaves to God, leading to freedom, holiness, and eternal life.

God, by his grace, picks us up and carries us. But he also teaches us, inspires us for good works, sets us on our feet to walk the path, accompanying Christ on the journey, focused on him, following in his footsteps.

The message of grace is both comforting and convicting. This message calls for some introspection and self-diagnosis, because only the individual soul knows what it needs to hear. Which part of the message do you need to hear? Maybe it depends on which day I ask. But let's take today, right now. If it is comfort that you need, forgiveness that you seek, then let God lift you up and carry you. You haven't done enough, and you never can. So receive his forgiveness. Be filled with the strength to persevere. Find joy in knowing God in Christ. Ask for the prayers and help of his people. Thanks be to God for his grace that saves!

But be honest. Maybe it is conviction and admonition that you need. I suspect this is the more common need among modern Western Christians. If it is, then take heart, because the abuse of grace, the presumption of forgiveness—this, too, can be forgiven for the sincerely penitent. You've been carried long enough now. By God's abundant grace, be empowered to change your will. Embrace the license, the freedom, to put childish ways behind you—to put behind you the person that you are not—and embrace the license to live and to be the person you were truly called to be. Thanks be to God for his grace that instructs!

In light of these truths, Romans 6 invites readers to ask some introspective questions. To what are you enslaved? To sin, or to God and to righteousness? How would you know? What are the indications? What are the signs that reflect what it is that you serve?

Discussion Questions

1. Do you agree that it can seem hard to be saved by grace? Why or why not?

2. Can grace cause us to take sin too lightly or be lazy in doing good works?

3. Which do you need to hear more—the *comforting* or the *convicting* message of grace?

4. What are the signs that indicate whether you are a slave to sin or a slave to righteousness?

13

Dead to the Law

Romans 7:1–6

IN THIS WHOLE SECTION of Romans, chapters 5–8, Paul is keen on contrasting life outside of Christ with life in Christ. Remember the point and
counter-point in Romans 5—Adam versus Christ. The gift, Paul said, is
not like the transgression. Where sin increased, grace super-increased,
super-abounded. In chapter 6, he said that believers are dead to sin and
alive to God and to righteousness. We are no longer slaves of sin, but
slaves of God and of righteousness, and therefore free. Paul has made the
point that something has changed—by grace, through faith, in baptism.
Throughout it all, Paul has emphasized the transition, the change.

This theme of contrasting one way of life with another continues
in chapters 7 and 8. We're going to focus now on the first six verses of
chapter 7, the burden of which is to set up the remaining set of differences and contrasts.

And these differences come to focus on the law. The law, or Torah,
that over the centuries had been so important to the Jewish covenant
with God and to Jewish identity. This law includes the ethical code that
even gentile Christians have been taught and have come to appreciate as
important in their life of covenant with the God of Israel. Let's just call it
the rules, the do's and don'ts. So where does this law fit in to the story of
salvation and Christian living?

86

So what is the change like? In Romans 7:1–6, Paul compares it to marriage, specifically, to the end of one marriage and the beginning of another.

A married woman, he says, is bound to her husband as long as her husband lives. For her to marry another, while he is still alive, would be wrong. If he dies, she is no longer bound but is free to marry another. The marriage covenant has been nullified. It is only an illustration, though what Paul says here about marriage is true. I'm assuming most marriage vows still include this agreement—only death parts marriage partners. It is the only prenuptial agreement that the Bible has to offer. And the survivor gets everything.

But it is only an illustration to get to his main point, which is laid out briefly here in 7:4–6. It concerns the law and the believer's relationship to the law. Paul uses the marriage analogy to say that we are no longer joined to the law.

But here's where it gets a little tricky. We might have expected Paul to say that the law has now died and so we are now free to marry another, namely, Christ. But that's not exactly what he says. Carrying on the language of the change that is wrought in us by grace and in baptism, Paul says that it is we who have died. As he declared in chapter 6, we are the ones who die to sin. The language in 7:4 is similar: "You died to the law." According to verse 6, we have died to the covenant that bound us.

It's interesting that he doesn't say that the law has died or that the law is nullified. Remember back in 3:31: "Do we nullify the law? No siree, Bob! We uphold the law." He uses that same Greek verb *nullify* here in 7:6—but in a strange sort of way. Literally, "We have been nullified from the law." The law has not been nullified; we have been nullified from *it.*

What in the world does that mean? Presumably, it means something like being "released" or "discharged" or "delivered" from it, as most translations have it. But still what's the difference in the law being nullified and we being nullified from it, dying to it?

It may be a bit confusing here because Paul seems to be both claiming the law and distancing us from it. In our new situation, there is continuity and discontinuity. Let's return to the marriage analogy that he introduces. Some who are reading this have, sadly, experienced the loss of a spouse. That experience will eventually be felt by roughly half of all people who are married. Some will marry again. In a new marriage, there is both continuity and discontinuity. The discontinuity is obvious. This is a different person, with a different background and story, different needs and desires and habits. The marriage is characterized by newness.

But there is also continuity with the previous marriage. Some things are the same. After all, forgive the tautology, but getting married is getting married, and it is a different action from, say, going jogging. (There are some similarities between jogging and marriage, but the similarities are highly figurative and not very deep.) Marriage is also different from a close friendship with someone of the same sex. This new marriage is, in some ways, like the previous one. They are both marriages. Some things do not change. Ladies, he's still a man. The way to his heart will likely still be through his stomach. Gentlemen, she's still a woman. You should still probably put the toilet seat down. The point is that there is continuity and discontinuity. But you could get yourself in trouble by assuming that something is the same when it's not.

And so it is with the law. There is continuity and discontinuity. It's not that the moral requirements of the law have died, so much as we have died to a certain way of relating to them. It is clear, based on 3:31 and other places, that we still have moral requirements, and that these moral requirements probably match up pretty well with what was spelled out in the law. As 7:6 says, we are still to *serve* or *be a slave*, the verb form of the same word he uses throughout chapter 6. We are slaves or servants of God, as 6:4 says, raised to walk "in newness of life." And so, as 7:6 states, we continue to slave or serve "in newness." That toilet seat still needs to come down, but now for a different person.

And this is why the subject of law is always a difficult one, especially in Paul's writings. In this changed situation, there is some similarity. But again, what is the newness? What has changed?

Even when we think about law, if we think about it long enough, we recognize that law can seem good or bad, and it can have different connotations and meanings, depending on a number of factors.

When we see "law" in this chapter, we should think "law-keeping." It's not just any law-keeping, but the method or spirit in which the law is kept. The idea is probably conveyed well by the notion of "rule-keeping." What comes to your mind when you hear *rule-keeping*? The rules may be good, as Paul later says (7:14), and keeping them is right. But what I mean by this is keeping rules for the sake of the rules themselves. That is, the rules become ends in themselves.

Paul uses two words here to describe the old way of relating to the law. The first is "flesh" (7:5). We have seen this word already in Romans, but it is about to become very prominent in chapters 7–8. Look ahead at how many times the word *flesh* appears. If you have an NIV translation, it will nearly always translate Paul's use of *flesh* as "sinful nature." Everywhere that the NIV Bible says *sinful nature*, the word is simply *flesh*. *Sinful nature* is not the best translation and could leave the wrong impression. We are not sinful by nature; sin is *unnatural*, a distortion of our created nature. We most fully reflect human nature made in the image of God when we are holy, not sinful.

The word here is simply *flesh*. At the same time, though, that literal translation is also incomplete, as is clear from the context and throughout Paul's writings. When Paul writes *flesh*, he does not mean the meat on your bones, at least not primarily. For Paul, flesh is humanity without Christ, broken humans without any aid from God. Brokenness, fallenness, domination by sin. To say the least, it is spiritual immaturity. Paul's point is that we are inclined, by the flesh, to break the good laws that God has given.

The second word that describes an old way of relating to the law is *letter* (7:6). Some translations here say "written code," but the word is simply *letter*. We sometimes talk about following the letter of a certain law versus the spirit of that law. Jesus definitely points to the spirit. Following the letter of the sixth commandment (do not murder) is pretty easy . . . on most days. Following its spirit (do not be angry [Matthew 5:22]) is, on most days, more challenging, especially while driving in heavy traffic. But that was the spirit behind the law in the first place. It is the immature and imperfect follower who boasts at the end of the day, "I guess I've got that sixth commandment down—I didn't murder anyone today."

Let's use that idea of immaturity or imperfection and think about different ways that law-keeping or rule-following can go wrong when someone is imperfect or immature. What can a good rule become when it is communicated to the immature, to the flesh? If you tell a five-year-old boy, don't jump on the bed, what is he going to start thinking about? Jumping on the bed! And depending on his upbringing to that point, he may even be *more* likely to jump on the bed than if nothing had been said at all.

The fault lies not with the rule. The rule is fine. It is not an end in itself, but it's a means for flourishing. It's meant to protect the bed, the furniture and things right next to the bed, and, yes, even the boy. A mature boy already knows all this. He has been taught it, or perhaps already learned the lesson the hard way. Paul says that when we were in the flesh (*"were,"* past tense), the rules themselves could actually bring the idea of breaking them—sin—to our minds and hearts and lives.

What about following the letter and not the spirit? Sometimes a written rule, intended to help people, can be followed to the detriment of those same people. If a teacher drills into her kindergarten class, "Keep your hands to yourselves," it is for their well-being. It is to teach them respect for the other person's body and space, to maintain their hygiene, to minimize distractions, and the like.

But imagine a child falls on the playground, gets hurt, needs help up, and no one helps. Why? The children are obeying the rule, keeping their hands to themselves. Well, they've missed the point. Likewise, Jesus taught that the Sabbath law was made for human flourishing—that should be clear to the mature. So it's permissible to heal on the Sabbath. The law is not the end in itself. The Sabbath is for man, not man for the Sabbath.

And this gets at a big question about Christian ethics. Mature Christian living is not a list of do's and don'ts. The moral perfection that is the goal, this perfect love, is the love of a mature agent, a mature lover. When we become mature, we do what is right not because we have to, or have to be told to, or are threatened with punishment so that we'll do what is right. No, the mature do what is right because that is what they want to do. The mature follow the good whether it's written down or not, whether there are consequences or not, simply because it's the right thing to do. They know what is right and do it, without need of rules or case laws.

The immature need rules. The immature follow a law because it is a written law. And if the maturity level is relatively low, more rules need to be posted and more cases anticipated. What is true on the playground is also true for society at large.

The immature, imperfect person hears, "You're saved by grace," and thinks, "I have a license for immorality." But the mature, perfect person that God calls us to be, hears, "No rules," and thinks, "I can do whatever I want, and all I want to be and do is the good." God gives us unlimited freedom to pursue the good, to become perfect. The mature person hears, "You're saved by grace," and thinks, "It is a license for morality, a license to live." A life of perfect, mature love is a life that thrives.

Now, of course, you shouldn't discard the rules; you can't just break a rule and claim that you're following the spirit. You have to start with the letter. We must begin at the basic level where all the immature begin. We have to know the letter, respect it, and follow it. Starting with the letter will help us know the reason—that is, the spirit of holiness—behind it, which is the most important thing. And to the degree that we remain imperfect and immature, we need the rules.

It is hard to know whether Paul has all this in mind when he con-trasts, on the one hand, flesh and letter with, on the other hand, spirit. But what he is after is showing how a good law, in the hands of the immature and imperfect, can become detrimental. What is needed to accompany the law is more maturity, a more perfect way of being a slave to God and to righteousness, a more holy Spirit. The truly perfected disciple acts from character, with virtue conformed to the image of Christ. She is not concerned primarily with rules or their consequences.

Both flesh and letter are opposed to Spirit. It is the difference be-tween something being imposed on you and receiving that same thing as a gift. It is the difference between following a rule because it has been written down and following it simply because it's good. It is the difference between obeying a rule because there are consequences for disobedience and obeying it because it leads to flourishing and reflects the nature of God. It is the difference between the law as an end in itself and the law as a means to a greater, nobler end. To oversimplify, it is rules versus relationship, when it should be rules that enhance relationship.

We are dead to the old way of keeping the law. The proximate, most immediate goal of being dead to this kind of law-keeping is that God's people might bear fruit for God (7:4). We are freed to slave or serve in "newness of the Spirit" (7:6). The ultimate goal, of course, is that we would be conformed more and more to the image of Christ, that we would reflect his glory (2 Corinthians 3:18), that we would live in endless fellowship with the God of eternal love.

What does that look like on the ground? What does it look like to be controlled by the flesh, bearing fruit to death (Romans 7:5)? As I asked in a previous meditation, what are the signs that someone is controlled by the flesh and by sinful passions that bear fruit for death? What are the in-dications in your life? What would we say are indications that someone is serving in the newness of the Spirit, bearing fruit to God? When we look at our own lives, which do we see? What do you think others would see?

That is the question that Paul puts to us, as we proceed through chapters 7 and 8. Are you joined to the law, to the rule-keeping of the letter, pursued with a fleshly mindset that despises the law and the law-giver? Or are you joined to Christ, with the spirit of the law written on your heart, eager to bear fruit for God?

Discussion Questions

1. How would you explain the Christian's new relationship to the law of God?

2. What's the difference between following the law by rule-keeping and following the law without or beyond the rules?

3. Can you think of cases where following the letter of the law clearly betrays or violates the spirit of the law?

4. What does it look like to bear fruit for God or to bear fruit for death?

14

Bearing Fruit for Death

Romans 7:7–25

WHEN I WAS A child, I was not exposed to any classic literature at home. What I was exposed to, every Saturday morning, was *Looney Tunes* cartoons. This was mostly the extent of my cultural literacy. One could do worse. There were some occasional references to the modern Western canon of literature and art. For instance, the "Rabbit of Seville," starring Bugs Bunny, brought me about as close as I ever came to opera.

It was also through *Looney Tunes* that I encountered characters and a story inspired by the nineteenth-century classic by Robert Louis Stevenson, *The Strange Case of Dr. Jekyll and Mr. Hyde*. In at least three cartoons, we find elements of this story being played out by *Looney Tunes* characters. What I learned about this story from the cartoons was this: a normal, mild-mannered character, Jekyll, often bullied by a stronger antagonist, drinks a potion concocted in a laboratory, and transforms into Hyde, a larger, scary monster.

In a couple of these episodes, the transformed monster, though grotesque, can now effect justice by getting back at the bullies. In one cartoon, it is Sylvester the Cat getting a little revenge against some dogs. In a later cartoon, it is Tweety Bird who gets to switch places and kick around Sylvester the Cat a bit. So, even though the monster is hideous, the viewer is led to root for that character. You want him to drink the potion. It's like Marvel Comics' the Incredible Hulk, who was also inspired by Jekyll and Hyde.

All this is quite different from Stevenson's original story, published in 1886, which I read later as an adult. Mr. Hyde, it turns out, was not someone you want to root for. In Stevenson's story, Dr. Jekyll indeed makes a potion that, when he drinks it, temporarily changes him, but into a hideous, *smaller* man, who, in disguise, is free to pursue his own lusts and violence in secret, with no regard for anyone else or even for his own moral conscience. It is not for justice or even personal revenge that he drinks the potion, but for pure lust. He begins to do this on a regular basis at night. And every time that he changes back to the respectable Dr. Jekyll, he always feels remorse for his actions.

At one point, he vows never to drink the potion again, never to become Mr. Hyde, never again to indulge those "pleasures" that he knows only cause pain to himself and others in the long run. But the temptation is powerful. What will he do? He articulates the dilemma in his written confession: "To cast in my lot with Jekyll [the good guy], was to die to those appetites which I had long secretly indulged and had of late begun to pamper. To cast it in with Hyde [the bad guy], was to die to a thousand interests and aspirations, and to become, at a blow and forever, despised and friendless." As Dr. Jekyll himself goes on to acknowledge, "Strange as my circumstances were, the terms of this debate are as old and commonplace as man; much the same inducements and alarms cast the die for any tempted and trembling sinner."

And it is indeed a common theme in literature, in art, and in philosophy, common enough perhaps to seem all too familiar to us. Do we sometimes feel like Dr. Jekyll? Do sin and its effects linger, rearing their ugly head when you don't want them to? Does your will feel pulled in two different directions? Is it possible to will two different, contradictory things—the good and the evil—at the same time?

As Jekyll said, the problem is as old and widespread as mankind. The second-century Stoic philosopher Epictetus spoke about the inner contradictions of a sinner: "What he wills, he does not, and what he wills not, he does." This raises an interesting question about the will. So, do you really will it the sin or not? When you sin, do you do something that you know is wrong, or do you make some excuse that seeks justification for the action? Or both? Do you will it or not will it?

The figure of Medea in Greek mythology provides a classic example of this knowing assent to the wrong. In Euripides's play from the fifth-century BC, Medea, who is about to kill her own children, says, "I learn what kind of evils I am about to do,/ But anger gets the better of my deliberations." In Ovid's later, first-century AD narrative, Medea, driven by desire for her husband Jason who abandoned her, says, "Desire persuades me one way, the mind another. I see the better and approve, but I follow the worse." She then kills her children as revenge on Jason for leaving her. She knew it was wrong, but still she did it.

For a more modern and less stark example, take a habit like smoking. Imagine you are a smoker, but you really want to quit. You know smoking is unhealthy. You go all day at work without smoking a cigarette. Yet you go home, and when no one is looking, you sneak into your backyard and light up! The temptation is powerful. The habit is powerful. Your body's reaction to the nicotine is powerful. You want to quit, yet you want a cigarette, too. Which do you want to do? Both? Which do you want more?

And if you cannot relate to smoking, then substitute a scenario you can relate to. Maybe it's not cigarettes, but it's those little cake donut holes. It reminds me of Augustine's prayer before his commitment to Christ: "Grant me chastity and self-control, but please not yet."

This is what ancient philosophers called weakness of will or unrestraint—when a weak-willed individual acts against his or her own better judgment. As Augustine described it, "Inasmuch as it [the mind] issues the command, it does will it, but inasmuch as the command is not carried out, it does not will it." Like Jekyll acknowledged, choosing one way means dying to a few evil appetites. The other way means dying to a thousand good hopes and aspirations and friends. The choice should be obvious. But the wrong choice is made anyway. This is weakness of will.

Paul writes about this very thing in the text under consideration here, Romans 7:7–25. After reading it, what do you think? First of all, remember the context. It is a continuation of the themes of Romans 5–8, contrasting life according to the flesh and according to the Spirit, life in Adam versus life in Christ.

Back in Romans 7:5–6, we have the contrast again, setting up the rest of chapters 7 and 8. Bearing fruit for God (Romans 7:4) versus bearing fruit for death (7:5). Chapter 8 will be about bearing fruit for God. What he's talking about here in the rest of chapter 7 is what it looks like to bear fruit for death. It is a picture of the flesh and sinful passions at work in one's members, serving in the oldness of the letter (7:6). What we have here is *not* a description of the Christian life, and its purpose is *not* to give comfort to people who continually lose the battle to sin. Let me explain.

Paul illustrates the life of the flesh by speaking in the person of someone else, someone that he simply names "I." You may have noticed a lot of "I" in verses 7–25, more than usual in this letter. First, let's take verses 7–13. Who is the "I" or *ego* (Greek for I) in verses 7–13? Who is this "I?"

Contrary to first appearance, the "I" in this section is not Paul himself. It is instructive that no Christian in the first 350 years of reading Romans thought this was Paul speaking about himself. Rather, early church fathers read this as a figure of speech. Paul is using a rhetorical technique of speaking in the person of someone else. We should think about it like a soliloquy being performed in another role or persona. Let's remember that this is the section that fleshes out the life of sinful passion.

According to verse 9, the "I" once lived without or apart from the law. Jews like Paul never describe themselves as living apart from the law, even in their innocence before the age of accountability. The "I" here in Romans 7:9 lived apart from the law until the commandment came. Not commandments (plural), but one commandment. As a result, he sinned and died. The commandment was good, but he was not. He coveted something, and his coveting was actually the first sin.

Who is it that Paul is describing? Who in biblical history lived at one time without the law, then was given one commandment, was deceived by sin, desired the forbidden object because it looked good, then transgressed that command and died? It was Adam. One can read back through verses 7–13 with Adam in mind and see how it fits. Paul is continuing the Adam/Christ typology begun in chapter 5. It is easy to forget what we encountered in chapter 5 if we read slowly and meditate on each paragraph (a practice I'm encouraging here). But, as the original audience heard this letter being read aloud in the assembly, it was only about five minutes ago. This Adam/Christ line of thought was interrupted briefly by the chapter 6 diatribe about how those who are dead to sin cannot live in it any longer. And now, back to unnamed Adam.

What was the purpose of the commandment, according to 7:10? It was for life and flourishing. But then sin personified (that is, the serpent from Genesis 3) deceives.

And then comes Romans 7:14–25. Paul uses the present tense now. Remember Mr. Hyde, Medea, and the smoker? This is the life that Paul is describing in 7:14–25. Life in Adam, introduced back in chapter 5. It is a terrible situation—this "body of death" (7:24). This life in the shadow of

Adam is summed up in verse 25b: "I myself in the mind serve the law of God but in the flesh the law of sin."

Remember from chapter 5 that the story of Adam is the story of us all? Isn't it? By the way, this may be one reason it is hard to tell at first that it was Adam here in chapter 7, because it sounds like the common human experience, which really is the function of Adam (the prototypical "man") in Scripture.

Again we ask, who is the "I/ego," now of verses 14–25? Once again, it can't be Paul. This person enslaved to sin does not fit with Paul's self-descriptions elsewhere—he is zealous, with a clear conscience, "according to righteousness that comes by the law, faultless" (Philippians 3:4–6). The "ego/I" of Romans 7:14–25 is *everyone* in Adam. Paul has shifted from past tense (Romans 7:7–13) to present (7:14–25). He was speaking in the person of Adam after the fall, but now he speaks in the person of all who remain caught in the Adam cycle.

Several possibilities present themselves. It could be a Christian or non-Christian trying in vain to keep all the rules. Or an orthodox Jew under the law, or a Jewish or gentile Christian in the same situation. It could be a non-Christian, perhaps on the way to faith, realizing at the end their need for deliverance. If it is a Christian at all, then this is a struggling, immature, carnal, or fleshly Christian: "The law is spiritual, but I am fleshly" (7:14). Remember what "flesh" means? It is not the ideal Christian. Not what a Christian should be. To be sure, it's not the worst person in the world. It's not someone with no moral conscience. This is not someone who doesn't care or can't see the difference between good and evil. This is someone who knows better, but just doesn't have the willpower to do it. Something is missing.

One thing is clear: Whoever is being described here, Paul is not intending to describe the normal expectations for the Christian life. This is not a justified person, under grace, in the process of sanctification. Paul is not recommending this as a model of normalcy for the Christian. Weakness of will characterizes life in Adam, a situation in which sin wins the victory.

As I noted earlier, everyone in the early church believed that Paul is talking in the person of someone else, and that "someone else" was either a carnal Christian or a non-Christian. So to say it is Paul after regeneration, after his new birth in Christ, goes against the early church's interpretation.

From the time of Augustine in the fifth century, however, many have read this passage as a description of Paul's struggle in the Christian life.

If you want to read it that way, go right ahead. But consider the implications. If this is a Christian under grace, then there is a normalcy to sin.

Without getting into too many details, there is only one main argument in favor of that interpretation: the argument from experience. This may describe our Christian life and how we feel. This may hit close to home.

Otherwise, if readers allow the text to speak for itself, that interpretation is right out! The immediate evidence is overwhelming. Notice the glaring differences between the descriptions. The description here in chapter 7 is directly opposed to the description of the Christian in chapters 6 and 8. For Paul, Christians don't live under slavery to sin as Romans 7 seems to describe.

Take note of some of the differences: "sold under sin" (7:14) versus "no longer slaves to sin" but now "set free" (6:6-7, 17-20, 22). Indwelling sin (7:17, 20) versus the indwelling Spirit (8:9, 11) or Christ (Galatians 2:20). Christ through the Spirit is the permanent resident in the Christian, not sin (Gal. 2:20). The only thing "spiritual" in chapter 7 is the law (7:14). Chapter 7 is all flesh ("I am fleshly," 7:14) and no Spirit (in 7:7-25, the word "spirit" does not appear). Chapter 8, after the great change, is all Spirit and no flesh (see 8:3-9, and throughout). In light of chapter 8, a Christian is not a "miserable man" (7:24).

Paul is not describing the normal Christian life here. The situation in Adam anticipates the need for the Spirit's assistance. If this is correct, what are the implications? Paul is showing Christians they ought to be better than this. This conclusion should not come as a surprise to anyone familiar with Paul's letters to believers. It is something he often does, presenting the ideal and insisting that sin should be in their past, even though it probably isn't, or he wouldn't have to talk about it all the time!

Other New Testament texts reflect a high standard of morals. But no other New Testament passage speaks of the members of Christ as "sold under sin" or with sin "dwelling" in them. Sin cannot dominate the life of a regenerate person as is described in Romans 7. Thinking that sin is constant and normal could undermine the process of sanctification. But if this is the Christian life, is this really life? Here is a person who doesn't just struggle, but struggles on his own and loses the struggle.

In all my teaching from Romans over the years, it is this interpretation that has met the most resistance. And it goes something like this: "Hey, you've taken away this one text that I could relate to; you've taken away my comfort." First of all, it's interesting that Paul doesn't engage an objector in diatribe or hypothetical dialogue. He worried earlier that people would think he was endorsing sin (6:1), so he immediately emphasized *death to sin*. After chapters 6 and 8, he does not seem worried about people advocating a life without sin. There's no counter-diatribe saying, "Hey, it sounds like you're endorsing a victory over sin!" That's the point. Death to sin is precisely what he is promoting.

Second, if we're comforted because we relate to a Paul who constantly lost the struggle with sin, then that tells us more about ourselves than it tells us anything definitive about Paul or this passage. On the one hand, far be it from me to take away someone's comfort. There's nothing wrong per se with being comforted by a biblical text taken out of its context. That happens all the time, and it is fine as long as the point being made is orthodox and clearly taught elsewhere in Scripture.

On the other hand, the comfort that we receive from a text should not be directly antithetical to the message of that text. So we must ask ourselves: If we're comforted because we relate to chapter 7, what is the nature of that comfort? Are we being comforted in our sin? I don't see how it could be otherwise, since the "I" in chapter 7 describes himself as "fleshly," in whom *nothing good* dwells, but *only sin* indwells. If we relate to that, then that should not be a comfort, but a wake-up call. I don't think Alcoholics Anonymous puts before its members, as models, people who openly get drunk every day, and say there's nothing you can do about it.

Let me suggest an analogy. Let's say you join a social group that emphasizes healthy eating. Not just a temporary diet plan, and not a diet as an end in itself, but a lifestyle as a part of healthy and happy living. The group is always talking about and giving advice for healthy eating. No one spoke and wrote more about the importance of healthy eating than the expert dietician and group founder—let's call him Paul (now deceased).

After confessing at one meeting your temptation for Blue Bell ice cream, you come to find out that no one in the group actually eats healthy or sticks to the diet. In fact, they claim that Paul himself was never able to resist a heaping bowl of Blue Bell every night before bed. He never ate vegetables unless they were deep fried. What kind of "comfort" do you take from this knowledge? Does that strengthen your resolve? Of course not! Pass the Blue Bell! I wouldn't even need a bowl; I'll just take the whole half gallon, thank you very much! It's just an analogy, and analogies break down. (For one thing, I would never want to equate eating Blue Bell with sin.) But you get the point.

Take it a step further. Let's say that scenario of unhealthy eating becomes the group's culture and deep habit for 1,500 years. It's the diet group that doesn't take the diet too seriously. But then a historian comes along and discovers that those claims about Paul were not true. He was in fact a very healthy eater. It can be done. Healthy eating is possible. In that one poem in which he described having Blue Bell every day, he was describing what it's like for people outside the group who are still enslaved to food, before they discover the power of healthy living in community. How do the group members take this news? Are they saddened and scandalized, their excuse gone? Do they feel abandoned, doomed to binge on Blue Bell all alone? Or are they encouraged and inspired to eat healthy, even when they have failed? Which reaction *should* they have?

What do we need to hear from all this? Does this change the way you see the Christian life?

Law is good, but not law alone. Something else must intervene. In chapter 8, we will learn that the "something else" is the Holy Spirit. God's empowering Spirit is literally missing in chapter 7.

Dr. Jekyll had vowed to put Mr. Hyde behind him. In his written confession, he immediately admits, "And it fell out with me, as it falls with so vast a majority of my fellows, that I chose the better part and was found wanting in the strength to keep to it." In fact, though he said he would be done with Hyde, he still holds on to the apartment where he becomes Mr. Hyde. He still keeps Mr. Hyde's clothes. He still retains the potion. It seems that Jekyll wants to put Hyde behind him, but he just cannot bring himself to forever get rid of the alter ego. He keeps that door open.

And sure enough, after two months of resisting, the temptation overtakes Dr. Jekyll. It becomes too powerful. He drinks the potion again, and, Jekyll confesses, "My devil . . . came out roaring." Mr. Hyde comes back in full rage. After more of these night-time rampages, it becomes habitual. Soon, Jekyll wakes up from sleeping and, without the aid of the potion, has already changed to Mr. Hyde in his sleep. He needs the antidote simply to become Jekyll again. And then, soon again, without aid of the potion, he becomes Hyde while he is still awake. Involuntarily, he is completely overwhelmed, and Jekyll eventually is gone, leaving only Hyde.

The story that Paul tells here is not only Adam's story, but the story of all those who are in Adam, bearing fruit for death. That is not the way it's supposed to be. This text is not for our comfort, if by comfort we mean affirming us in the status quo of sin. It is a description of humans *without God*, anticipating the solution in chapter 8—the help of God's Holy Spirit to overcome sin. The Christian life should be characterized by struggle yes, but not defeat. Believers may lose some battles, but not the war. It is a struggle that leads to victory in chapter 8, as Paul goes on to say, by the power of the Spirit, "the Spirit of the one who raised Jesus from the dead" (8:11). "There is now no condemnation for those who are in Christ Jesus. For the law of the Spirit of life in Christ Jesus has set you free from the law of sin and death" (8:1-2).

If we feel like we have made no progress in the spiritual battle, let us allow God's Spirit to work within us. If our story is one of weakness of will, then let us call on the aid of the Spirit-led community of faith. We are not in Adam, but in Christ, by his death and resurrection, by the eternal love of the Father above. Sin does not indwell us; God's Spirit lives in us. Through God's grace and the Spirit's power, may we find the strength needed to engage the battle in this life of testing.

Discussion Questions

1. Do you think it is possible to will—on some level—two contradictory things simultaneously? Can you give an example? Do you really will it or not?

2. Before reading this reflection, who did you assume was the "I" in Romans 7? Why?

3. What are the different implications if the "I" is a Christian or not?

4. If the "I" is not a Christian, does it change the way you think about the Christian life? Do you feel saddened or do you feel empowered by this interpretation?

5. Is there a difference between being comforted by grace and being comforted in sin?

15

Life in the Spirit

Romans 8:1–17

IMAGINE THAT A NON-CHRISTIAN questions you about your beliefs. "Why do you believe in God? Who is Jesus? Tell me about the Bible." Do you have answers to these questions? How about these: "Who or what is the Holy Spirit? What does the Holy Spirit do?" Do you know what you would say? If you do not know, you're probably not alone. But why don't we know more about the Holy Spirit?

One reason is that, particularly in non-charismatic or non-Pentecostal fellowships, churches don't talk about the Holy Spirit very much. In an undergraduate class on the book of Acts, I once assigned my students to go to their own church and listen during worship for any mention of the Holy Spirit—in a song, prayer, sermon, or anything—then to write it down, who said it, what was said, and so on. I kept track mentally for about a month, and I must admit that the Spirit was mentioned more than I anticipated. But still not much.

What would Christians think of an entire worship service that failed to mention God the Father? What about a worship period where Jesus Christ was ignored? Hopefully, we would notice that something is wrong or the focus misplaced. I have also attended a church that had composed a wonderful confession of faith and purpose, and, on occasion, the congregation would recite it together during the worship assembly. Despite the appropriate centrality of the Father and Son, however, the confession made no mention whatsoever of the Holy Spirit. It was thoroughly binitarian, and the omission was glaring. Since we believe and confess that the Holy Spirit is divine—that is, equal in power and glory and to be praised together with the Father and Son—it seems to me that we shouldn't let a worship service ever go by without proclaiming this belief.

Obviously, one cannot read Romans 8 without considering the Spirit. Much of what Paul says about the Spirit here was anticipated in chapters 6 and 7 and has therefore been raised in our previous reflections. Indeed, this meditation will not be anything like a theology of the Holy Spirit. Many issues will have to remain untouched: for instance, the personhood of the Holy Spirit, his place in the Trinity, his work in creation and in the inspiration of prophets and Scripture, his empowering for special tasks such as miracles, the sin against the Holy Spirit, all the various images and names that the Bible uses to refer to him. The list could go on and on. Instead, the point here is to leave readers with something concrete to say to someone about the Holy Spirit—something you can take with you, based especially on the account in Romans 8:1–17.

The main point for us now is that the Holy Spirit is the *presence of God among us.* The whole purpose of God's creative act is that we might obey God, glorify him, and enjoy him forever, that he might share his love with his people, and that he might dwell among them. He does this now through the Holy Spirit. For those who have faith, have repented, and have received baptism, the gift of the Spirit comes as God's saving presence (Acts 2:38). God's special presence is still in his temple—the temple is not a man-made building, but the temple is us as individuals and corporately as his church (1 Corinthians 3:16; 6:19–20). God's Spirit brings to completion what was planned by the Father and initiated by his Son. This is the main point: God is present with his people. But what does God's presence mean in our lives?

Romans 8 is a good place to go for answers. Paul used the word "spirit" only five times in the whole first seven chapters of Romans—and never in Romans 7:7–25. The last time he used it was in 7:6, contrasting service in "the oldness of the letter" with "the newness of the Spirit." But here in chapter 8 alone, Paul uses the word spirit twenty-one times. The theme has clearly changed from chapter 7 to chapter 8. Based on Romans 8, I want to mention three things that the Holy Spirit means for us.

First, God's presence means our justification. God is present for our justification. That is, the past act of being declared righteous before God. Justification is a legal term. A justified person has been declared "not guilty." Justified, as I mentioned previously, means *just as if I'd* never sinned. The Holy Spirit is the one who brings about the necessary union with Christ.

There is a mistaken notion among some churches that one can be a Christian without having yet received the Holy Spirit and that the Holy Spirit comes as a later gift of blessing. But see Romans 8:9: "If anyone who does not have the Spirit of Christ, this one is not his." The Holy Spirit is not for special, first-class Christians only. Even before our turn to God, his Spirit opens our hearts to receive him (Acts 16:14). When we are joined with Christ in baptism, the Spirit enters our lives in a special way, a redeeming way. Just as the mark of the beast (Revelation 13:16–18) brands people who belong to Satan, the Holy Spirit seals God's people for salvation. We are adopted into God's family, and now we have the right to call on God as our "Abba," our Father (Romans 8:15). The Holy Spirit bears witness that we are God's children (Romans 8:16), beloved members of his family, that we have been made right.

Second, God's presence through the Holy Spirit means our sanctification, the process of becoming holy. Just as we can't save ourselves apart from the Holy Spirit's help, we can't become more holy on our own. The Holy Spirit lives within us to aid us in our struggles against sin. He helps us carry out those duties that God requires of us. As it says in Ezekiel 36:24–28, God gives his people the Spirit for the purpose of walking in his statutes and obeying his ordinances. We walk "not according to the flesh but according to the Spirit" (Romans 8:4).

This same point is made here in Romans 8:5: "For those who are according to the flesh set their minds on the things of the flesh, but those who are according to the Spirit on the things of the Spirit." The fact of the Spirit's presence living within us spurs us on to keep ourselves from sin. In addition, the Spirit helps us in our weakness by interceding to God on our behalf (Romans 8:26–27). In short, the Holy Spirit renews the image of God in us, conforming us to the likeness of Christ, and deepening our love for God—all things we can't do on our own.

That's the difference between Romans chapter 7 and chapter 8. In chapter 7, "The law is spiritual, but I am fleshly" (7:14). In other words, the fleshly person is not worthy of the law, not on its level. But in chapter 8, we are no longer fleshly; we are now, by God's grace, "spiritual," walking "according to the Spirit" (8:4), able to follow the good! It is the difference between following a list of do's and don'ts as a means of spiritual transformation—but continuously and ultimately failing—versus Spiritual transformation that enables and empowers for holy living.

Paul is not promising there will be no struggle. But when we confess our sins and struggles to one another, as we should, there are two vastly different approaches. On the one hand, we could say, "Thank you for sharing your struggle and that you have fallen to temptation. Sharing it helps us help you and all of us. We know what it's like. But we also know that, with the Spirit's help, you can overcome temptations. Let's talk about how to do that." On the other hand, we could say something very different: "Sinning is totally normal; don't feel too bad; you're just like the rest of us." If we enter the struggle with low expectations, then we will probably fulfill them. If we aim at nothing, we will hit it. But if we are confident in the Spirit's power and want what God wants for us, then we have a goal to mature toward. If we have been truly "set free from the law of sin and death" (8:2), then our language and expectations ought to reflect that reality.

In the Gospel according to John, Jesus refers to the Spirit as our *parakletos* (*paraclete*) (John 14:16, 26; 15:26; 16:7). This Greek word paraclete is variously translated as *helper, comforter, exhorter,* or *encourager.* The most literal translation is "advocate." It is used to describe *Jesus* in 1 John 2:1, the believers' "advocate with the Father." The best translation is probably "advocate" or "counselor." They both retain the wide meaning that the Greek word has. In its legal context, a counselor is the one set for our defense. In its more personal setting, a counselor or advocate is the friend we call on to help, comfort, and encourage us when we're down, and who urges us to do better. In this way, the Spirit is on our side, helping us in our sanctification, the process of becoming holy.

Third, the Spirit's presence within us means assurance. We are assured of the authority of God's word. We are assured of God's love for us. We are assured of our salvation and glorification. This "blessed assurance" does not come from us; it doesn't come from intense study; it does not come from knowing more Bible facts than our neighbor. This assurance comes from God's Spirit.

It is an assurance that gives us hope for the future. When you buy a house, after you've made the first down payment, you own that home. Not in the same way you'll own it after you've made the final payment, but it is the first installment, and it is yours. In 2 Corinthians 1:22, Paul says that God has given us his Spirit as a "down payment." Like earnest money, the Spirit is that first installment of the glorious inheritance that awaits us. A similar idea is expressed here in Romans 8:11: "If the Spirit of him who raised Jesus from the dead dwells in you, he who raised Christ from the dead will give life also to your mortal bodies through his Spirit who dwells in you." The Spirit indwells God's people now for the future. Thus, in 1 Corinthians 15, Paul talks about the future "Spiritual body" God will give us when Christ returns (1 Corinthians 15:44–46). The Spiritual body is a body filled with and animated by God's Spirit.

The person who submits her will to God's and the person who lives his life trusting God—these are the people who know the work of God's Spirit in them and are assured by his presence. Everything has changed in Christ and with the Spirit. The point again is not to be sad that we find ourselves in the state described in chapter 7. Rather, the point is the exuberant joy in chapter 8, that, by the Spirit, we are given new life, we are being sanctified, and we are assured of God's love for us and our final salvation.

After noting now these three things that the Holy Spirit means for the Christian life, one may ask, "What is the practical difference for a person who now has the Spirit?" Or, put more negatively, "Why is my experience of the Spirit incomplete?" In other words, how can we detect the Spirit's work in us?

First, what is evident about the Holy Spirit's work is that there is a past, present, and future dimension. We might like to ask where we are in that process. We have been justified, we continue to be sanctified, and the Spirit assures us that we will be glorified with Christ. Our experience of the Spirit can be called an "already/not yet" experience. By God's Spirit we *already* have his presence for salvation and assurance.

At the same time, we anticipate the *not yet*, the fuller salvation and experience of God's presence that await us all. The Spirit's presence is about the gift of life and communion with God. That life-giving Spirit that hovered over the waters of chaotic emptiness in the beginning and breathed life into the first man is the same Spirit that will continue his work of re-creation. His work of re-creation in his people every day may not be sudden or self-evident, but it is evident to the eyes of faith. God's work of re-creation in us will be fully realized when he raises us to live with him forever. But, in sum, there is still the "not yet."

And that's connected to the other reason that someone may not perceive the presence of God's indwelling Spirit—sin. Inasmuch as we sin and put our selfishness above God and others, or to the extent that we have low expectations for God's work in us, the Spirit will not be evident. The fruit of the Spirit will wither and die to the extent that we cease to give attention to sanctification. If we don't care, we limit the Spirit's activity. We can quench the Holy Spirit's fire. As Paul says in Romans 8:6, "The mind of the flesh is death, but the mind of the Spirit is life and peace." We would do well to ponder what it means to set our minds on the flesh and what it means to set our minds on the Spirit.

Whenever we speak about God, we may feel like the thoughts and words are inadequate. It is an appropriate feeling, and it may apply to the present reflection. Our own sinfulness renders us inadequate to speak about things too wonderful for mortals; perhaps no one is quite up to snuff. Praise God that the Spirit works even through inadequacies. The bottom line is this: God desires a people who will commune with him in a mutual relationship of love, made possible through the death and resurrection of Christ.

John 4:23 says that God "seeks" worshippers who will worship him in Spirit and in Truth. God wants worshippers who will open their hearts to him. He wants to send his Spirit to us for our salvation, and he wants us to experience the Spirit's comfort and assurance. However, God will not force his Spirit into our lives. He will not override or compel our wills. To thrive in holiness, we must seek the God who seeks us first, accept his supplies of grace, and then utilize the grace we have received.

But as long as we insist on putting our will and our pride above God's will, we may continue to wonder where God's Spirit is. In fact, he is wondering where you are. He is seeking you. God wants to perfect you, but will you let him? It is the Holy Spirit seeking, tugging at your heart. Allow him to infuse your spirit, to rule your life, and to cleanse you of your deepest sins.

May God grant the saving, comforting, and assuring presence of his Spirit. May God help us to live our lives so that we keep in step with the Spirit and are conformed to the image of his Son Jesus.

Discussion Questions

1. How is the Holy Spirit described in Scripture?

2. Read Ezekiel 36:24–28. What was the purpose of the giving of the Holy Spirit?

3. What would you say the Holy Spirit does for you or in your life?

4. In what ways or circumstances have you experienced the "blessed assurance" of God's Spirit?

5. What does it mean to set your mind on the Spirit?

16

Groaning for Redemption

Romans 8:18–27

I AM NOT A scientist, and I don't know much about the laws of physics, but here's the best I can do with the second law of thermodynamics. It says that "the entropy of the universe tends to a maximum." "The entropy of an isolated system always increases." Okay, so entropy increases. "What's entropy?" you ask. I'm glad you asked. Basically, entropy is the measure of disorder, chaos, and randomness in a system. This goes for everything, including the entire universe. The universe, when regarded as a closed system, which is how physicists view it, is increasing in chaos and disorder. From a purely observational perspective, the universe is winding down and will eventually come to an end.

This is bad news, but it's not really news. We know this is happening. For instance, the older a car gets and the more it is used, the harder it is to keep it clean and running properly. Chaos increases. The older we get, the harder it is to keep in shape. And we see it all around us—sickness, death, decay, dis-integration. Physics tells us this, but we don't need a science textbook to know it. Not only do we see it all around us, but it's also perfectly consistent with Scripture. Scripture confirms that we, like the universe of which we are a part, experience what Ecclesiastes calls meaningless and life "under the sun" (Ecclesiastes 1:2–3). From this perspective, life is meaningless vanity. As the famous song by Kansas puts it, "All we are is dust in the wind. Everything is dust in the wind." Maybe this is where you find yourself right now. So it might not feel like a day to rejoice in or a wonderful day for worshiping God. Maybe you barely drag yourself to church or to the reading of Scripture.

The apostle Paul has some things to say about all this in Romans 8:18–27, which, in some ways, is a commentary on the opening verses of Ecclesiastes, a perspective from another angle. Paul intends to contrast the suffering of this age with the glory of the age to come. The context of these verses is suffering.

Paul knows what it means to suffer specifically for the cause of Christ. He has endured suffering on all his missionary journeys. As he writes this letter to the Romans, he is nearing the end of his third missionary journey. He is heading back to Jerusalem to face persecution. He does not know exactly what will happen, but, in the book of Acts, he does say that he is ready to be bound and even to die in Jerusalem (Acts 21:13). At any rate, he knows he will suffer.

Not only does Paul know about suffering, but also the Jewish Christians in Rome have gone through some specific distress. They were exiled from their homes in Rome for five years. They have just returned to their city, only to find themselves at the center of unrest in the church. They know suffering.

But the suffering here in Romans 8 is not merely about specific, voluntary suffering for Christ. It is more about the kind of suffering that is common to humanity and to all creation, and it leads Paul to contrast this present suffering with future glory.

In this passage, there are at least two levels of reality that are evident, and Paul uses different words to describe each one:

First, what does it feel like to live on this side of the fall into sin? What is it like to live in a world that has lost its innocence? Which words does Paul use here in Romans 8 to describe the human predicament of *fallenness*? He speaks of *flesh, suffering, groaning, bondage, decay, weakness*, and *frustration* or *futility*. These are the words that characterize life in a fallen world. And then he personifies all creation (that is, subhuman creation). The whole creation was subjected to futility or frustration (Romans 8:20). What is this futility? It is the same word used in the Greek translation of Eccl 1:2 and throughout that book—*mataiotes*. This word means not so much meaninglessness or vanity, but futility and frustration. Frustration characterizes life under the sun in the fallen world. It is the slavery of corruption (Romans 8:21). What the Preacher in Ecclesiastes describes is what Paul is alluding to here. It is creation experiencing futility and frustration. Futility is like the predicament of Sisyphus from Greek mythology. He rolls a heavy boulder up a hill, and before he reaches the top, the boulder rolls back down. He is cursed to repeat the process eternally. That is *futility*. Frustration is when things just aren't right, and there's nothing you can do about it.

Here is one thing "we know" (8:22). We may not know everything, but we know that creation groans together, collectively. This is an interesting personification. Just like creation sings praise and declares the glory of God (Psalm 19:1), it also groans or sighs. The word here indicates an audible "sigh" or "groan." What does that sound like? It's hard to spell. Ugh . . . ! It is wordless, almost inexpressible. When things aren't going your way. Ugh . . . ! Well, things aren't going creation's way, so creation groans. The present world is not the way God created it to be. Why did God subject the creation to frustration? It was a punishment for a purpose: to teach dependence on God.

Not only creation in general but humans in particular also groan (8:23). In the fallen world, everything leads to sickness, decay, and death. But, like creation in general, we also are to learn a lesson. It is in this situation that we are to learn complete dependence on God. We are not sufficient ourselves. We are not able to save ourselves. We are reminded of these perennial truths when we face our situation in a fallen world. And thus, like creation, we also groan (8:23). As the Preacher in Ecclesiastes puts it, this is life "under the sun."

Second, there is another moment still in the future—a reality not yet here. Which words in the text of Romans 8 describe this experience of the last times? What is it that believers are waiting for? Paul speaks of *glory*, *adoption* or *childship, freedom*, and *redemption of our bodies*. The futility that the Preacher in Ecclesiastes sees all around him will be overturned!

We get a small hint of what this future will be like. Just as the whole creation was subjected to frustration or futility, Paul indicates that the whole creation will be *liberated* or freed from its bondage to decay (Romans 8:21). The future end time, the goal to which all this is leading, is not that creation will be overcome or done away with. Overturning the frustration to which creation was subjected does not mean overturning creation itself! It means restoring it. What does that mean for us humans? The adoption for which we groan and wait is the redemption of our *body* (8:23). It's not just a soul that never dies. Not an ethereal spirit floating on a cloud or absorbed into the cosmos.

I don't know exactly what should be imagined here, but whatever it is, it includes an embodied existence. If it is the body that dies, then resurrection to life means resurrection of the body. The soul is at home in the body. Just like Jesus, who was the "firstfruits" of the general resurrection (1 Corinthians 15:20). When he was raised to eternal life, it was not as a spirit or a ghost without a body. The tomb was empty—empty of a body. Why? His body was raised. Likewise, although transformed into a "spiritual body," it is nonetheless a located body, animated and sustained by the Holy Spirit.

And, yes, this redemption of the body obtains not simply for us humans. We are not the only ones who groan for liberation. Remember, all creation groans, but all creation will be liberated from the slavery of decay to the freedom of glory. All creation will be redeemed and restored to what it was supposed to be . . . and some! No more "death or mourning or weeping or pain, for the first things have passed away" (Revelation 21:4). In the language of Ecclesiastes, there will be no more vanity or meaninglessness, no futility or frustration. In the language of physics, no more second law of thermodynamics, for the old order of things has passed away. The universe, as it turns out, has never been and never will be a closed system.

What this affirms is the truth that we find way back in Genesis 1— that what God created was good, even very good. Created matter, human and otherwise, is not inherently evil and not irredeemable. What God created, he will restore. It also affirms that there is nothing out of reach of God's goodness and power and love. There is nothing, and there is no one, no matter how corrupted and how far from God right now, that cannot be restored to their rightful place in God's presence. What may appear now as meaningless and vain finds its meaning and its fullness in God.

But this full redemption has not yet happened. Remember "already/not yet" from the previous meditation? It is characteristic of this in-between period. It is not the old period of fallenness. Christ is risen indeed! The new age has already been inaugurated. But neither has the kingdom fully come yet.

In one sense, we can say that we are already saved, but also not yet fully saved; we are already redeemed, but not yet completely redeemed. So, after the coming of Christ and the sending of the Spirit, what does it feel like still to be on this side of the future glory? Which words does Paul use in Romans 8 to describe the *present* or "already/not yet" experience of Christian life? Paul speaks of Spirit, prayer, waiting, hope, and expectation. And, again, this goes for all creation. The creation eagerly awaits (8:19). Creation is not alone in this. Like creation, we, in the Spirit, groan and wait (8:23) for adoption and redemption.

This in-between time is characterized by hope. Hope is not only the desire but also the expectation of receiving. If we hope for the unseen, then we wait more eagerly in perseverance (8:25). This is how the future shapes our present—how the eager expectation affects the way we live here and now. One of the activities of this already/not yet situation is prayer. So let's consider prayer as it is addressed in 8:26-27.

1) In the already/not yet situation, *what* should God's people pray for? (Thus the NIV.) "We don't know" (8:26)! Some things we do know, as Paul said in verses 22 and 28, but not this. Has there ever been a time in your life when you didn't know what to pray for? Sometimes we just don't know. In the midst of suffering, sickness, sorrow, death, sometimes we don't know what to pray for. If we pray for healing, and someone is healed, it's just postponing their death. This is something we all have to come to grips with. As I've heard many old people quip, "Growing old is not for wimps." I agree: "Life is not for wimps." My grandmother suffered for many years with advanced Alzheimer's, and it was difficult to know what to pray for. Should we pray for her brain to start functioning better? For her pain and suffering to go away? Certainly, and for God's will to be done. Life "under the sun," in a fallen world, is not for wimps.

2) *How* do God's people pray? (Thus the NRSV.) We may not know this either. But I'd say we have some clues about the proper attitude or disposition in prayer, especially in prayers of groaning.

First, we pray in weakness (8:26). It's okay to bring our angst and dread and fear and questions to God. Guess what? He can handle it. It's okay not to know what to pray for or how to pray. And it's okay to be vulnerable in prayer. Whether it is the tax collector in the corner beating his breast or Jesus in the garden weeping, Scripture teaches that the prayer in weakness is heard. When I am weak, then I am strong (2 Corinthians 12:10).

Second, we pray in hope (Romans 8:20, 24–25). In that sense, we pray boldly. We have reason for hope. If God is for us, who can be against us (8:31)?

Where does the confidence lie? If we don't know what to pray for, and we're not too sure how to pray either, then where is our hope? Why do we continue to pray? Read on to see the good news: "The Spirit helps us in our weakness" (8:26). First of all, before we even get to how God's

Spirit helps, just imagine that concept: The Spirit helps us. The verb Paul uses for *help* is *synantilambanomai*. Clearly there is much going on with this word, and to translate it as *help*, though it is a permissible gloss, seems to shortchange a verb with two prepositional prefixes. The word connotes taking on someone else's part or burden, "with" them and "for" them. God, by his Spirit, takes on our part, our burden. He lifts the weight, which makes the yoke is easy (Matthew 11:30).

How does God help? What does he do? God's Spirit intercedes for his children with inexpressible (or unexpressed) groans (Romans 8:26), wordless sighs. Here is the connection. It is not just we and creation who groan, but God also groans with us. In other words, God is not too happy about this fallen situation either. Have you ever heard or said yourself, when you were about to discipline a child, "This is going to hurt me more than it hurts you"? By the way, I don't think that's true. I never have said that, because I doubt that "more" part! But it does hurt. It gives a loving parent no pleasure to punish. But the parents will go through with it, if they are moved by love and the purpose is for instruction and reform.

But this may be a true instance—it hurts God more than it hurts us. God looks at the fallen world, and *he* groans. God sees sickness, suffering, decay, death, futility, and frustration, and God says "Ugh." Believe it or not, that is the best news we can hear: God himself cares, God himself, who has the power to restore creation, also has the will to do it. God knows about our suffering, and he knows suffering personally.

When the Word became flesh, God experienced all the frustration and the futility that life under the sun has to offer. In Christ, he suffered and died for his children—good news for sure! And the one who brought creation out of nothing has the power to heal it and restore it from its brokenness; the one who gave his own Son and raised him (8:32, 34) is willing to do the same for us. That's what makes this day worth rejoicing in, a wonderful day to worship God. We have reason for joy. What we believe, what we know, is that the love that moves the sun and all the stars will win.

So let's pray in weakness. But let us also pray in the strength that comes from God, knowing that the Spirit intercedes for us. Let us pray, in hope and anticipation, the prayer of the early church: "Maranatha, Come, Lord Jesus."

Discussion Questions

1. Would you characterize your life right now as one of order and stability or of disorder and chaos?

2. What light does this passage from Romans 8 shed on the problem of suffering?

3. How would you describe the "already/not yet" experience in your own words?

4. What does it feel like to be on this side of future glory?

5. How does that experience shape the life of prayer?

17

God for Us

Romans 8:28–39

IN ROMANS 8:28–39, PAUL continues his reflections on God's eternal purpose. Everything that he says in this passage is built on what he said in the previous verses: As all humans and all creation are groaning for redemption, God's Spirit also groans with us and will bring about that full redemption and liberation for which we hope. Well, as we will see, Paul is not finished talking about that hope and the assurance we have of God's love. And it's an important point to remember; it helps to frame what Paul goes on to say here at the end of chapter 8. But, in the meantime, we still suffer.

What are we to make of suffering? We still face death. What does it mean? Does it mean that God has neglected us or is ignoring us? What about when we suffer not just as all creation does, but when we suffer specifically for doing good? What if we suffer for following God? Does it mean that God doesn't love us, his own people?

This is the question of Psalm 44, which I would recommend as a companion text to our discussion. The people addressing God in this psalm are not just lamenting about suffering in general. Suffering *per se* seems to be a problem on its own, but there are two more concerns in Psalm 44.

First, they are suffering not because they did something evil or disobeyed God, but because they obeyed God and did what was right.

Like Joseph, like Daniel and the three Hebrew children, they are being persecuted for doing good. It is not for their faithlessness, but for their faithfulness to the covenant and to the God of the covenant. That's one problem—suffering for doing good.

Second, unlike Joseph and Daniel and his friends, the psalmists feel like God is not listening, that he has abandoned them, that he is far from them, that something has separated them from his love. God rescued Joseph from jail. God protected Shadrach, Meshach, and Abednego in the heart of the fire. God shut the mouths of the lions for Daniel. God is the one we have depended on to crush the enemies, the Psalmists say.

But what has God done for his people lately? Now the enemies plunder us. We are covered with shame, the psalmists cry, brought down to the dust. But to return to the first point, we suffer not because we have forgotten God; we haven't. This is the question, indeed, the complaint, of Psalm 44.

And has it ever been your question, your complaint? Have you ever felt *that* pain? It's one thing to suffer and be able to trace the suffering back to sinful or foolish decisions. It's still painful, but you kind of get it. It's another thing to suffer and not really know why. No one is perfect, but you've been as good as you can. You go to church. You pray, and you give. You love God. So why did you get laid off? Why the money problems? Why do you suffer stress and distress? Why did you get sick? Why did your loved one die? Paul has more to say about these and other things.

In Romans 8:28–39, Paul begins by declaring something that we know. He is perfectly comfortable confessing when we don't know or understand (as in Romans 8:26). But here, "we know" that God works things out for the good of those who love him (8:28). This is good news!

First, what this does not mean: This is not a promise of physical health and wealth. That much is clear because of what he goes on to say beginning in verse 35. It is not that "all things" are good, as some translations might imply. Rather, God takes all things, even the bad ones, and works them out for ultimate good! So it is not a promise that God will eliminate all suffering and hardship for us in this life. Just as parents work out the good for their children or physicians for their patients, it doesn't always mean immediate alleviation of physical pain and suffering.

What it *does* mean, then, is that God can bring something good out of suffering. This claim—that God can bring good out of evil—should not be too hard for us to fathom. We can surely recall instances in our lives when we went through something bad—when we experienced some discomfort or pain, physical or emotional—and came out with a blessing on the other side. You wouldn't have wanted to go through the suffering. You wouldn't have planned it that way. But you came out stronger as a result, often discernible only in hindsight. As Kierkegaard wrote, "The school of sufferings educates for an eternity."

If we can easily see how kites fly highest in a strong wind, how a hardship can make us stronger, and how suffering can teach us a valuable lesson, then how much more can God, from his eternal perspective of love and his infinite resources of power, make the wrong right! Now, don't misunderstand. It's not that God causes suffering. He allows it, he permits it—which is different from directly causing it. He groans over it and laments it. But he takes that trouble and pain and makes it into gain, or at least into an opportunity for growth. Sometimes we are privileged to see the good result. At other times, we may not see it.

This brings us back to our question from Psalm 44. How do we know that God still loves us? He did not quite defeat our enemies in the way we had hoped or planned. So what has he done for us? Yes, "If God is for us, who can be against us?" But how do we know that God is truly for us?

He gave his Son for us (Romans 8:32). That's how much God hates sin and its consequences, and that's how intense his love and his mercy are for us. "What has God done for us?" the psalmists ask. He gave up his Son. Look at the great lengths to which God has gone in order to redeem and rescue us. "God is for us."

In light of this truth, in light of what God has done for us in Christ, then, Paul asks, "Who can accuse you?" Who can accuse me? We're not justified because *we* did anything. We're not made right by our own goodness. We are justified, made right, because *God* did it. Christ, who died and was raised to life, intercedes on our behalf (8:34), as also does the Spirit (8:27). So we can rest assured that, if God is for us, no one and nothing of import can possibly be against us. Not even the fanciest lawyer in heaven or hell can bring a successful case against us, as long as God is on our side, as long as God is for us.

And the overriding question for the rest of this passage appears in 8:35: "Who will separate us from the love of Christ?" Well, one candidate surely is all this suffering. What about all these sufferings? Do they separate us from the love of Christ, that is, Christ's love for us? Are sufferings an indication that we have done evil and are being punished? Or, as opponents of God's people have often assumed, do the sufferings of God's people mean that God is not real? On a more personal level, what is your hardship? What risk or danger are you in? Notice that the sufferings mentioned in verse 35 are probably the voluntary sufferings for Christ. These are persecutions that are endured for the sake of Christ. "Famine" can just mean hunger. Persecution is the context. Now, in verse 36, Paul quotes the concern from Psalm 44. God's people constantly face persecution and death for the sake of God; they are sheep for the slaughter.

The answer to this concern was anticipated back in Romans 8:17. Paul has already answered it. We are children of God, "co-heirs" with Christ of the inheritance, if . . . what? We are God's children, if we "co-suffer" with Christ, in order that we might also be "co-glorified." Suffering for Christ does not mean that God has abandoned us anymore than it means that God abandoned Christ in his suffering. Instead, God loves us and sticks with us through the suffering. Because of God's vindication of Christ's life and suffering, because God raised him from the dead, then our sharing in his sufferings means that we will also share in his glory.

Just as a valuable reward does not come without real, hard effort, the glory doesn't come without the suffering. We might like for it to come without suffering, but it never does. The glory for Christ didn't come without suffering. Instead, glory comes *through* the suffering, as resurrection comes after death. James and John wanted to sit at Jesus' right and left in his coming glory. He said, "Fine, but can you drink the cup of suffering first?" Ananias and Sapphira sought glory and honor without the sacrifice. It did not end well for them. It is the purging, purifying trial that teaches necessary dependence on God for everything. This is why Christ pronounces curses on those who have everything, but blessings on those who mourn, who hunger and thirst, who are persecuted and insulted because of righteousness.

So, in verse 37, it is not despite these things, not despite these sufferings, but in these sufferings that we conquer. And there it is again: Paul makes up another word, adding that prefix "hyper" to the verb here, which most translations turn into a noun. Remember how grace "superabounds" (5:20)? Here Paul says, "We hyper-conquer, we super-conquer, we overwhelmingly conquer" (8:37). Paul's excited. We have special words when we're excited, too.

From the time we were kids at home until now, when my brother and I play ping-pong, a game is to 21. We reserve a special word for a victory of ten or more points. That's a "whoop!" Paul's word is super-conquer, but it's the same as whoop. That's what it means to "hyper-conquer." We're not defeated by suffering. On the contrary, we whoop the enemy. But, again, not because of how powerful we are. "We whoop," Paul says, "through him who loved us" (8:37). We super-conquer through the power of God.

This passage and this point are instructive in many areas. One area relates to the idea of lament. Biblical scholars and now churches have rediscovered the value and the place for lament in Christian worship. "Lament" is a word that means crying out to God. It's okay to cry out to God, to lament. We see it throughout Scripture—God's people crying out to God for vindication, for release and salvation, for relief from enemies. Lament is when God's people cry out in their suffering with questions like "Why?" and "How long, O Lord?" We see this most often in the book of Psalms, where about one-third of the individual Psalms can be classified as lament.

There is certainly a place for lament to God, in our individual prayer lives and in our corporate worship assemblies. Jesus himself cried out on the cross, quoting the words of Psalm 22:1, "My God, my God, *why* have you abandoned me?" As the previous reflection noted, the lament is fine, because God can handle our questions and even our complaints. Psalm 44, which Paul quotes here in Romans 8:36, is a lament to God. To paraphrase: "Where are you God? Why are you letting us suffer for doing the right thing? Why don't you do something about it?"

Again, those kinds of questions are okay. But Paul, in Romans 8, is reminding us of an important truth not available to the lamenting psalmists or, in some ways, even to the lamenting Jesus. We stand on the other side of Jesus' resurrection. We have the answer in a more concrete way than they did. The God who loved his Son also raised him from the dead. The God who loves us in Christ will do the same for those of us who are in Christ.

What Paul is doing here is setting a limit to the lament. Again, to lament is okay. But it should not turn into excessive complaining. And it cannot turn into despair. No, Paul says (8:37). We are super-conquerors, in the sufferings and trials. The power of the lament, the strength of the complaint, should never obscure what God can do—and is doing—with us in the suffering, in the midst of the fire. If we keep our eyes open and expect a blessing, we may find one. Suffering with Christ? Yes. We don't stop having trouble and affliction. But that's a pretty good place to be. Because to suffer with Christ is to be glorified with him. As the lament of Psalm 22 ends in words of victory, and as Psalm 44 ends by urging God to arise and act, so Paul reminds us that God has indeed acted and he does guarantee the overwhelming victory—the whoop!

"Who will separate us from the love of Christ?" There are enough enemies that would lead a person without Christ to a sad and dismal outlook—despair, really. But who will separate *us*, God's people, from Christ's love? The answer is clear in verses 38–39. Because God is for us, and because God brings his children to glory through the apparent obstacle of suffering, then nothing can separate us from God's love for us.

Your hardship cannot separate you. Not the marginalization, the ostracism you endure for Christ. Not your lack of resources. Nothing can tear you away from God's love. Not your illness. Not your ignorance. Not Satan or your past sin. Nothing today. Nothing tomorrow. Not your worry about either one. Nothing can separate us from God's love. Not that big black hole out there. Not the vast measure of space and time in all its magnitude. Christ Jesus is Lord of it all. So *nothing* can separate you from him! Not your impending death and physical disintegration. God restores it all. Thanks be to God! In the sufferings of life, we overwhelmingly conquer through God, from whose infinite love nothing can separate us.

If we, like Paul, "know" this, and if we are "convinced" of these truths, then whatever we lament—and there is plenty to lament—must be kept in perspective. How will we then live, except in joy and gratitude, for the God who loves us so? Let us live, then, even through suffering, not as the victims but the victors, not as the defeated but as super-conquerors.

Discussion Questions

1. In light of this passage in Romans 8, what do suffering and death mean to a Christian?

2. Have you complained or lamented to God? What was the reason behind the lament?

3. Have you ever been punished or penalized for doing the good?

4. How do we know that God is for us?

5. What does it mean to be a "co-heir" with Christ?

18

God's Promise and Purpose

Romans 9:1–33

Does it sometimes feel like the word or promise of God has failed? Do you find yourself looking around and saying, "I don't really understand what God is doing"? It is not that we don't trust God. We have faith. We are truly committed. But our faith seeks understanding, and we fall a bit short on the understanding. What do we do?

One thing we do is go back to Scripture. This is why it's important to read the Bible and know the stories. We can see times in Scripture when God's people were going through the same things we go through and were wondering the same thing that we wonder: "What is God doing?"

When God promised that Abraham would have a son, and then he let Abraham and Sarah sit and wait for about twenty-five years, I'm sure they wondered if God's promise had failed. When God told Moses that he would free his people from Egyptian slavery, what happened? First, Pharaoh said no. And not only did Pharaoh say no, but the work load was increased. I'm sure that got all the Israelite workers wondering. Then the plagues started, and Pharaoh continued to say no. The people, and probably Moses himself, wondered what God was doing. In hindsight, with stories like these, we can imagine their confusion in the midst of the story, while they waited for who knows what, for who knows how long. And we can see how things have turned out. And so we have a clearer perspective, or at least a longer perspective, on God's plan and purpose.

Scripture teaches us to take the long view when we ask these kinds of questions about God.

In Romans 9–11, it is Paul who is raising the tough questions about God's promises. It is Paul who is wondering what God is up to. It is Paul who goes back to his Bible in search of answers. In these three chapters (9–11), we see a greater concentration of Old Testament quotations and allusions than anywhere else in Paul's writings. He is searching the Scriptures for answers. What we should be doing when our faith goes in search of greater understanding—this is exactly what Paul does here in Romans 9–11.

In light of Romans 9 in particular, I want to spend a few moments explaining some basic things about this perplexing and notoriously difficult passage, pointing out what it is saying and what it is not saying. Think of chapters 9 through 11 as one section with one extended point. It has often been considered as a separate section that has little to do with what comes before and after. For some, this is Paul's discourse on the doctrine of predestination. But, since Romans is not just Paul's systematic theology, we would do well to see how this section relates to the issues going on in the Roman church.

These three chapters, like the whole letter, have everything to do with the gentile/Jewish problem in the Roman church that Paul is addressing. That is, the occasion of Romans, which I have mentioned in previous chapters, also illuminates Romans 9–11. Remember that Paul is writing to a gentile majority in the church that has dismissed the Jewish minority in the church. This section is about the place of Jews in that congregation and the place of Israel in salvation history.

And the Jews are asking, "If the Messiah is the hope of Israel, if the coming of the Holy Spirit was prophesied by Israel and for Israel, then why is it that the Jews mostly are *not* accepting Jesus as Messiah, whereas gentiles seem to be taking over?" The fact that gentile Christians are increasing while Jewish Christians are decreasing seems to contradict the promises made to Abraham (beginning in Genesis 12). The gentiles seem almost boastful about their standing, and the Jewish Christians don't understand what has happened to their people. This is an issue for Paul himself—a Jew who calls himself the "apostle to the Gentiles." He is speaking here for Jewish Christians and for himself. If God's blessing is for Abraham's seed or offspring, then why is Abraham's seed on the outside looking in?

Romans 9–11 is a continuation of and further response to questions brought up in 3:1–9. "What advantage has the Jew?" (Romans 3:1). "Is God unrighteous?" (3:5). "Why does God hold us accountable if sin is part of the plan?" (3:7). "Are we better then they?" (3:9).

Chapters 9–11, though a distinct section, are not an excursus or tangent. This section is indispensable to Romans. This is the most sensitive and important concern of Paul in the letter. He takes a while to build to it, wanting to set the context and build rapport with a church that is not naturally under his authority (he did not establish this church, and he has never visited this church). With churches he established, Paul comes to the point more quickly. (In his letter to the Galatians, he tears right into them.) Here in Romans, he has been very patient.

In these opening verses of chapter 9, we get a glimpse of Paul's personal agony, an important factor that frames this whole section. As an apostle to the Gentiles, his own concern for Israel has probably been questioned by critics, so he begins with a vow of sincerity in the name of Christ and the Holy Spirit (9:1). Paul is sincerely in anguish that ethnic Israel, the Jews, have, by and large, rejected Christ. After just saying that nothing can separate us from the love of God that is in Christ Jesus our Lord (8:38–39), he says that he wishes that he could be "anathema" and cut off from Christ for Israel's sake (9:3). It is reminiscent of Moses, who, in the wake of Israel's idolatry, offered himself in place of the people (Exodus 32:32–33).

This section is full of pathos. Paul's pain is evident, as is his pride. Look at all the blessings that belong to Israel (Romans 9:4–5). But there is a responsibility and even peril that must go along with the privilege (cf. 3:1–3). These first five verses are essential for understanding the motivation behind chapters 9–11. Paul is in anguish, and he's speaking out of the anguish, and he's searching through Scripture to understand and articulate what's going on and why. Thus the heavy concentration of quotations from the Old Testament in these three chapters. Paul is trying to discern the meaning and nature of God's promise to Israel, and in so doing, he models how to think through tough questions with the aid of Scripture, still trusting in God's infinite wisdom.

The situation in the church is looking bleak for Jews, because fewer and fewer are turning to Christ, and more and more gentiles are. What does Paul find in Scripture to address this question? Has God's promise failed?

Paul begins by affirming that God's promise to Abraham has *not* failed (9:6). It could be that our understanding of his promise has missed the mark. Here's how. The promise was never meant to imply that each and every descendant of Abraham would be chosen or would always be the direct recipient of the promise. After all, Ishmael was a son of Abraham, but God says that the promise will be through Isaac. Esau was a son of Isaac, but the promise will be through Jacob.

So it's not just about biology; otherwise, Ishmael and Esau would have been chosen, too. God's elective process was on the side of Abraham's son Isaac and Isaac's son Jacob (9:7, quoting Genesis 21:12). Paul's point here is that, already in the Old Testament—in fact, already in Genesis—we can see that not all of Abraham's descendants are really part of true Israel. Paul is saying that, we shouldn't be any more dismayed about the situation now than we are about the situation depicted in Genesis. From the beginning, God chooses certain people.

With this distinction between those who are selected and those who are not, Paul has introduced two categories of people. And he names the categories: "Children of the flesh" and "children of the promise" (Romans 9:8). (Again, some translations obscure the word "flesh" here.) Remember that Paul is not talking about literal flesh. All four sons were "natural" children of the literal flesh. But these individuals serve as *archetypes*.

Ishmael and Esau serve as types or paradigms of children of the flesh. Isaac and Jacob are paradigms or patterns of the children of the promise. So verses 12 and 13 refer to the working out of the promise through the Israelites (descendants of Jacob) and not the Edomites (descendants of Esau). At times, the Edomites literally became Israel's servants (as in 2 Samuel 8:14). In Malachi 1:2-3, when the Lord says, "Jacob I loved and Esau I hated," it is the nations of Israel and Edom—and ultimately the archetypal categories—that are in view (Romans 9:13).

Some further observations are in order. First of all, this text is primarily about *groups*, not individuals. As we know, again from the Old Testament, an individual from the group of Israel can reject God, just as an individual from a pagan nation can turn to God and obey him. And it is that latter point that shows how it all relates to the Jew/gentile question that Paul raises. Paul uses Genesis to prove that not all of Abraham's descendants are heirs of the promise. Then he uses other passages from the prophets to prove the converse: Some who are not Abraham's literal descendants will be heirs of the promise. These prophets say that those who were not God's people will be called "children of the living God."

They show that those who are not God's people can become his people, and that *his people* can become *not his people*. At the same time, a remnant from Israel will remain.

Paul is well on his way to proving the point that, regardless of how the promise to Abraham has traditionally been interpreted, the Old Testament itself teaches that being selected as part of God's plan, like being saved, is not now, and never has been, simply a matter of physical descent. The ethnic categories that Paul raises at the beginning are fluid and not of ultimate importance.

Let me take a moment also to clarify a common misunderstanding of chapter 9. Some have taken this chapter, especially the business about the potter and the clay (9:20–22), to be saying that God chooses people to save and others to destroy with no regard for their own choice. Unconditional predestination is a central doctrine of Calvinism or Reformed theology—that God saves some individuals and condemns others without them having any choice in the matter. In this system, those elected for salvation are no better than the reprobate. All are sinners and equally deserving of condemnation. According to this view, humans can meet no condition to become elect. God has his reasons, but, from the human perspective, the predestination is unconditional, individual, and concerns one's eternal destination.

Is Paul saying that? Does Romans 9 teach the doctrine of unconditional predestination? In short, no. The question is complex, but some points are clear. First, the selection of the *group* is about God's choosing a *people* to represent him, to be a light to the world. That choosing or calling is, in some ways, unconditional. Abraham and Israel did not ask to be chosen. But Abraham and Israel had a choice to respond to God's choosing.

Second, to the degree that this relates to individual salvation, it is appropriate to ask, "How does one become a child of the promise?" Is it because God chooses someone, regardless of that person's faith or unbelief? If we've paid attention to Romans so far we know that one becomes a child of promise not by doing good works. It is by faith. How do we know? After all the examples and analogies and proof texts, look at the summary statement in 9:30–32. The gentiles found righteousness by faith, but the Jews pursued righteousness through the law. Those who have been rejected are responsible for their own rejection. As for those who were accepted, they were accepted through their faith; they had a say in the matter.

Israel chased after righteousness, but in the wrong way. Despite all Israel's advantages, they had stumbled over the stumbling block (9:32). As Paul writes elsewhere, the cross was a stumbling block to Jews (1 Corinthians 1:18–24). The gentiles weren't really looking for it, but they found righteousness through faith. So it's not an arbitrary or mysterious decree of God about who's in and who's out. Paul is not saying that everything is determined by God without us having any choice in the matter. This is not about unconditional predestination.

Faith, our free acceptance of God's gift, is the condition of the covenant of grace. Thus the pagan gentiles are in, and the monotheistic Jews are out. The gentiles have attained righteousness by faith. Certainty of salvation, the assurance that Paul reiterated at the end of chapter 8, rests on God's purpose to save believers. If we have faith, we can be certain of our salvation. What cannot be resisted here (Romans 9:19) is that God will save penitent believers and punish impenitent unbelievers. Clearly, faith is the condition of salvation.

It is also evident that God has a plan to show his mercy through both Jews and gentiles. He bears patiently with the unrepentant (9:22) to show his mercy to the repentant (9:23). He wants all to see his glory. Even with the unrepentant, God is merciful. He inclines toward mercy and not wrath!

Before we plunge into chapters 10 and 11, then, we need to pause and consider what we see so far. Not all Abraham's descendants (for instance, Ishmael and Esau) are heirs of the promise or part of the line of the promised seed. God's larger plans can, for a time, exclude some descendants of Abraham. But this does not mean that God's word has failed.

What about us? What do we take from all this? First, it is interesting that, right after one of the most lovely and assuring passages in all of Scripture (8:28–39)—a statement of conviction that God works all things for the good of those who love him, assurance that nothing can separate us from God's love—immediately after all that, we find Paul in agony, asking the same questions that his fellow Israelites ask.

Being convinced about the big picture does not necessarily mean we understand all the details or have them all figured out. It also doesn't mean we can't investigate the details. That's what Paul is doing: Rather than concluding that God has failed us, he lets the big picture—about who God is and what he has done for us in Christ—inform his handling of the hard questions. He searches the Scriptures and finds; he knocks and the door opens. Let us be equally busy in the Scriptures, in God's revealed word, seeking guidance, instruction in righteousness, and wisdom concerning God's plan and purpose.

Another important point we should not miss is that God is not answerable to us for what he does. God's in charge, and that's okay. In fact, it's better than okay; it's wonderful. It's a good thing God doesn't feel the need to consult us about his plans. Nothing good would get done. So we need a healthy respect for God's sovereignty and our submission to him, even when we don't understand everything about the plan. But that does not mean what he does, when it comes to salvation, is irresistible, or that he has determined destruction for specific individuals apart from their choice. What are God's plans for Israel? Paul will have more to say in chapter 11.

Finally, we again see Paul, through the wisdom gained in Scripture, relativizing human loyalties. This is a challenging word, especially in a day when the culture teaches people to see everything through their own preferential lens. We are told by the media that our identity is found in race, ethnicity, gender, sexual preference, and so on. To be sure, those factors cannot help but color the way we see the world and ourselves. But those categories do not constitute our loyalties; they are not our primary identity markers. Here, after recounting all the great things about being a Jew (9:4-5), Paul relativizes ethnicity; elsewhere, he relativizes all the rest. Our primary identity is in Christ. What binds all of us to God, and all of us to each other, is that by faith we are in Christ, died and risen for us. That's it. That's the only question that matters.

Romans 9 forces the question: Are you in Christ? Do not chase after another kind of righteousness or fulfillment that will leave you empty at the end, on the outside looking in.

Discussion Questions

1. Do you think the biblical characters ever wondered what God was doing? Who and under what circumstances?

2. Have you ever wondered about God's plan and what he is doing? What puzzles you?

3. Is sin part of God's plan? If so, would it be right for God to hold us accountable?

4. Does Romans 9 teach the doctrine of unconditional predestination—that humans have no say in salvation or condemnation? Why or why not?

5. According to Romans 9:30–32, how does one become a child of the promise?

19

The Word Is near You

Romans 10:1–21

CAN YOU RECALL A time when you were desperately looking for something and just could not find it, only to discover that it was there right in front of you all along? It's pretty common, and I hear it gets more common as we get older. We all know the feeling. We say, "If it was a snake, it would have bitten me." It is like looking around for your glasses while they're resting on your head.

One of my wife's favorite stories is an instance of this. Many years ago, my oldest son and I were sick at home with the flu. He got it first, and his symptoms were improving, while mine were getting worse. It was time again to take some ibuprofen for my fever, and I couldn't find it anywhere. We were out! My fever was over 103, pushing 104, and I was miserable. My body was aching, and I could barely move from the bed. I called my wife. There was no answer. (She was at work or something!) I texted her. Nothing. She finally called back and said that we weren't out of ibuprofen. It was in the kitchen somewhere. I said I couldn't find it. She insisted. So I hung up and dragged myself to the kitchen. My son and I both looked for it. The kitchen counters were a bit cluttered, and it really could have been anywhere. But it was nowhere to be seen. This cabinet, that cabinet. Unfortunately, even when it is in the "right" spot, medicine in our house could be in one of about five places. But it was in none of them.

I called her back, desperate now. "It's not here; please buy some on your way home." She really took her time coming home. After what seemed like an hour, the garage door finally opened. And instead of, "Here sweetheart, let me bring the pills to you," I was greeted with, "Look, the ibuprofen was right here in the kitchen where I said it was!" Everyone was laughing, but I failed to see the humor. She and my other kids insist that, indeed, the medicine was right next to the stove all along. They made great fun of me that day, and they still do. I still say they were wrong and it wasn't there. (I will concede that they may have been right, but I will blame it on the delirium that accompanies a high fever.) At any rate, this meditation will proceed on the assumption that they were right and that the medicine was actually in front of me the whole time.

This is a frivolous story, and perhaps a common experience, to illustrate a serious thing that Paul says happened to the Jews. While reading Romans 10, look for the theme of, "The medicine was right there in front of you," as it were, "right next to the stove."

Remember what Paul is discussing in this section of Romans, and, to some degree, throughout the whole letter—namely, what is God doing with the Jewish people? He made a covenant with them, but they have rejected the Messiah through whom the promise was to be fulfilled. Now what? This is the larger question, but it is also the question on the congregational level, in a church where the gentile Christians, now the majority, are arrogant toward their Jewish Christian brothers and sisters. What is going on?

Recall a couple of points that Paul made in chapter 9. First, physical lineage is not decisive when it comes to being reckoned as God's people. Ishmael and Esau were descendants of Abraham, but not "heirs of the promise" or part of "the chosen." Second, the people of Israel are responsible for their own rejection. If they were rejected, it is only because they rejected the Messiah. They stumbled over the stumbling stone (Romans 9:32). God did not want that for them, and God sure didn't cause it to happen. Part of that stumbling stone, as it turns out, is the news that salvation is for all, not just for ethnic Jews.

Paul continues the same themes and builds on them now in chapter 10. Paul, an Israelite himself, continues to open his heart to the Romans, even as he opens his Bible, our Old Testament, and searches the Scriptures for answers. He says that his heart's desire is for Israel to be saved (10:1). But what he said at the end of chapter 9, he reiterates here in 10:3: Pious Jews who don't accept God's righteousness (revealed in

Jesus) are pursuing, in reality, a *works-based* righteousness. They should have opened their eyes to Jesus Christ, who, Paul claims is "the end of the law" (10:4).

What does he mean by saying that "Christ is the end of the law"? The explanation has to do, in part, with the ambiguity of the Greek word *telos*, translated "end." As in English, *end* can mean the termination of something or the goal of something. Christ is the end or the termination of law-keeping for its own sake. As Paul has made clear already, it's not that law-keeping is wrong. We are, in fact, called to keep the laws of God. The law is not nullified (3:31); indeed, it is spiritual and good (7:14). It is a good means to a good end. But the law is not an end in itself. As Romans 10:5 indicates, that pursuit of the law is the kind of righteousness that reduces to a list of do's and don'ts. It was never God's intent that law-keeping alone should be equated with righteousness itself. Law-keeping alone does not bring transformation. In this sense, Christ marks the end or termination of that kind of law-keeping.

At the same time, and more importantly, Christ is the end or goal to which the law pointed; he is the righteousness that the law could not produce on its own. The Jews sought righteousness through law-keeping rather than through the Messiah himself. As the goal of the law, Christ is also the focus of the law. "Law" in the Old Testament, moreover, does not mean just the do's and don'ts. Law is the Hebrew word *Torah*, "instruction"—the five books of the law, the foundation of what Paul calls "Scripture."

Especially in hindsight, Paul and other faithful Jews could look back at Scripture and read it through the lens of what God has done in Christ—the sending of his Son the Messiah, the Messiah's death and resurrection, his ascension and session at the Father's right hand, his pouring out of the Holy Spirit. When the Old Testament Scripture is read through the lens of all these events, then the events themselves inform what one finds in the Scripture. In hindsight, then, Jewish Christians could see that, even though Jesus of Nazareth is never mentioned by name in the Old Testament, Christ really is the center and theme of the law. When read on the spiritual level, the law, the Torah, really is about Jesus, who is the end of the law.

And that is how Paul interprets it. As he does throughout these three chapters (9–11), we especially see Paul's method in 10:6–10. He is quoting Scripture, then interpreting and applying it to his own day. The words that he uses in his own explanations are often taken straight from the texts he is quoting. He is showing that God's people could have seen all this—that they should have seen all this—in their own Scriptures. In this case, starting in verse 6, Paul quotes Deuteronomy 30.

The point of Deuteronomy 30 is this: Do we have to go around the world and across the universe to find out God's will? How hard this would be! Do we have to find a way to get ourselves to heaven to discover God's word? Do we have to plunge into the depths to bring up God's message and hear it? How far do we have to go to retrieve the righteousness that we have forfeited by sin? Is the cure for our disease forever beyond our reach?

No! "The word is very near you," Moses says and Paul quotes (Deuteronomy 30:14; Romans 10:8). (Paul uses the Greek word *rhema*, "something spoken," but usually translated as "word." He picked up that word from Deuteronomy, and it is very important throughout his discussion.) You do not have to go out and hunt for this word. It has come to you. It is accessible. And if I may say so, it is obey-able. It is not too hard to find, nor is it too hard to keep. The choice between life and death has been set before you (Deuteronomy 30:15). The choice is here, available, and clear. It has been placed right in front of you, placed within you. The word, he says, is in your mouth and in your heart (Deuteronomy 30:14; Romans 10:8). The medicine is right there, next to the stove.

Paul takes over from there, and, now commenting on this good news from Deuteronomy 30, he says that this word is the message of faith, the good news about being set right by faith in Jesus Christ. Do you have to go up to heaven to find this word? No. Christ has come down to us. Do you have to plunge into the depths of the earth to find this word? No. Christ has been there, too, and has been raised up from it (Romans 10:6–7). The word that is on the *mouth* and in the *heart* is the Christian confession.

What should be done with that word on your mouth and in your heart? Paul clarifies. "If you confess in your mouth Lord Jesus and believe in your heart that God raised him from the dead, you will be saved" (Romans 10:9). The word is there on the heart and mouth. Just believe it in your heart and confess it with your mouth. The law, the Torah, which includes Deuteronomy 30, *points to Christ* and is for everyone. This is the controversial word over which the Jews stumbled. Here is the news: "Everyone who calls on the name of the Lord will be saved" (Romans 10:13; from Joel 2:32). It was all there in the Old Testament. This is the good news: Salvation is for everyone, for the Jew first, but also for the gentile.

But how? They have to believe first, and to believe, they must have the good news proclaimed to them. We love it when someone delivers good news. How beautiful!—Paul says—how beautiful are the feet of those who bring good news (Romans 10:15; from Isaiah 52:7).

And then, Isaiah 53 begins, and Paul quotes, "Lord, who has believed our message?" (Romans 10:16; from Isaiah 53:1). This question, asked first by Isaiah, applies in the first century—this is the question Paul is asking about the Jews. Who has believed? Who has had the faith by which we are made right? It is also a question we may yet ask in the twenty-first century. It also shows the connection between hearing and faith. As Paul says, translated quite literally: "'Lord, who has had faith in our heard message?' [Isaiah 53:1]. Faith is from the heard message, and the heard message through the word of Christ" (Romans 10:16–17). It is a condensed summary of Paul's interpretation of Deuteronomy 30, with a little help from Isaiah 52–53.

Readers can anticipate the question posed by the interlocutor: But the Jews haven't heard, have they? (Romans 10:18). Yes, they have. Remember, they had the law, and Christ is the focus of the law, the Torah (10:4). Again, to quote from the old Scriptures: Their sound has gone out, their "words" to the end of the world (10:18; from Psalm 19:4), that is, to Jews and to gentiles. The cure is available.

Paul goes on to say that Israel should have known that God wanted other nations, too (Romans 10:19–20). Jews will become envious that God found a people who were not seeking him. Paul will pick up this theme of envy again in the next chapter.

But for now, chapter 10 serves as a good reminder that, if we are rejected by God, it is simply because we rejected him. We are responsible, because it is not impossible. In fact, God has set life and death before us. Which will it be? As Paul says, we have heard the message. That's right, isn't it? Have you heard the message? Then what stands in the way of faith?

Paul said in Romans 1 that we also know the difference between right and wrong, but we suppress the truth, or we simply ignore it. That's right, isn't it? Do we always pursue the good and choose what is right? We don't always. But why? It's not because we don't know the good. In Romans 2, he said that the law has been written on our hearts, and it has been revealed to us in God's word. Have faithfulness and the moral life been modeled before us, even if imperfectly? Yes. Do we pursue our own selfish desires or think harmful thoughts, when we should rely on the power of God's Spirit? Do we feel like giving up? We shouldn't. It is not impossible. As Moses and Paul declare, the word is near you, in your mouth and in your heart, if you open your eyes and ears to receive it.

Romans 10 also reminds us that sometimes even God's people can fail to see what God is doing. This is what Paul claims about his own people, the Jews. There was the law, the Torah, pointing to Christ, focusing on Christ. Then came the Messiah (Christ), in the flesh, but despised and rejected. "He came unto his own, and his own received him not" (John 1:11). They missed out.

Likewise, could it be that the people of God still miss out? How is that? For instance, we may be set in our ways and mistake our customs, traditions, and preferences for *the* gospel truth. "This is the way we have always done it" becomes effectively equivalent to "this is the only way to do it." We think we have already arrived, and so we refuse the opportunity to dig deeper and to climb higher. And we miss the opportunity to be stretched, to be challenged, to grow. We didn't set out to miss out, but we in fact miss the opportunity to be molded and further shaped by Christ. We don't want to miss the medicine, but we sometimes do just that.

The good news is that God has not left us in the dark, wondering what his will is for us, or what his intention is for creation. It would probably be impossible to know, except he has brought the truth down to us. The Word, made flesh, is very near. He descended to become man. He was raised from the grave to reveal the new man. He is right here in front of us, through the Holy Spirit, in the bread and in the cup, in the water, in the word (New and Old Testaments), in his Spirit-filled community, in our heart and on our mouth. If only we would open our eyes to see and our ears to hear, then the message and the decision become very clear.

Do we have to go far to attain to God in Christ Jesus? No, Christ the Word has come to us. He was there all along, as it were, right next to the stove. He is there, in the good times and the bad, in creation, in the Torah, in the gospel, in the church. And he is there for you.

He is there for you in the good times and bad times, in your trials, pain, and despair, in your joy and in your victories, before your very eyes and ears. Our prayer, then, is that God's Spirit would continually open the eyes and the ears of our hearts to see and hear what God is doing in our lives. Look! Listen! The Word is near you! God is calling you today to put your trust in him and to be conformed to the image of his Son.

Discussion Questions

1. Can you recall a time when the solution you were seeking was right there in front of you? What happened?

2. What spiritual goals have you ever felt were beyond your reach?

3. What reasons (or excuses) do we give for not attaining those goals?

4. Why do you think people don't believe the message today? What are the obstacles to faith?

5. Do God's people still miss out on opportunities? Why? What good things do we fail to see?

20

God Keeps a Remnant

Romans 11:1–10

WHAT DO YOU THINK about leftovers? Some people do not like them. But some leftovers are really good. Especially if it was great the first time around. In fact, I can name a couple of dishes (casseroles) that my wife makes that are wonderful the first time around, but even better leftover. I'm not sure about the science, but it seems to take a day or so for the juice and everything to soak in and all the ingredients to come together. These are leftovers you look forward to. Sometimes you can be creative with the leftovers and do something more exciting with them the second time around. For instance, I've noticed that most leftovers can be heated and wrapped in a flour tortilla to great effect. In these cases, you want the leftovers, the survivors. We wouldn't dare throw them out. There is a good purpose for them.

For now, let's remember what's going on in the book of Romans. We'll get back to the leftovers later (which is quite fitting). Remember that, throughout the letter to the Romans, and especially in Romans 9–11, Paul has on his mind the destiny of God's chosen people. The main point of chapter 10 is summarized pretty well in its closing verse: "But God says to Israel, 'The whole day I extended my hands to a disobedient and obstinate people'" (Romans 10:21, from Isaiah 65:2). In other words, God actively seeks his people, but they repeatedly say, "No thanks." If God seems to be rejecting Israel, it is only because they have rejected his works among them. As it is with all people, it is no different for Israel: They are responsible for their own rejection.

Then comes Romans 11:1–10. Paul continues his line of reasoning and questioning in the first verse. Has God rejected his people Israel (Romans 11:1)? No siree, Bob! (Paul is again engaging in the method called "diatribe," where he imagines what an objector or opponent might say, and then he answers it.) And the force of the question here is, "Has God rejected *all* Israel or the Jews as his people?" The answer is, "Of course not!"

There is not a wholesale rejection of Israel, because some have come to faith. Paul himself is living proof that not all Jews have rejected their Messiah. Paul is a direct descendant of Abraham through Benjamin, and he is not rejected. He is a believer. Jewish Christians exist in the Roman church. Remember Aquila and Priscilla (16:3) and others like them. They may be the minority in that church, but they are not forgotten.

And this is when Paul brings up the famous story of Elijah from 1 Kgs 19. Elijah has just come from a triumph at Mt. Carmel. The priests of Baal were defeated in a contest over who was the true, living, and powerful God. Elijah was vindicated (see 1 Kings 18). But then, immediately, came the despair. His enemies, like Ahab and Jezebel, still sought his life, and maybe even more now. He felt like he was the only one left who remained faithful to God.

Do you ever feel like you're the only one? The only one committed to Christ? Do you ever have the feeling that you're the only one left who does what is right? This would have seemed like an absurd question to ask Americans just fifty years ago. North American culture—not necessarily the culture that was portrayed in the media, but actual American people—were "Christians" by default, if there could be such a thing as "Christian by default." The point is that most people in the US identified as Christians.

Sure, there were denominational differences, and certain groups have always been able to get very worked up about these differences, but we all mostly worked with, went to school with, and did business with believers in Christ. Even those who didn't describe themselves as Christians generally assumed a Christian social ethic as the norm, even if they personally veered from it. Fifty years ago, you might have felt like the only one at work or school committed to transubstantiation, or *a cappella* worship, or "TULIP," or entire sanctification (fill in your denominational distinctives), but not the only one committed to Christ.

And it could be that this question about feeling like the only one still strikes some people as absurd. Maybe, because of your region and circumstances, you're blessed to be surrounded by believers and constantly encouraged and even pressured to do the right thing, to be the right kind of person. Well, this is closer to how it was for everyone fifty years ago.

But it is not the typical case today. Since the vast majority of people, including Christians, consume a vast amount of media and their messages (which are often anti-Christian), it's safe to assume that most of us Christians feel bombarded. Even if you are sane enough not to watch the news and be consumed by the media and their messages, if you dare to step foot outside your door, you can't help but notice a more overtly non-Christian and even anti-Christian environment and culture.

Like Elijah, maybe the cultural turn hits us a little harder because it comes on the heels of what seemed like a great victory. Beginning with the post-war evangelistic fervor of the 1950s, there was unprecedented growth in many conservative churches that lasted for decades. Everyone, it seemed, was a Christian. Again, for some believers, maybe there was doctrinal correction to be had, and there is always moral progress to make, but we all (mostly) claimed to be "Christian." And then . . . What happened? Where did everyone go? Now, at work, you may be the only Christian, or at least the only one who speaks up as one. Now, at school, you may be mocked or even hated for defending Christian ethics and a Christian way of life.

This was Elijah's despair. "There is no one left but me" (see 1 Kings 19:10). Paul calls the famous story to mind. Because the Jewish Christians, including Paul himself, are thinking the very same thing: "There is no one left but me. The Jews have rejected the Messiah, so has God rejected them?" The answer is No. Recall God's answer to Elijah: Even when things look bleak, God preserves a remnant. What is a "remnant?" It just means leftovers. You know that food you couldn't finish for dinner last night, now sitting in the fridge with plastic wrap over it? That's a remnant: the good leftovers, the remainder, the survivors.

It's an important concept throughout Scripture. The remnant is the smaller portion that has made it through some trial or suffering and that God has preserved safe on the other side. The remnant is in Noah's ark, saved to return to the land. There is a remnant of people in Elijah's day who are persecuted but faithful. A remnant that survives destruction and Babylonian exile, and they return to the land. For the remnant, there is always something better waiting on the other side of the trial, though they cannot always see that in the midst of the trial.

In Elijah's day, the remnant was 7,000 strong. By looking back to the Scriptures, Paul can make his point here in Romans 11 that God has not abandoned the Jewish people and that there is a remnant of Jews who remain faithful to God—who have accepted the Messiah, who have been restored by the Spirit that he has poured out, who will be saved through their faith in Christ. It is a small group now, indeed. But the fact is, God has not abandoned Israel. And those who know their Scripture know that God has something good waiting for the remnant on the other side.

A number of implications may be considered, and they all have to do with this idea of the bad times we now live in. It is true: This seems like a particularly tough moment to live in Western society and, moreover, globally. It's a tough time to be a human. I noticed during the last couple of years that my oldest son was in high school, when we would see insane things on the news or on social media, he would often say something to the effect of, "How stupid is this culture! What a crazy time to be alive!"

As it goes with children, I think I know where he got his inclinations. I don't have to look too far. A part of me is proud of his reaction. I like the resistance; I would rather see that than blind acceptance of cultural values. But when we start going down the road of how bad things are, we need to avoid a number of temptations. In other words, how should we proceed, based on texts like 1 Kings 19 and Romans 11?

First of all, just as we must resist the crowd, the world, we also must resist the temptation to despair. If you're like me, pessimism is a strong temptation. But there is no place for despair or pessimism. In his 1981 classic, *After Virtue*, a thorough diagnosis of today's dire moral situation, Alasdair MacIntyre comments, "Do not however suppose that the conclusion to be drawn will turn out to be one of despair . . . But if we are indeed in as bad a state as I take us to be, pessimism too will turn out to be one more cultural luxury that we shall have to dispense with in order to survive in these hard times." We do not have the luxury of pessimism.

In times like these, the remnant needs to pull together and pool resources. We need a vision for how to be the people that God wants us to be in difficult times. We need to roll up our sleeves and get to work. We need to think outside the box. We need to be creative and use our imagination. We need a vibrant community that models the good life.

Pessimism about the future is not going to help us accomplish any of that. Pessimism is crippling. It restrains and restricts. It diagnoses the disease without offering a remedy. Optimism is what we need. Not a blind optimism that ignores or can't understand the challenges. But a realistic optimism that sees the best in God's creation, that finds in the crisis an opportunity. An optimism whose hope is in the God who preserves his remnant for a greater purpose. We need an optimism, a hope, that accepts our place in this challenging world, not just with Stoic resignation, but with Christian joy, and looks forward to what God is doing with it and with us.

And, connected to that point, do not be fooled by a nostalgia that whitewashes the past. The good ol' days weren't always and everywhere all that good. For instance, the second century seems to have been pretty rough, as Polycarp of Smyrna (ca. 70–156) often lamented: "O good God, for what times have you preserved me, so that I should endure these things?" Indeed, in the old days, there were still sins and sinful people. There could be cruelty. There was hypocrisy. There could be injustice. Let's not idealize and thus idolize the good ol' days. Nostalgia can be good, but, like despair, it can also keep us from the work we have before us. Pining away at the past is no plan for the present and the future.

And now, back to the present, back to work, back to school. When you are being singled out and questioned and mocked and persecuted for your faith in Christ—or if you are watching TV or surfing the Twitter feed and you see anti-Christian propaganda, usually as brainless as it is offensive—you may wonder, "Am I the only one left? Shouldn't we just give in? Don't we want to be on the 'right side of history?' Isn't it easier just to conform?" As Paul says, "No siree, Bob!"

Remember, God has preserved a faithful remnant. God keeps and guards the leftovers, and he's going to make something very good out of them. Seven thousand have not bowed the knee to Baal. There are untold numbers who have not bowed the knee to our politics of division and our culture of death—who will not give in and who will not despair.

Finally, we learn from these texts that we should not judge by appearances alone or what we see before our own eyes. Who are the 7,000? Elijah didn't know in his day. Paul didn't know in his. We may not know in ours. We don't see them all. They are in this city, in this state, and in this country. They are around the world. I don't know who or where they all are.

But if and when we start thinking that we are the only ones, we will need to enlarge our vision of who God is and what God is doing. For, even as the number of Christian adherents is declining in the global West, the gospel is increasing throughout the global South, throughout

Africa and Asia. It is not easy in those places. Persecution against Christians rages in parts of Africa, throughout southern and eastern Asia, and elsewhere. But God is working his wonders, as he often does, in the midst of the suffering. The 7,000 are out there, even if we don't see it before our eyes on a daily basis. In light of this good news, we can be hopeful about God's action and our place in the world.

For now, may the gospel increase in our spheres of influence, which is to say, where we can actually do something about it. But it's not going to happen by doing nothing or maintaining the status quo. The optimism, or, let's just say, the hope, that relies on God's Spirit who brings dry bones to life (Ezekiel 37)—may this hope inspire us for necessary being, thinking, and doing to which we are called. Cooperating with God to preserve that remnant faithful—in our lives, in our families, and in our churches—to be the holy and flourishing body of Christ for our city and for the world. Will you stand with Elijah and Paul, with the saints and the martyrs, trusting the God who raised our Lord from death to life for our salvation?

Discussion Questions

1. What is your opinion of leftovers? Are there any really good leftovers you look forward to having again?

2. Do you ever feel like you are the only one left in your sphere of influence who is committed to Christ? At work? At school? In your neighborhood?

3. How does the Elijah story (1 Kings 19) inspire you to press on and remain faithful?

4. Who and where are the 7,000 today?

5. What kind of creative work does today's remnant need to come together and do?

21

Holy Envy

Romans 11:11-24

IMAGINE A DATING COUPLE. Things seem to be going along well, until one day the woman decides to dump the man, for whatever reason. Actually, she has a reason. She has found someone else. The grass was greener on the other side of the hill. The man she abandoned, in the meantime, found someone else, too—a beautiful, loving woman who really appreciates his love and does not take it for granted. The original girlfriend, as it turns out, finds out about it and is now a little jealous. Her new relationship was not all it was cracked up to be. If she could only go back to her first love.

What does this have to do with Romans? Recall the situation of heavy tension between the Jews and gentiles in the churches there. The Jewish Christians, who have recently returned to Rome after five years of exile, are being marginalized by the gentile Christians. And, since the beginning of Romans 9, Paul has been fixated on this question of what God is doing with the Jewish people, Israel. The gentiles perhaps do not naturally care about this question regarding the Jews' status. It is a question about Jewish believers and their relationship with God. Maybe the Gentile Christians have tuned out for the last few minutes while this letter from Paul was being read to them. Well, if they don't care, Paul wants to help them care, which should also help us care.

In Romans 11:11–24, Paul gives two reasons why the gentile Christians ought to care about the Jewish people—and this includes all Jews, Christian and non-Christian.

We can get at the first reason by asking the question, "Why is Paul ministering to gentiles?" Besides being called by God to this ministry, what else is motivating him, and what does this have to do with the Jews? The rejection of the Messiah by the majority of the Jews means salvation for gentiles. But why must Paul talk so much to the Jews about what God is doing among the gentiles?

Paul, ministering to the gentiles, hopes to rouse his fellow Jews to see the truth. He wants to create in them a little envy. He hopes that the gentiles' inclusion will make the Jews jealous of the gentiles' new relationship with the Jewish God. The Jews, largely now on the outside looking in, will want to come back in.

This envy theme goes back to Deuteronomy 32, which Paul quoted back in Romans 10:19. In Deuteronomy 32, God's people have turned their back on God. God is a jealous God. But don't get hung up too much on the word "jealous." God's not petty or insecure. It's just a metaphor, as is the whole scenario. The point is that God loves his people so much! As they abandon him, God says he will go and find—and be found by—another people. He will be in a relationship with them. What will happen? His original people, who abandoned *him*, will become a little jealous themselves. Impelled by that new jealousy, they will do what it takes to restore that original relationship.

It is all there in Deuteronomy 32. Then in Romans 10:19, Paul quotes from Deuteronomy 32:21. Paul is reading Scripture and applying it to his own day. And again, here in Romans 11:11, 14, he picks up that same word that he quoted back in 10:19—to be envious or jealous. You can see Paul putting two and two together as he sees what is happening in the church in light of Deuteronomy 32. God just might be doing that same thing now. As predicted back in Deuteronomy, Jews will become jealous of the gentiles' relationship with God. Paul sees himself and his work as a fulfillment of Deuteronomy 32. He and his ministry are the instrument through which God makes his people Israel jealous, leading to their salvation.

But it's really a backhanded compliment to the gentiles. Paul claims that the motivation for his ministry to the gentiles is primarily to make Jews envious in order to save Jews (Romans 11:13–14). Paul's mission to the gentiles ends up really being about the Jews: gentile salvation is for the sake of drawing the Jews back in. The Jews' acceptance of the Messiah will mean "life from the dead" (11:15). He is putting the gentile Christians in Rome in their place—these gentiles who have acted arrogantly toward the Jewish believers in the congregation. They are a means for helping the Jews reconsider what God has done through his Messiah, Jesus, and how they can still be a part of it.

The second reason that the gentiles ought to care about the Jews is that they need the Jewish people, the "olive tree" (11:17–23). Paul addresses the gentile Christians directly: "You Gentiles, who came out of paganism, with no knowledge of God, are dependent on the Jewish people." Think about all the ways that the gentile believers, former pagans, are dependent on the Jews, in ways they do not even recognize.

The Jews have modeled for these pagans what it means to be in covenant with the God of Israel, to be devoted exclusively to the one, true, supreme God. They have taught these gentiles what it means to read, interpret, and apply Scripture. The Jews have modeled for these former pagans what it means to follow the moral law and to live counter-culturally in a pagan, polytheistic society. As Paul will say later, the gentiles have shared in the Jews' spiritual blessings (15:27). "So you gentiles ought to respect these Jewish Christians who were there before you. Yet you boast!" (see 11:18).

The Jews are the foundation of the building, or, to use a more natural, earthy metaphor, they are the root of the "olive tree" of salvation. If the Jews are the root, then, according to Paul, what are the gentiles? "You Gentiles are not even part of the same plant. You are wild branches." Branches from another tree, a comparatively worthless, wild plant, that have been brought in and attached—ingrafted—to the olive root and tree. The new branches are in need of the root that the Jewish church provides, and not vice versa. Without that root and tree, the branches would wither and die. "You Gentiles," he says, "don't naturally belong here on this tree of Israel, and you are easily cut off." Room has been made for the gentiles by the Jews who have temporarily fallen off. If the gentiles ever fall into disbelief, they'll be cut off in a second. As it is, they are drawing nourishment from the root without returning any gratitude or respect.

As with all of Romans 9–11, there is a very specific issue being addressed here that involves the Jew-gentile tension in the Christian congregations. Paul has a message for the Jewish Christians and also for the gentile Christians about how each group should relate to their brothers and sisters in Christ.

Directly related to and flowing from Paul's first-century message, there are two questions that may be considered in our own context.

First, how can we show greater respect for those who have come before us? The gentile Christians, Paul insists, are very much dependent on the Jews who have come before them. They are in debt to the Jewish people. But they don't act like they are. They don't seem to acknowledge any debt. Not only do they not show respect for the Jewish Christians in their midst, they are treating them like inferiors. Maybe the gentile believers do not really think about this debt, or they aren't really aware of it. So Paul reminds them. If anything, they should be deferring to the Jews.

Who has been our foundation? Who is the "root" in our midst? Who is our olive tree? On whom did we depend for our knowledge and practice of the Christian faith? We depend on our parents and their parents and on ancestors whom we never met: Bible class teachers, preachers, and other ministers, as well as their teachers and ministers. We owe a debt to elders and deacons, to fellow sisters and brothers who now sit, or in the past have sat, in our church pews. All those who have come before us who taught us about the Bible and the one to whom it points; those who modeled for us a life of holiness and faithfulness to God.

Now, in what ways do we fail to acknowledge or show proper respect to those same people? How do we, like the gentiles, boast (11:18–20)? Rather than deferring to or showing proper respect for them, do we ever find ourselves disrespecting those who came before us? We do live in a culture that glorifies youth and, as a result, tends to overlook or even disrespect those older and wiser than we. Maybe we feel like we are more enlightened than they were, that the current generation has such a better understanding of the world, of Scripture, of God, and of the Christian faith. So we fail to learn anything from them.

We should stop and think about where we would be, if not for those who came before us. We would be branches without support, without a tree trunk, without any roots. Branches without nourishment wither and die. The branches that receive that nourishment should return respect and thanks to their roots. We should consider how we may do that.

Now, another question that this text prompts us to ask: How can we instill a little healthy envy, even holy envy, in others? What do I mean by holy envy? Isn't envy or jealousy bad? Envy is bad when it causes us to despise someone else. Jealousy is bad when we are jealous of something that we shouldn't have, or something that doesn't make us better. If we are envious of someone's position or circumstances, and it causes us to hate them, then that's bad. If we are envious of someone's possessions—their house, their car or truck, their job—then that's a sin.

But there is also a kind of envy—or, let's just call it desire—for what is good. And in this sense, there are some things that we should be envious or desirous of, and so much so that we can never get enough. We should want more faith, hope, and love of God and proper love of neighbor. We should desire more joy in the Lord. That's what is meant by healthy desire or holy envy.

According to Deuteronomy 32, God wanted his new covenant relationship with pagan nations to rouse his original covenant people to holy envy. "Hey, that used to be us living that good life. See now what we're missing! Let's return to God." That's the holy envy. Paul says that this is what he hopes for Israel in his own day.

Well, what does that look like in *our* own day? How could we instill in unbelievers a little healthy envy? What would those who are "not the people of God" see in us, "the people of God," that would move them to a kind of holy jealousy or envy? What do we have that they would want? Consider it on your own for a minute. What should others see in us as Christians and as the church that they would want to be a part of? Think on that for a moment, because whatever it is, three conditions have to be met if it's going to work at all: 1) we have to want it, 2) we have to have it, and 3) we have to show it.

So what are those things that will make others envious, that might make others want what God's people have? What will they see that they just have to be a part of? We can think of plenty of negative examples. I don't want to dwell on these. But, suffice it to say, if an outsider's understanding of Christianity is based on what they learn from the media, then what picture will they have of Christians?

They may suppose that Christians are anti-intellectual and that their faith is irrational. They may think that Christians are anti-science. They may believe that Christian living is defined primarily by all the stuff you can't do. They may have in their minds that Christians are probably bigots and haters. They may have the suspicion that many Christian leaders are power hungry and greedy, or perhaps even sexual predators.

The anti-Christian media certainly exaggerate all these things. But if we look around hard enough at some Christians and some Christian groups, we may find that there is a kernel of truth to some of this. You can find Christians who are like that. In which case, then, people may be forgiven for associating those negative characteristics with Christians.

And no one is going to be envious of that. People can find plenty of sexual misconduct outside the church, plenty of greed, plenty of anti-intellectualism and hate. They don't have to come to church for that. We don't want people to find these things associated with Christians, and if they actually do find this, then they will not want what we have. So it's our responsibility to be the kind of people who counter those stereotypes.

On the positive side, what will lead others to look at disciples of Christ and say, "Yeah, I want that"? What are those things? Joy—infectious joy and gratitude that remain constant in any and every circumstance in life. A community of people who really love each other and really love the outsiders who are not yet a part of their community.

In a world where people are by far the most "connected" we have ever been, but at the same time the most isolated we have ever been, people want to belong. These others want to see a community they can belong to. It should be clear that this is not about attracting people with new fads, the latest technology, or a popular church growth gimmick. I mean genuine people being the genuine body of Christ.

To extend Paul's argument a bit, outsiders want to see Christians who have a genuine desire to help those who need it—to feed the hungry and clothe the naked. People want to see families that stay together no matter what, that don't break up, but are stable and faithful. People want to be welcomed as they are. They want to be part of a community that will take them as they are and help them to be better. In a world of death and despair, people need hope; in a world of conflict and bickering, peace; in a world that is plagued by divisions, unity; in a world of competing allegiances, people seek meaning in something truly worthwhile; in a world of distractions, people need direction; in a world of brokenness, wholeness. In a world dominated by bad news, people need good news, the gospel of Jesus. These are the things that ought to characterize God's people and will draw in those who long for such community. They want to experience these things. They want hope and wholeness.

Back to the three conditions. First, do we even want it for ourselves, whatever the "it" is? Do we actually *want* families that stay together, which is to say, do we want to do our part in ensuring that it happens? Do we want sexual purity? Do we want to take the trouble to welcome people as they are and journey alongside them on the straight and narrow? Do we want to love all people? We have to want these characteristics for ourselves.

Second, we have to have it ourselves. Outsiders will not be attracted to something we don't already have. Do we have the joy? If not, what's robbing us of it? Do we have the community that an isolated world full of isolated individuals seeks? If not, how are we going to be that kind of community? We need to have that sense of belonging with one another before we can begin to invite outsiders into it. If we do not want to appear ignorant to the world, then we certainly should actually have something intelligible and attractive to say about our faith to the skeptics.

Finally, we have to show it. We may want it and even have it, but we also have to show it. We have to demonstrate that we are a people actually ruled by peace—the peace of Christ. Talking about it and saying nice words won't cut it. It has to be clear where our allegiance lies. We have to show that our life of morality is in accord with the moral law built into creation and is more do's than don'ts.

Above all, we want to show to others the changed lives of a family who loves because Christ has loved us first. We must demonstrate that we are a community who gives everything because Christ has given everything for us. Because of his death and resurrection, we have good news to share.

Of course, holy envy by itself is not an evangelism strategy. But it is permissible to create a little holy envy in others. The envy is holy if it is desire for the good and leads to a good life and good end.

Let's seek to do that. But, again, I ask: Do you want the good, do you have it, and do you show it to others? The God of love, who wants all people to be saved, has chosen us as his instruments to proclaim and to share and to model that love.

Discussion Questions

1. What all can be learned from Paul's analogy of the root, tree, and branches?

2. Who has been the root or tree on whom you depended for your knowledge of the Christian faith?

3. Have you ever experienced holy envy for someone else's virtues or relationship with God? Did it have a positive effect on you?

4. How can the church do a better job of creating holy envy in outsiders?

5. Do our actions ever undermine our good witness to the world? In what way(s)?

22

Mercy for All

Romans 11:25–32

ROMANS 9–11 ARE NOT the easiest chapters to read, understand, and apply to one's Christian life. As we draw nearer to the conclusion of this section, we finally get answers to the questions Paul has been asking and digging through the Scriptures to find. Well, we'll get some of the answers and, frankly, more questions. Let's do just a little review to get our momentum back.

Beginning in Romans 11:16, Paul introduced a couple of metaphors. The first was a batch of dough. Then he quickly left that one behind and went with another: the olive root and tree, and the branches connected to it. The root is Abraham and the covenant that God made with Abraham—the covenant that Abraham had been chosen for a purpose, that through his seed all people would be blessed. The tree is Israel, the covenant people of God throughout history.

This tree, of course, has branches. The branches are the Jewish people who have come along and grown on the tree and been nourished by their connection to the tree. It is this association to the tree and its root, then, that links someone to the covenant. Being connected to the tree is of utmost importance.

Paul went on to say that many of the natural branches have been cut off. Why? Because of unbelief, indeed, but also to make room for other branches (Romans 11:17–20). These other branches were wild branches of a whole different species and genus from the olive tree. But they were grafted onto the tree. Paul's not trying to give a lesson in agriculture as much as he is asking his readers to use their imagination a bit.

I'm picturing a tree that has chopped off branches lying on the ground around it. And we look up at the tree trunk, and it has stubs where the branches were. Those natural branches were chopped off in order to make room for new ones, and now those other branches have been brought in. And they're attached, being held onto those stubs with duct tape wrapped around the point of contact a few times. They're attached, but barely. You can't hang or swing on these branches. At least not yet. It is not a natural attachment. These wild branches from a wild plant are of a different nature than the tree, and they need much nurture and cultivation and training to remain as a part of that tree. Maybe that wild, different wood will begin to merge into the olive trunk.

These wild, ingrafted branches are the gentiles. Paul's warning to the gentiles (as in 11:13) is that "you are these unnatural branches, newly grafted or taped on. You're not really a natural part of the tree, the covenant." If the *natural* branches could be chopped off—and it takes some effort to saw them off—how much more easily can the taped-on branches be torn off, with just a little effort! So, "Watch out!" he warns, "Do not boast; do not be arrogant about your connection to the tree or your standing with God and in his covenant" (see 11:18, 20).

Maybe a better modern-day analogy is an organ transplant. The original organ has gone bad and has been cut out. A transplanted organ is a foreign element that, without proper care and medication, the body could swiftly reject.

Paul has in view more than just new branches; there is more than an organ transplant. The old has not been permanently discarded. Verse 24 tells us that the old organ will be restored. Or, to return to Paul's metaphor, the natural branches, right now separated, lying there on the ground, can be easily grafted back in. Those branches that have been cut off in order to make room for these new, wild branches—they can be restored to their place.

What does that mean? I'm not exactly sure, but those natural branches are naturally close to the covenant and to salvation. Again, if the wild, unnatural branches can be taped on and survive, then how much more easily can the natural branches be restored and grow onto their mother tree.

And that's what Paul anticipates. When the fullness of the new, wild branches is finally grafted in, then room will be made once again for the natural branches. That is, branches were cut off to make room for new branches, but room will be made once again for the broken branches. This is the "mystery" (11:25), which brings us to the next section (11:25–32).

The mystery is something once concealed, now revealed: A "hardening" has happened to Israel (11:25). Paul mentioned this earlier in the same chapter (11:7–10). The "fullness" of gentiles must come in first (11:12). Of course, this won't happen without the gospel, which is the power of God for salvation (1:16). Gentiles are connected to this tree through the Messiah, and this is what Paul sees happening in his day. If by "fullness" Paul means a full number, which is how some translations take it, then it is a number known only to God. And so after that happens, or along with that happening, "All Israel will be saved" (11:26).

This assertion has been historically controversial and puzzling. Are all Jews going to be saved? Paul does say, "all Israel." What does he mean by those two words, "all Israel"? Consider the word "Israel" first. Who is Israel?

We can imagine two main answers to who Paul means by "Israel" when he says that all Israel will be saved. The possible answers are very different. 1) He could mean spiritual Israel. This is what we Christians usually think of when we say "the church" or God's people. That is, Israel could refer to Jews and gentiles who are in Christ, in which case "Israel" is not an ethnic or physical category. 2) He could mean physical Israel. That is, Israel could refer to ethnic Jews, physical descendants of Abraham. Which is it here?

The trouble is that Paul uses the word "Israel" in both ways, even in this letter to the Romans. Back in Romans 2:28–29, he said that a person is not a Jew who is one outwardly, but inwardly. Sometimes, Israel is meant as a spiritual reality that can include gentiles and even exclude some Jews. But it's different here. Paul is not saying that just spiritual Israel will be saved. First of all, it would be redundant. If "Israel" just means the church or the saved, then Paul is saying that the saved will be saved. That's not a mystery, and it hardly justifies the big buildup to this revelation. It's great news—that the saved will be saved—but the mystery here is that even those who don't appear now to be saved will be saved.

A second reason that this cannot refer primarily to spiritual Israel— particularly if spiritual Israel excludes some Jews—is that it does not do justice at all to the context of chapters 9–11. It might be an easy answer to say it is spiritual Israel. But it is clear that, throughout these three chapters, Paul has been contrasting ethnic gentiles with ethnic Jews or Israel. Paul's question from the beginning of this section was not, "What is God doing with spiritual Israel?" which, in the church at Rome, is composed largely of gentiles. That is not the question. The question all along has been, "What will happen to ethnic Israel?" He has asked about their relationship to the covenant. It is ethnic Israel that Paul is hoping will become jealous through his ministry to the pagans. Likewise, it is ethnic gentiles that he distinguishes and addresses in passages like 11:13.

So it is evident that the concern here is with ethnic or physical Israel. Now, what does he mean by "all"? Well, that seems pretty clear, right? Maybe, maybe not. Once again, I see a couple of possibilities, and the answer to this question is less clear in the context. A very straightforward interpretation would be that he means every individual ethnic Jew. Another possibility is that "all" means ethnic Israel with some exceptions. Even when Israel was on the inside, even when the branches on the tree were all natural and naturally attached, not every individual chose to obey God, and not every branch remained intact. Many times in the Old Testament, "all Israel" does not mean each and every Israelite. So that could be the case here.

At any rate, why does Paul use the word "all"? He is contrasting "all" with the few, the "remnant" that he spoke of earlier in chapter 11. And he is contrasting it with the previous verse, which speaks of the hardening "in part." The idea is that right now, there is a tiny number of physical Israel—a remnant, the leftovers—who are in the covenant relationship. After the fullness of gentiles enters, though, it will no longer be a small number, but a great multitude. God will have mercy on all, including ethnic Israel.

Paul is answering the question he raised back toward the beginning of the letter: "Will their lack of trust nullify God's trustworthiness?" (3:3). Again from earlier in this section: God has mercy on whom he wants to have mercy (9:15). But on whom will God have mercy? Is the hardening of hearts the final word? Has God made Israel to be vessels for destruction? Paul keeps asking the question, and the jury is still out. Again, Paul's "good pleasure," his heartfelt desire, is that Israel will be saved (10:1). Well, will they be? Did God reject his people (11:1)?

The answer to all of these questions is finally given here in 11:26. And he extends that salvation not simply to physical Israel but to all (11:30–32). You all were disobedient but now have been shown mercy.

God imprisoned *all* in their disobedience, so that God "may have mercy on all." What an amazing assertion—mercy for all!

In some ways, we're left with as many questions as we started with. For instance, Paul does not say when the Jews will be saved. If it's through faith in Christ, then we haven't clearly seen this yet. Is it a gradual thing? Will it happen in the middle of history? Will it be a sudden thing? Conversion of the Jews may be an end-time, eschatological event. Paul may be thinking of this as a sign of the end times.

Paul also does not say how the salvation of the Jews is going to happen. We do not know. He doesn't say exactly how all Israel will be saved. Is it something that we can help make happen?

Whatever he means to say, Paul is not teaching unconditional salvation for any group of people, Jew or gentile. He is not saying that one way to God is just as effective as any other. If people will be saved, it will be through their joyful trust in Jesus Christ joined with their obedience. That much Paul has made clear throughout this letter. The gospel is the power of God to save, to the Jew first and then to the gentile (1:16). What God has done for us in Christ matters. Our response to the good news of what God has done in Christ matters. God will not forever unconditionally bless any group of people. Paul is hoping that Jews will realize just how near salvation is, the salvation that was intended first for them. If all Israel will be saved—and he says they will be—if "all" people will be saved, it will be because of what God has done in Christ.

Paul is not advocating what today is called Zionism. He is not here suggesting a separate plan for Jews outside of Christ. He is certainly not suggesting a literal return of Jews to the physical land of Israel.

Jews will be saved in the same way gentiles will be: through their coming Messiah, who is also the Messiah having come and coming again. God's elective process once favored physical Israel but was then opened up to physical gentiles. But, Paul is telling us, that's not the end of the story of redemption. Once that number is complete, it will be increasingly open again to Jews.

Despite many ambiguities, the message to the gentile Christians in the Roman church is clear—get off your high horse. You were once disobedient but have now received mercy. Most of the Jews are now disobedient. You gentiles have benefitted from this. Guess what? The Jews, even those chopped off branches, will also be shown mercy. The end result is that God will have mercy on all. So think about how you actually treat your Jewish Christian brothers and sisters, and then consider how you ought to treat them. You should be grateful to them.

Ours is a very different situation than the one in the first century, so it is somewhat difficult to apply, and the application requires extending Paul's argument into a new context. Readers should at least come away with a better appreciation of God's infinite mercy for us all. As I wrote above, we should have respect for those who came before us, who taught us the gospel, who are *our* roots and tree. We may not agree with them on everything. That is fine. We ought to appreciate and respect our elders.

Furthermore, even non-believing Jews are beloved of God "on account of the fathers" (11:28). It is as true today as it was then. We share Paul's hopes for ethnic Israel, but we also expect that people will come to salvation through Christ, the Messiah, whose death and resurrection is the atonement for sin, sufficient for the whole world. The Messiah is the true vine and we are the branches, if we remain in him (John 15:1, 5).

Again, to extend the exhortation, do we love those outside of Christ as much as Paul did? No matter who they are or what their background, is it our "good pleasure," our heart's desire and delight, to see people come to Christ? There is mercy for all. As the body of Christ, as humble agents of God, we offer his divine mercy to all.

Discussion Questions

1. What do you think about Paul's statement that "all Israel will be saved"? Do you think it means each and every individual physically descended from Jacob? Why or why not?

2. Do you believe the salvation of Israel is something we can help accomplish?

3. In light of Romans 9–11, what kind of relationship do you think Christianity has or should have with Judaism?

4. How would you compare your love for those outside of Christ with Paul's?

23

Deep Wisdom

Romans 11:33–36

WHEN I WAS AN undergraduate student at a Christian university, I was in the university choir. On the Spring Break tour one year, the first stop was on a Sunday morning in Garland, Texas, on the northeast side of Dallas. We attended a church that morning, and they had us sing a couple of songs in the sanctuary between Sunday school and the worship assembly, which basically meant we were the first featured thing that morning. I'm from Dallas, so I knew a lot of the people in that church. And since I am not tall, I was pretty much front and center. I felt a little added pressure.

One of the songs we did that morning was Johannes Brahms' setting of "O Heiland reiss die Himmel auf." The entire piece is in German. It's a fast-tempo, complex, five-and-a-half minute, *a capella* song, and it ends with an intricate chorus of Amens, with each part executing its own string of melismas until all end on the same Amen. On that morning, the first stop of the tour, we bombed the concluding Amens. Throughout that conclusion, since everyone was singing "Ahh" (prior to the final "men"), if you got lost or didn't keep up or know where you were, it was not easy to find your way back by listening to the other parts. Many of us didn't quite know where we were until it ended. The whole song was a little rough, but the worst part at the end lasted probably about ten seconds, at the most. But it seemed like ten minutes. It's one of those things that probably was not noticeable to most listeners, but it was to us. And for me, it was personally very embarrassing in front of the home crowd.

How did this happen? It wasn't because we didn't have the music. We held the sheet music in our hands. We had to have it. It was full of German words, six stanzas of four lines each. That's twenty-four lines of German poetry, with different melodies and notes for each stanza. But we worked all semester on it, and it sounded great in rehearsals. What went wrong?

After the church service, we ate lunch, got on the bus, and traveled to our next destination. We were to do a full concert at a church in Fort Worth later that same evening. We arrived mid-afternoon, unloaded our things, and assembled in the empty sanctuary for our warm-up. The director was not happy with our performance of that one song that morning. This was not a surprise. No one was happy with it. What was surprising was his solution.

He said that he wouldn't allow us to use our musical scores for that song anymore, for the rest of the tour, starting tonight . . . in about two hours! With all due respect to this teacher, who had been conducting the chorus for over twenty years at that point, I thought this was the dumbest idea. "If he thinks we bombed this morning, just wait! He knows that we don't know this song by heart." I thought he might try to wean us slowly off the music. But no! Was he trying to make us fail again?

In our travels through the book of Romans, we have recently been wading through chapters 9–11. At the crescendo of this section, in response to God's dealing with Israel, Paul breaks out in praise of God.

> O the depth of the riches and wisdom and knowledge of God; how unsearchable his judgments and inscrutable his ways. For who knew the mind of the Lord? Or who became his counselor? Or who gave in advance to him and it will be paid back to him? Because from him and through him and unto him all things; to him the glory forever. Amen (Romans 11:33–36).

This passage is an ode to God's deep knowledge and ways. It is almost poetic. In fact, most modern translations take the liberty of indenting these verses, setting them off into poetic lines, and, of course, adding verbs to the final sentence. Paul begins by praising three attributes of God. First, God has deep wealth or riches. In other words, God possesses infinite resources. He has very deep pockets. His power, ability, or capability is beyond imagination. God never starts a job he cannot finish.

Second, with God there is profound wisdom. Third, to God belongs inexhaustible knowledge.

What is the difference between knowledge and wisdom? Knowledge begins with the raw data, "just the facts, ma'am." Wisdom is taking the knowledge and putting it to good practical use. Someone has said that knowledge is recognizing that tomatoes are a fruit. Wisdom is never putting tomatoes in a fruit salad. This distinction is an oversimplification, for true knowledge includes insight that goes beyond mere information. Wisdom then builds on the body of knowledge. And with God, there is no shortage of knowledge and facts, no insufficient data. He is not surprised by anything that happens, and there is no possibility that he has not accounted for. He knows what to do with his infinite knowledge. He knows how to achieve his ends and goals, despite our ability to mess things up. His ways are infinitely wise.

As for creatures, we lack all these things, and so our finitude—our limitedness—in all these areas negatively affects our calculations and judgments and actions. How many times can we look back on our lives and say, "If I had known then all the facts that I know now, I would have acted differently? If I had only known it was appendicitis, I would have gone to the doctor sooner!" Or, "If I had only known it was nothing, I would never have gone to the doctor and wasted all that money on tests!" We did what seemed intuitive and best at the time, given our limited perspective.

Paul goes on to exclaim how "unsearchable" are God's judgments and "inscrutable" his ways. One reason God's decisions and actions are unsearchable and untraceable is our limited perspective. It would have seemed weird and uncaring not to go to the doctor with that much pain, but, lo and behold, it was nothing! Or it would have seemed strange and paranoid to go to the doctor for what looked like the common cold, but, lo and behold, it was pneumonia! Because of God's infinite riches, wisdom, and knowledge—and our finite understanding—what God does for humanity's good in the long run can seem to us very odd in the moment. It is not the way we would do it. And so, from our point of view, his ways are unsearchable and inscrutable.

Next, Paul asks three rhetorical questions, corresponding to these three attributes, but in reverse order. "Who can know the mind of the Lord?" No one! God has infinite *knowledge*; we don't know what he knows. "Who can be his counselor?" No one! God has infinite *wisdom*; he doesn't need advice or counsel from us. "Who can give in advance to him so that it might be paid back to them?" No one! God has infinite *riches* and resources; he doesn't need anything from us. We cannot put him in our debt.

If we think we can understand God and put him in a box that we can wrap our minds around, then we are sorely mistaken. God is always greater. Whatever we think or say about God, God is always greater. However we choose to describe God, that concept or description is at best incomplete. God is always greater than our thoughts and words can indicate. We should not confuse our concepts about God with God himself. Because of our finitude, there is always and necessarily an inaccuracy in what we say about God. The words we use, even the words that God has given us to use about him, are like an accommodation to children, the notes for beginners.

In light of the context of chapters 9–11 and of the entire letter, Paul is making a very particular point. It's not merely in praise of God's greatness, though it is that, too. It's about the greatness and incomprehensibility of God's plan, at least from the limited human perspective. We may sit back in confusion and wonder, "What is God doing? Is God trying to make us fail?" Even more specifically, Paul is emphasizing the greatness of God's plan to extend mercy to all, even when it looks like all have been given over to disobedience (11:32). The theme here is God's grace and mercy.

Whatever God is doing with gentiles, whatever he is doing with Jews, the answer to the question culminates with emphasizing the *mercy* of God on all (11:32). Then 12:1 begins, "Therefore, through the compassions of God . . ." Thus, after the answer has been given, and before he goes on to spell out some more of the implications in chapter 12, Paul pauses to praise the plan of God to have mercy on all, a plan that we have yet to quite figure out. His thoughts are higher than our thoughts. His ways are higher than our ways.

Now, the fact that we don't know everything about the outworking of God's plan doesn't mean we don't know anything about God's will or the goal of his plan. God has revealed certain things and made them plain. He created us. He loves us. He has redeemed us. He will have mercy on all.

How those things will play out and the means through which God will bring about his purpose—these things are not always clear. In fact, if there's one thing we can be sure of in Scripture, it's that God often has a surprise up his sleeve for his people. We may not know how it's going to be true that he will have mercy on all, but it is true. Don't put limits on God's love.

Back to the chorus concert and the infamous song. Our director said we couldn't use our music, and that if we don't know the song yet, we better get to it. And that's what we did for the next hour or so. We had to trust him. In the past, he usually seemed to know what he was doing. At any rate, we really didn't have much of a choice.

What happened that night? We nailed it. And every night of the tour, we nailed it. The problem was never that we didn't know the song. We knew it. We didn't know that we knew it, and so we had messed it up. But he knew that we knew it. During the failure that morning, we were looking down at our music at "Amens" that we knew, instead of looking up at the conductor who was directing us with his hand and guiding us. Because he forced us to, we did work hard that afternoon to tighten it up and remember things that we had always relied on the sheet music for. Once we stopped looking down at ourselves, however, and we looked up at the conductor, we were able to see clearly.

There are many lessons we could draw from this story. But the one I want to emphasize is the one I think about most when I remember that day. Before we sang that night, I truly wondered whether our director was crazy, and I thought that taking our musical score away was the worst thing he could do if the goal was to perform the song well. More generously, we could say that I found his judgment to be "incomprehensible." Instead, his plan was masterful. He motivated us to learn what we could learn and should have known already. He motivated us to do something we didn't think we could: sing that complex song by memory. I already had respect for him as a teacher. But after we succeeded, that day I gained a whole new level of respect for his teaching technique. His way of getting us to the goal was not the way I would have planned it. But he knew better, and it worked out.

It is a common experience: In the moment, you doubt the means, but it turns out to achieve the intended end perfectly. The plan looked foolish, but it was in fact wise.

God is the director, and we are the choir. We don't always understand what the director is doing, especially after we mess things up. But we can look to the past and see his success with previous choirs. We trust that he has prepared us well and given us what we need to succeed. He calls us to receive that gift, to step out in faith and participate in the great story of redemption, to keep our eyes on him and become more than we thought possible.

These words in Romans, and this story and others like it, remind us that if a human's judgment can sometimes be wiser than we know or expect, then how much more is it true about God! God writes the play differently than we would. Be careful when making judgments about God's intentions from an uninformed, finite human perspective. The more that our conclusions or someone else's conclusions are limited by time and space, the less we should trust those judgments.

But we tend to rush to those judgments. For instance, note how we often think about missions and evangelism. "Look what's happening to the church in this city over the last fifty years! God must be doing . . . *x*." Chill out, and take a deep breath. Maybe God *is* doing that in that specific time and place. But add to that myopic viewpoint a wider perspective that encompasses a larger region and more history. How does our sliver of personal experience fit in with a historical and global perspective? How does that fit with Scripture? How does it all fit with God's eternal plan revealed therein? The hardening of one group or one part of the world—even our own city, perhaps—may mean acceptance elsewhere in the world.

Wow! We can't really know it all. Paul doesn't have it all figured out. Paul is simply trusting in the trustworthiness and power and love of the God who made a covenant with Abraham—the God who brings the dead to life and calls non-being into being. God will keep his word, sometimes in surprising and unpredictable ways. God will deal not only righteously, but also graciously, with his people, with those not yet his people, and with his entire creation. It is our job to be faithful here and now. God the Father is to be praised for his deep, inscrutable wisdom and power, as well as his mercy toward all. His mercy has been shown in the incarnation of his Word, in the death and resurrection of Jesus Christ, and in the pouring out of his Holy Spirit.

Discussion Questions

1. As with the choir and its director, have you ever questioned the actions of a leader, only to understand later the wisdom behind the plan?

2. Based on Scripture, what things can we know about God's intentions?

3. When we question God and his plans, how can Scripture come to our aid?

24

Living Sacrifice

Romans 12:1

LIFE IS FULL OF questions, some more important than others. The questions are ubiquitous: on tax forms, exams, applications, polls, and so on. Sometimes the questions make me laugh. Some are very strange. When a friend of mine got a fish hook stuck deep in his hand, he went to the doctor's office. After he was brought into a room, the nurse came in, looked at her clipboard, and asked, "When did the pain start?" "When the hook went in my hand," he replied. "Do you feel safe at home?" she continued. "Yes, except for when I'm fishing." "Who is the current president?" And on she went with the protocol.

Years ago, when my wife took our little kids to play at a city park, she saw some illegal drugs on a nearby bench. She called the police to report it, so they sent someone out to her. For their report, among the questions they asked her was, "How much do you weigh?" No good deed goes unpunished. Sometimes we do the question-asking ourselves.

But most of the time in life, we simply go through the motions without bothering to ask any questions at all. Especially the thoughtful, provocative, and penetrating questions. It's easier that way. We avoid those; our society generally doesn't encourage them. Usually the most important, thoughtful, penetrating question we can ask is, "Why?" I remember when my oldest son learned the word "Why." He went through a phase, when he was about three years old, asking this question all the time: "Why?" After we answered to the best of our ability, he would ask again, "Why?" Did you know that you can pursue that question for a long time? It's as if the kids know they can drive their parents and teachers nuts by asking them "why" over and over again.

Well, in my attempt to be a good dad, I was patient with my son's interminable question-asking. I realize that this is how kids learn. So I tried to answer, and sometimes got caught up in the moment. I remember very well one time, we were turning at a signal light, and my little son said, "Why is the light red?" "That's a good question," I replied. Then I got carried away. "Do you mean what makes it red and not white or green? I don't know. Is the color in the bulbs themselves? Or are the bulbs all the same color and perhaps there's a tinted barrier that makes them appear red? Or do you mean what is the purpose of having a red light? Well, sometime back when cars became widespread, people didn't know what to do when they came to an intersection with other cars. Someone invented a color-coded light system, and red is a recognized color that means stop." The *why* question can be answered in many ways. Of course, my son had stopped listening long ago. If your kids try to drive you nuts by asking why, you can drive them bonkers by giving an unusually long answer that makes no sense to them. They *may* stop.

Why. Much can be done with this little word. Once, during that same time in our lives, we were sitting down at the table about to eat dinner, and my son asked, "Why are we here?" It was a profound question for a three-year-old. I was proud. I began to wax eloquent about how our ultimate purpose in living is to glorify God and enjoy him forever, when he interrupted and said, "No, we're here to eat!"

At any rate, the *why* question is really important. It's a good way to examine and evaluate your life. Let's give it a try. "Why do you work where you do? Why do you have particular rules and try to enforce or follow them? Why do you spend your money the way you do?" I remember discussing with some students in class: "Why are you going to college?" There may be many reasons—some good, some lame. "My parents made me come." That would be a lame reason. "To receive a quality education." That would be a good reason. I also reflected with my Christian students about another question that applies to just about everyone reading this book. "Why go to church? Or why participate in the work of the church and contribute money? Why spend your week in service to others?" Again, there may be many good reasons and many lame ones.

One good answer for all these questions is found in and around Romans 12:1–2:

> Therefore I urge you, brothers, through the compassions of God, to offer your bodies as a living, holy, God-pleasing sacrifice, your thoughtful worship. And do not be conformed to this age, but be transformed by the renewing of the mind, so that you may discern what God's will is, that which is good and pleasing and perfect.

The first noteworthy thing about this passage is that we are entering into the middle of a long conversation here. When Paul says, "Therefore," in Romans 12, we know something important has come before. Much has come before, but he is mainly speaking about God's mercy. Before we say anything about a "living sacrifice," we have to say something about what precedes this—God's mercy and compassion. Recall what Paul has just written about God's mercy in Romans 9 through 11. The overriding question that Paul asked is, "To whom does God show mercy?" God has mercy and compassion on whom he wills; it does not depend on the one "willing" or "running" (Romans 9:15–16, 18). God prepares his "vessels of mercy" for glory (9:23). The last thing Paul wrote before coming to his doxology and now chapter 12 is that the gentiles have received God's mercy, Israel will receive it once again, and God will have mercy on all (11:30–32). That is the answer to the question, to whom does God show mercy? He shows mercy to all. And then, at the end of chapter 11, Paul breaks into praise of God for his wise plan to show this infinite mercy. God's mercy is the reason for everything that follows here. It is the answer to every *why* question. Why? Because of God's mercy and compassion.

So now, in light of God's mercy toward us in Christ, in light of the fact that he has saved us, not because of our inherent goodness, but despite our sin, what is our response to God's mercy? We respond with *sacrifice*. First of all, since Paul is using the language of worship ("sacrifice"), it should tell us something important about worship. God is the one who initiates worship. Our response of worship is just that—a response to what God has already done. He has shown us mercy and called us to worship. We respond to his super-abundant grace with sacrifice.

When Paul says we should offer a sacrifice in gratitude to God, he is saying nothing new. Israel had different types of sacrifices they could make in worship to God—some for sin, others for uncleanness, and the like. Many sacrifices *had* to be made to be right with God. But there was a type of sacrifice called a "peace" or "fellowship" offering that was made voluntarily, out of sheer gratitude for God's blessings (see Leviticus 3 and 7). The main category of this type of voluntary fellowship offering was called *todah* in Hebrew, which means "thanksgiving." In view of God's mercy, the response of God's people has always been to offer a sacrifice of thanksgiving.

Do we still offer sacrifices today? Yes. Physical sacrifices? Yes. Not animal sacrifices, but they are physical sacrifices, the sacrifice of our bodies. Not sacrifices for sin. The once for all sacrifice of Jesus Christ—his death and his resurrection—has bought our redemption and cleansed us from sin. So what sacrifice is left for us? The voluntary sacrifice of thanksgiving.

Paul describes the sacrifice that we are to offer, the sacrifice of our bodies, in three ways—it is living, holy, and pleasing to God. First of all, this sacrifice should be a *living* sacrifice, in contrast to the slain animals. Your body, your whole life—this is the sacrifice. Your life in self-sacrifice is what God wants. Second, the sacrifice is to be *holy*. Just as the offered animal was to be without blemish and the sacrifice of a crop was the pure firstfruits, the life offered in sacrifice should be holy. Third, a *God-pleasing* sacrifice could mean many things. But it certainly means that this sacrifice, in order to be pleasing to God, must cost us something, or else it's not really a sacrifice. It should be something more costly than the animal from your herd, something more precious than whatever you put in the collection plate at church. Now, God is interested in what we give financially. But he is interested in so much more. Indeed, Paul is saying no more than what God spoke through the prophets long before Paul. "I desire mercy not [animal] sacrifice" (Hos 6:6). In exchange for the sins of our souls, God has revealed the kind of sacrifice he requires from us: "To do justice, to love mercy, and to walk humbly with your God" (Micah 6:6–8). This sounds like a living sacrifice.

Paul goes on to say that this living, holy, pleasing sacrifice is "thoughtful worship." By "thoughtful" he means rational and spiritual, not worship or sacrifice that requires a beast. What about the next word: Is it "service" or "worship?" The Greek word here (*latreia*) can be translated as service or worship. But it is clear from the context that Paul is talking about true *worship*. He has been speaking in the worship language of Israel about offering a sacrifice; sacrifice is an act of worship in a holy place, at the altar of the tabernacle or temple. Like the prophets before him, Paul is reminding readers of something often forgotten. Worship is not just something we do one or two hours a week.

Now, that one or two hours a week in the assembly is of first importance. Don't get me wrong. Paul isn't saying, just be a good person during the week, and that's all you need. It is a common thought these days that the horizontal dimension of our service to one another and even the vertical dimension of private worship throughout the week supersede the assembly. The thought is that if service during the week is worship, then the Sunday assembly is optional or unnecessary. But this is incorrect. He isn't saying that, any more than the Israelite prophets were encouraging people to stop worshiping in the temple. When God's people assemble together to receive the gifts of bread and cup in the presence of Christ in the power of the Spirit, we are doing what we were created and called to do.

The corporate worship assembly is where the body of Christ together confesses and celebrates God's mercy, what he has done for us in Christ through the Holy Spirit. Out of that worship assembly flows the living sacrifice of gratitude during the week. These two aspects of worship are intimately tied together. Without the vertical attention to God, the acts of service are empty. And conversely, without this horizontal dimension of worship, the vertical dimension is incomplete and means nothing, and it is not pleasing to God.

The vertical and horizontal dimensions of worship—and their mutual relationship—are assumed throughout Scripture. To offer one very clear example, Jesus says that one's sacrifice to God is not pleasing as long as there is a breach on the horizontal level (see Matthew 5:23–24). We can probably think of many instances of this connection between the vertical and horizontal being broken. All God asks is that we do our part in repairing a horizontal breach. But can we think of an example of all of this going right? It looks something like this: coming together on the Lord's Day to remember the death and celebrate the resurrection of our Lord, to confess our common faith and praise God for his mercy, and in the power of the Spirit to encourage each other as fellow believers; and then we go out and, out of sheer gratitude, spend ourselves in sacrifice to others, serving others in ways that reflect the love and grace that God has poured out on us.

We return to the *why* question. Why give oneself to God? It is about thanksgiving. Because of God's mercy, we offer ourselves. That is the ultimate answer to nearly all the important why questions—to show our gratitude to the God who created and redeemed us, and to glorify and enjoy him forever.

So do we as Christians still offer sacrifices? Paul would affirm, "Absolutely." Even physical sacrifices? Yes. Offer your bodies. I've given some hints about what it means to offer yourself as a living sacrifice. How do we know what Paul means by a living sacrifice? Again, the context helps. As you look down throughout the rest of Romans 12, it is clear: show to one another the love that God has given to us.

God has given his Son—his all—for you. In view of God's compassion, his mercies, what have you sacrificed for him?

Discussion Questions

1. Would you agree that our society does not encourage asking thoughtful questions? Why or why not?

2. Why do you work where you do? When is the last time you asked yourself that question?

3. Why do you go to church (or not go to church)?

4. Are we Christians still to offer sacrifices? What sacrifices have you made to be a Christian?

5. Why give yourself as a sacrifice to God? Could you persuade someone else of the importance of making such a sacrifice?

25

Transformation by Renovation

Romans 12:2

CONSIDER A TALE OF two cars. Both vehicles were decades old. They both sat in an old covered carport for years. Neither one ran. It would take a great deal of work to get them going again. My dad was given one of them.

It was a 1960 Chevy Impala. He restored it. He transformed it by renewing it. First under the hood: new battery, new belt, new hoses, new plugs. It started running again. But he didn't stop there. From the very inside, he moved to more cosmetic features. He re-did the upholstery and then the exterior. It got a new paint job: two-tone, turquoise and white. He finished it off with white-wall tires. Now the car sticks out for all the right reasons. Now it's nice, well-maintained. Now it's parade-worthy. Now it shines. The other car? Well, its story is short; it was still in the old carport the last time I saw it.

Recall Romans 12:1–2:

> Therefore I urge you, brothers, through the compassions of God, to offer your bodies as a living, holy, God-pleasing sacrifice, your thoughtful worship. And do not be conformed to this age, but be transformed by the renewing of the mind, so that you may discern what God's will is, that which is good and pleasing and perfect.

In the previous discourse on verse 1, we really dealt more with the *why* question. "Why offer our bodies as a sacrifice?" We offer our sacrifice

168

to God because of God's compassions toward us. Here we will deal more with the *how* and *what* and *for what purpose* questions.

Let's focus on verse 2. Let's take up the first part of the verse: do not be modeled after this world or age, or, as J. B. Phillips translates it, "Don't let the world around you squeeze you into its own mould." The word *world* is a word that really should be translated "age." In Latin translation, it is *saeculum*, from which we get the word "secular." An *age* (by itself), long or short, implies a span of time that won't last forever; "this age" is temporal and passing away.

Part of Paul's point is the futility of seeking to conform to this (secular) age—an age that will soon be obsolete. It is like rearranging the furniture on a sinking ship. What's the point? Keeping up with this age is perhaps like trying to keep up with fashion. What's in fashion today will be out of style tomorrow.

It is not shocking to those who know me, but I've never been overly concerned about fashion. If I have any fashion principle, it is this: It is futile to try to keep up. In fact, fashion is cyclical. If you hang on to things long enough, they eventually come back into fashion. The wide lapels on blazers from the early 1990s have made their way back in the late 2010s. Around 2017, someone complimented my shirt, calling it retro and noting that it looks very mid-nineties. I said that's because it *is* from the mid-nineties!

Again, Paul is saying that this world, as it exists right now, is just one age that will not last, and this is one reason we should not conform to it. It has been said that "whoever marries the spirit of this age will find himself a widower in the next."

Second, and more importantly, we should not be modeled after this age, not only because it is temporary, but also because the values of this world are, by and large, antithetical to the values of God. Surely this point is obvious to us all. Secular society is not founded on the pursuit or enjoyment of God, but instead is centered on self. We are probably aware of so many ways in which the values of the world and of God clash that it is unnecessary to try to list them all.

What is not so obvious to us, though, and in fact is a little scary, is how much we are modeled after this age without even realizing it. The language of being formed or molded suggests that a shaping takes place. Don't let the world squeeze you into its mold or image. A little shaping here, a little there. No single change was big enough to notice. But a thousand little tweaks later, and our form becomes unrecognizable, but we never even knew it. Sometimes we don't realize, until we travel cross country, how thick our accent is. Are we so enmeshed in this world and so conformed to this age that we don't even know it? So, metaphorically: Do we have a secular accent and fail to realize it? "Do not be conformed to this age."

Sometimes the differences between the Heavenly City's accent and the Worldly City's accent are so subtle that they go unnoticed, but the differences mean everything. For example, the world's emphasis on tolerance sounds good, and it *is* derived from Christian principles. When pushed to an extreme, however, it undermines the very concept of truth and the will to proclaim it. It obscures the real meaning of love and hinders the will to exercise it.

This age is trying to shape us into its form, and it's doing a pretty good job. So we must be alert to these attempts. For instance, if you've ever watched the Super Bowl, then you know what I'm talking about. The advertisements are almost a bigger attraction than the game. Those advertisements come with messages, and we should be alert to those messages. And we receive the messages—some of which are frightening, some are just untrue, and some are antithetical to the gospel that we profess.

I sometimes get tired of being the media critic in my house, so I was mostly quiet during Super Bowl LIV. A Google ad came on that showed an old man talking, and his computer knew everything about him, down to the most minute and intimate details. It was clearly supposed to be sentimental. About five seconds into the ad, it was the eleven-year-old among us who spoke up and said, "That's scary! How does Google have all those pictures and know everything about that guy?" A little later, Facebook had an ad promoting the platform's ability to unite everyone together and create a sense of loving community. That ad wins the award for most ironic—or unintentionally funny—since Facebook is much more successful at creating hostility and division than unity.

The present age is full of such propaganda. Some of the messages are simply untrue. At other times, the messages are not virtuous. In a consumerist culture, marketing aims to make you discontent and want something you never dreamed of wanting, and the marketers are more than willing to deceive to make it so. Today's new desire then becomes tomorrow's necessity.

When we allow ourselves and our children to be enamored by celebrity—especially the "fifteen minutes of fame" variety—or technology for its own sake, then we have conformed to this age, succumbed to its values, and have ourselves to blame. When we waste hour after hour of our short lives in front of a TV watching things that can never produce anything virtuous, we have yielded the advantage to the enemy. Not that things like TV or smartphones are evil in and of themselves, but they become subtle means for molding us into the image, not of Christ, but of the world. They make our brains and our souls into passive recipients of all the worst the world has to offer—from the merely inane to the positively wicked. "Do not be conformed to this age."

Look to the next part of the verse. Before considering transformation, we must think about what makes transformation happen in the first place. "Be transformed"—how?—"by the renewing of the mind." Transformation (of life) by renovation (of mind).

In verse 2, Paul coins a new word, used for the very first time in Greek literature: renewal. That's what renovation means, renewal. Other words we sometimes think of as churchy, like justification, sanctification, baptism. But those were fairly common words to Hellenistic pagans. Here, however, we encounter a genuinely and uniquely Christian word, a real churchy word—renewal.

Have you ever renovated something? Maybe a house. Perhaps you have renovated or restored an old car. How does one renovate or renew an old house or car? Depending on the state of disrepair, it may not be easy. You can't do it in one hour or even one day.

Even though it is a process and doesn't happen overnight, there will be a real, objective moment when you can step back and say it has been renewed, renovated. Once renewed, does the renovation stop there? No, it does not. You have to maintain the job that has been done. You keep the car running on the inside and clean on the outside. The point is that things that have once been renovated need to be maintained. They will require some sort of continuous care, maybe constant care.

And the care doesn't stop with one aspect of the car. When one part has been renovated, it opens your eyes to the car's potential. It's a constant process that involves not just one aspect of the car but the whole thing, inside and out.

Some of you may own a home that's a permanent fixer-upper. Although there is satisfaction with the progress that has been made, if you look hard enough, you can always find something that needs improvement. Maybe your "to-do" list is never empty.

The apostle Paul is not talking about the renewing of a car or a house, but the renewing of the mind. How is the mind renewed? It is an inward renewal, a spiritual rebirth. It begins when we give our lives to God, when we are regenerated by the Holy Spirit. Like the house renovation, there is a point that you can look at someone and say, this person has been reborn. The conversion is internal. Like the house or car, this initial conversion demands constant, ongoing attention. There must be a continual process of renewal. No maintenance-free siding here. Such is the renewing of the mind.

If the mind is renewed by that initial conversion—the reception of grace, turning to God in faith, repentance, baptism—then how is this renewed mind maintained? How do we keep our minds renewed?

As with the renovated house, it requires constant care. There is a children's song that's very simple, but also correct: read your Bible, pray every day, and you'll grow. It is worth mentioning, because not all Christians do it. Daily being in the word, attending to prayer, and seeking God's face. This is Mind-Renewal 101. Although basic, it's a different way of thinking, enabled by the Holy Spirit. What are you doing, then, to maintain the renovation?

In other words, once the mind has been renovated, that renewal is not maintained by neglecting it or by conjuring some big spiritual high once a year. Annual spring cleaning is good, but it takes more than that. It is more mundane. It's the regular rhythm of a life lived in the presence of God. It's a daily submission of our will to his. It is a daily vigilance that is wary of any dirt or external influence that could compromise the renovation. It means being cautious and thoughtful and ready to evaluate what we watch and listen to, our attitude, our heart. Constant renewal means looking at our lives and seeing where we need improvement. Although we may be satisfied with the progress we have made by the help of the Spirit, we are not yet perfect. We are works in progress. The "to-do" list is never finished.

If the mind is renewed and it stays renewed, then the body follows—which we offer as a living sacrifice. The obvious result of the renewal or renovation is transformation. This gets to the *what* and *for what purpose* questions. What is the goal of renewal? Transformation.

What does Paul mean by transformation? The word he uses is *metamorphein*, the verb form of "metamorphosis." In English, we think of metamorphosis as the process by which the caterpillar becomes a butterfly. By transformation, Paul means change, of course, but what does the change look like?

Paul places transformation in direct opposition to being conformed to this age. So it is change *from* something that is conformed to the world, like the world, modeled after the world, *to* something that is now distinct from the world. Distinctness is the key concept. The renovated and now transformed person is not made in the mold of the world, of the crowd. A difference, a distinctness, is present. It is not about separation or removing oneself from the world, but distinctness. It is to be in the world, but not of the world.

The transformed person is like a house that, in the midst of a neighborhood of decay and dilapidation, is restored, renewed, and transformed. It shines now with that new coat of paint. It catches your eye as you drive by because it is distinct from its surroundings. In the neighborhood, but not of the neighborhood. So the renewal of the mind is inward, but the transformation shows; it *shines*. "Be transformed."

The idea of being transformed is interesting to pursue in the New Testament. The word appears only on two other occasions in the New Testament. On those other occasions, transformation is related to glory.

First, the word "transform" or metamorphosis appears in Matthew 17 (and the parallel in Mark 9). Jesus takes his three closest disciples, Peter, James, and John, up on a mountain (see Matthew 17:1–6). The word "transfigured" is the same verb in Romans 12:2: "He was transformed before them." The main purpose of this event is to show the superiority of Jesus over Moses and Elijah.

But focus on the transformation. Jesus' face shone like the sun. White light was emanating from his clothes. This is a brief glimpse of the *glory* of God in the flesh. That's what 2 Peter says in recalling the majesty of that moment. The transfiguration was the sign of Jesus receiving glory from the Father (2 Peter 1:17). In other words, this is a sneak preview of the glory of the Lord—his resurrection and exaltation.

Do you know what "glory" means? It is not a common word nowadays. It seems like a churchy or "Bible" word. But what is glory? One of the meanings of glory in Hebrew and in Greek is simply *brightness* or *radiance*. When you walk out of a dark movie theater into the afternoon sun and you're blinded by the light, that's a lot of glory.

When Jesus was transformed, he was shining like the sun. And what did the disciples do when Jesus was transformed and they heard God's voice? They fell facedown! They collapsed not only because he was too bright for them to look at but also, Scripture says, because they were terrified. Rather than basking in his glory and hearing God's word, they hid their faces from the Messiah, as if veiling themselves from the light of the world.

The final passage in the New Testament with this word "transform" is 2 Corinthians 3:18. Paul, in a mysterious passage, is discussing the covering or veil that Moses sometimes wore when his face was shining brightly after speaking with God. Paul then mentions that the old covenant is read, in a certain sense, with a veil or covering or barrier, and he contrasts that reading with the removal of the veil (see 2 Corinthians 3:16–18). Paul says that when we hear God's word and recognize its proclamation of Christ and the Spirit, "we all with unveiled face reflect the glory of the Lord" (2 Corinthians 3:18). This encounter transforms us from what we were into the glorious image of Christ. With what? Ever-increasing *glory*. "Changed from glory into glory." Brighter and brighter we shine. Transformation is about glory, about shining forth. Like mirrors, God's people reflect the depth and magnitude of God's glory, shining his light.

Unlike the disciples on the mountain, who saw the glory and heard God's word, and hid their faces, turning away from the Lord; instead, when we turn *to* the Lord (2 Corinthians 3:16) and hear God's word, we have seen his glory. That's the transformation. Our minds are renewed; we become like Christ. He shines; we shine. He was not conformed to the world, nor are we. We are transformed to look like and be like him. Then we can discern God's will for us—we know what is good, pleasing to God, and perfect. We know it, we pursue it, and we do it. By the power of the Holy Spirit, we become the good, pleasing, perfect sacrifice he desires. "Be transformed."

So why, for what purpose, are we renewed? For transformation. Again, what is this transformation, in light of all these passages? It happens when we turn our face toward the face of God. It happens when we turn to God's word and through it gaze upon his true Word, Jesus Christ. It means being transformed into his brightness and becoming like Christ, being changed into a daughter or son of God. It means distinctness. Just like my dad's newly-painted car shines. It's noticeable. It stands out in the crowd. It's different. The transformed person emanates bright light. When we are turned toward God, like a mirror we reflect the profound depth of the goodness and beauty and radiance of God's face.

But, we confess, it's easier to hide our faces and to put up the veil. Sometimes we don't want to be noticed—at least not for Christ's glory. We don't want to be different from the crowd. It's difficult. Do you hide your face from God? Has your light dimmed? Do you need renovation and renewal?

Everyone who has been touched by God's love is looking for renewal. The simple practices mentioned earlier—reading the word and praying, looking to Christ, following the guidance of the Holy Spirit—along with the prayers and fellowship of Christians, are a good place to start. By the Spirit, may God transform us into the image of the Son, so that Jesus Christ, the light of the world, may shine his beauty and glory through us.

Discussion Questions

1. In what ways do Christians betray a secular accent?

2. What do you think "renewing of the mind" means? What does it look like?

3. When Jesus was "transformed" in the presence of the disciples, why did they hide their faces? Why were they afraid?

4. Do we ever hide or turn our faces away from God? Why? What are the consequences?

26

A Christian Handbook

Romans 12:3–21

AS MENTIONED EARLIER, IN 2017, I bought a car to replace my deceased Toyota Corolla. My new pre-owned vehicle was a 2015 Ford Fusion. One of the first things I did when I got home was check out the owner's manual. It's not that I don't know how to drive a car. It's that this new car had all kinds of gadgets in the front and on the control panel, things that I thought I'd like to try out and get a handle on. After all, my Toyota had no CD player but a cassette tape deck, if that tells you anything about its age and the state of its technology.

So I pulled out the owner's manual. There were actually two versions: the regular version and the abbreviated version—the "quick reference guide." The quick reference guide was not very helpful. It was full of features that had asterisks next to them, such as "Adaptive Cruise Control," "Push Button Start," and "Remote Start." When I looked to find what the asterisk meant, it said, "If equipped." Mine was not thus equipped.

Then my questions became more specific. For these questions, the regular car manual was a pretty good help. In the midst of all the intuitive instructions, there were other things not so intuitive to me. I dog-eared the pages "Keyless entry," "Audio system," and "Connecting the Phone to Bluetooth."

With an owner's manual, we expect certain things. It is a how-to guide in the sense of how one does it, which buttons you should push. It is full of practical instruction. If I want to know how a combustion engine works, I'll have to go elsewhere. If I want to know what the vehicle's computer does, I won't find it in the manual. The manual does not discuss the inner workings of the car. Not too much about what's happening behind the scenes. It includes no physics or engineering technicalities. Just practical tips for how you operate it. Those instructions, of course, are based on all the technical details. The practical how-to's all assume the basics, the foundations.

Sometimes even the practical instructions can be a bit confusing, and help is required. It sometimes takes someone who has done it all before to model how it is done. After reading the instructions about connecting my cell phone to the Bluetooth, I still didn't do it right. It took my wife showing me how to do it.

When we come to Romans 12, we are introduced to this notion of a living sacrifice. We are to offer our bodies, Paul says, as a living, holy, God-pleasing sacrifice. The natural question arises, "What is a living sacrifice? What does it look like to give your body as a living sacrifice?"

For the specific details of what it means to be a living, holy, God-pleasing sacrifice, we read on in Romans 12:3–21. This section is a manual or handbook for Christian living. From *manus*, the Latin for "hand," we get the word "manual." It is a handbook, a book you can carry with you and have at hand when you need it. A book of practical instructions.

Many commentators divide the letter to the Romans into doctrinal and practical: chapters 1–11 are doctrinal, and 12–16 are practical. It is not that nothing to this point in Romans has been practical or that nothing hereafter will be doctrinal. That is the beautiful thing about Paul's writings, and really, all of Scripture. The doctrine and the practice go together. Theology and ethics together. Believing, knowing, and doing are all necessary for Christian faith. How we live necessarily flows out of what we believe God has done for us in Christ. What we believe and what we love are the basis of how we behave. How we behave reflects what we truly love and believe (which we hope matches what we *say* we love and believe).

In his commentary on the epistle to the Romans, the Swiss theologian Karl Barth put it this way:

> [In Romans 12] we are not now starting a new book or even a new chapter of the same book. Paul is not here turning his attention to practical religion, as though it were a second thing side by side with the theory of religion. On the contrary, the theory, with which we have hitherto been concerned, is the theory of

the practice of religion. We have spoken of the mercies of God,
of grace and resurrection, of forgiveness and Spirit, of election
and faith, of the varied refractions of the uncreated light. But the
ethical problem has nowhere been left out of account. The questions "What shall we do?"—"How are we to live?" have nowhere
been excluded. We have not been searching out hidden things
for the mere joy of so doing.

In other words, the practical instructions in the rest of the book of
Romans are intimately connected to the doctrinal truths that Paul has
explored in the first 11 chapters. In fact, doctrine and ethics, head and
heart, understanding and relationship—they all go together, and you
can't have one side without the other.

Let us recall that these practical instructions are intended primarily
for the Roman church. That doesn't mean they won't apply to us. They
will apply to us, but even more so when we understand the situation Paul
was addressing. Remember that the gentile Christians had been arrogant
toward their Jewish Christian brothers and sisters. There has been a tension in the congregation, especially upon the return of the Jewish believers who had been absent for five years. For both groups in the church,
Paul has a message. Here—in this church—here is what it means to be a
living sacrifice to God.

As I considers the situation of the ancient church in Rome vis-à-
vis today's social and perhaps even church situations, I can't help being
struck by the similarities. In a highly charged political atmosphere that
seems never to subside, and in a time when social divisions and tensions
threaten to seep into our Christian fellowship and to divide us, too, these
instructions from Paul are as timely in the twenty-first century as they
were in the first.

What do you hear in this passage? Which practical instructions
stand out to you—for yourself and for your church community? I'm a bit
overwhelmed with all the instructions, as in a car manual, though most
of the things covered we may already know. Here are the things that stand
out to me, the phrases in this manual that I dog-eared, and maybe the
things I need help with, to be modeled for me. Here's what it means to be
a living sacrifice.

Do not think of yourself more highly than you ought (Romans 12:3).
Do not be proud or think you are superior (12:16). It's not that there's no
place for self-esteem. But it's that every person, not just you, is made in
God's image, too. It has been said that being humble doesn't mean to

think less of yourself, but instead to think of yourself less. The best way to avoid thinking of yourself too highly and to avoid sinful pride is simply to think of others. Put yourself in their shoes. Think about their situation. Think about them. For a church that was playing identity politics—Jew versus gentile, us versus them—this instruction is a good place to start.

Another instruction that I dog-eared in this Christian manual is that love must be sincere (12:9). "Sincere" is a fine translation, but the literal word used here is "unhypocritical." "Agape-love unhypocritical." Remember the word "hypocrite" simply means "play-actor." If we want to know how love must be unhypocritical, then we must ask, how can love be hypocritical? What is fake love?

In many ways, modern society has re-defined and watered down the meaning of love. One way society misconstrues the concept of love is to overuse the word to try to convey a reality that is not there. In the process, we render the concept and word meaningless.

When I think about the misuse of the word "love," I cannot help but recall a particular movie that depicts a dystopian future in which nothing but heartless and joyless addicts to technology live—if you can call it living. And one of my favorite scenes in this comedy shows the characters walking into a massive, sprawling Costco. As the shoppers enter the building, there is an employee greeting them, who mechanically repeats, with no expression or eye contact, "Welcome to Costco; I love you."

The language of love has been hijacked, so it now means nothing. The greeter at Costco "loves" all of us. The corporate workplace is a "family." And on Facebook we may have "friends" whom we do not know from Adam and couldn't pick out of a lineup. We go along, but it's a joke, fake, hypocritical, insincere. It's a fake because we don't show any actual love, we don't treat our coworkers like family, and we've never sat down and had a discussion with some of these social media friends. Is your co-worker from across the building, that you said "hello" to once at the water cooler, going to drop by your house for Thanksgiving dinner? You hope not? Then you're probably not family.

Society has certainly watered down these terms. In light of this biblical text, we must ask ourselves, how does this same language function in the church? Is it any less fake? When we in the church use the language of love and family and friends, does it mean anything more than in these other social contexts? I hope so.

If love is to be unhypocritical, genuine, sincere, then, if we say we love each other, it must be shown. If we are family, then we do drop by the house. If we are friends, then we talk about important things outside of one hour a week in the assembly. Only when we in the church get our act together can we then extend that real family love to those not yet among us.

The final thing that really stands out to me is the prohibition against revenge. Imagine what this world would be like if this instruction were followed. If we all gave up our "rights"—our "right" to be offended, our "right" to be right, our "right" to set things right? It is a sacrifice, after all, that requires giving up something that we think belongs to us. What would happen if we let God handle it? What if we take the evil, the wrong, that has been done to us and "overcome evil with good" (12:21)?

All the instructions in this manual go together. Consider it negatively: If someone thinks more highly of himself, then he is going to be conceited. If he is conceited, then he will think he is superior to everyone else. He will then be easily offended when someone does not treat him the way he thinks he should be treated. Then he will repay that perceived evil with real, intentional evil. Love for others will be fake, not sincere. As all of these things could make our love for one another grow cold, our spiritual fervor can then be quenched. Ours is a society that is overcome with evil and answers the evil with more evil.

Put negatively like that, it may be a fitting description of the Roman church or any church experiencing similar tensions. And this is why Paul gives the instructions he does. I know of no better description of our society. So we must hear and heed the same instructions.

In light of the tense situation in the Roman church, when I take in this whole text from Romans 12, this handbook for Christian living, I would sum it all up thus: Lay down your arms. In 1918, on the eleventh hour of the eleventh day of the eleventh month, the Western world came together to mark Armistice Day, a laying down of arms, the end of the bloodiest and most pointless massacre the world had ever known, up to that time. The truce and its subsequent peace treaty lasted for about two decades, not long enough. The world was overcome once again by evil.

To a church racked by festering divisions, where they are all at each other's throats—Paul's message is that they lay down their arms and show genuine love and regard for one another. "Overcome evil with good."

Do you have a disagreement with someone? Lay down your arms; let it go. Do you have a right to be angry with that same someone? Maybe so. That is fine. Lay down your weapons, Paul says. It is not your place, but God's, to punish (12:19).

So Romans 12 begins the Christian handbook, the how-to manual, for the Roman church and for us, teaching us how to be a living sacrifice. And the instruction is: Lay down your arms, and love without retaliation. Because we are all members of Christ's one body. Honor others more than yourself. Rejoice and mourn with each other. Even when you're the recipient of evil—and you will be—then overcome evil with good. Sometimes we need others who have done it before to model it and show us how it's done.

Discussion Questions

1. Which instructions stand out to you in Romans 12:3–21?

2. Does the language of love and family ever seem fake or artificial when used in society? What about in the church?

3. Describe a time when someone you know overcame evil with good.

27

God's Servant for Good

Romans 13:1–7

ROMANS 13:1–7 RAISES THE question of civil government, a perennial question for Christians whose citizenship is in heaven. A disciple's ultimate allegiance is to King Jesus, and we are his subjects, citizens in his kingdom. But the questions arise: Do we have dual citizenship? Are we not citizens of our country, too? As Christians, can we pledge our allegiance to a secular nation? How are we to live in society? What is our responsibility, as Christians, to human civil authorities?

When Paul wrote this letter to Christians in Rome, the government regarded believers in Christ as just another sect of Judaism. Since Judaism was a legal religion, the earliest Christ-followers were also officially protected (whether or not local officials honored that protected status). And when Jewish leaders living in Rome were exiled under Emperor Claudius, that included Jewish Christians. Those Jews and Jewish Christians were probably angry with the government. But now the new Emperor Nero had lifted the edict and allowed the Jews to return. Perhaps there was still some resentment against the Roman government.

To those who might be angered with the government—if it's possible for us to imagine such a scenario today—Paul reminds them who establishes government, what the government is for, and what our Christian responsibility is to the government. We should find good reminders for ourselves as well.

Paul is not providing a political philosophy or full-blown theory of "church and state." So he does not supply clear answers to every possible question. He is vague enough that some very different philosophical approaches look to these same verses for support. But some questions and answers recommend themselves.

1) From where does the civil government derive its authority? It is ordained by God. On the one hand, from the Christian perspective, Paul seems to exalt civil authority by saying it is from God. Doesn't that seem exaggerated? Really? The emperor is from God? This emperor? Or we might say, this White House? This Congress?

Look at the words Paul uses to describe the authorities. God's *diakonos* (servant or deacon; 13:4) and *leitourgoi* (ministers or servants; 13:6). These are the same kinds of words used to describe church workers. So the civil authorities appear to be on God's team; they are God's servant for good. They are in God's cabinet, so to speak. This is high language and high regard for secular authorities!

On the other hand, from the Roman perspective, Paul puts civil authority in its place by saying it is from God. Civil government is not independent, but answers to a higher authority. The emperor is not all-sovereign. His authority owes its very existence to God—namely, to the God of the Christians. The government is therefore to be in submission to its higher authority.

What exactly does it mean that civil government is established, ordered, or ordained by God? It could sound like God determines particular rulers for particular regions. According to this opinion, in effect, God voted for Joe Biden in 2020, just as he voted for Donald Trump in 2016. He will appoint whom he will appoint. It would seem, since God's decision is the only one that matters, why vote? This is not what Romans 13 is saying.

What Paul means is that God is sovereign over it all. God has established human society—for humans to live in community. This divine action does not mean that human means are pointless or that we shouldn't waste our time voting or getting involved because God established it and "God's going to do what God's going to do." Not at all. Because God created humans to live in community, then some sort of civil arrangement or social contract on the human level is necessary. God is the prime cause. He has established human society, and he has ordained that human authorities should govern those communities. But he allows secondary causes; he allows us to decide how best to order our life together.

So to acknowledge that the civil authority is God's servant does not necessarily mean that the government is godly or that everything the government does is somehow right. As we know from reading the Old Testament, God sometimes uses instruments and servants despite their own evil intentions. Nebuchadnezzar's Babylon, for instance, was a "servant of God" to punish the evildoing of Judah. That did not mean Nebuchadnezzar was good or that the Babylonians were good. On the contrary, Babylon was an idolatrous nation and worse than Judah, a point raised by the prophets.

2) What does government do? What is government's main job? At its core, what is the government for? According to Romans 13:3–4, it is to punish evil. Before government took on the job of providing health care, retirement benefits, or even fixing potholes, its task has always been to punish evil. Paul does not opine about whether government is inherently good or evil. It is a necessity, especially given human fallenness. Citizens need protection from wrongdoers, from within and without. Law and order, police and military. In this case, the Department of Justice and Department of Defense, and their subsidiaries, are at the heart of what government does. If a government cannot protect the citizenry, then there is no real point in having good roads. The sword is a symbol of punishment. This is the threat of physical punishment and perhaps even the reality of capital punishment.

Vengeance, or just punishment, is whose? To answer this question, we must consider the end of chapter 12 together with the beginning of chapter 13 and notice two sets of connecting terms or hook words that join these two paragraphs—*wrath* and *vengeance/avenger* (12:19; 13:4). (By the way, we often associate the English words "vengeance" and "avenger" with excessive force or uncontrollable violence, but the Greek words simply convey "just" punishment. An avenger is one who punishes justly.) These words join these passages together logically.

In fact, we must connect chapter 12 with chapter 13 if we are to understand why Paul seems to interrupt himself for these few verses to talk about the government. Why is he talking about civil authorities here? It's not that he thought now is the time in the letter to give his political philosophy. He is talking about how the Christian community should behave and show love to one another. Look back at 12:19: Vengeance is whose? First of all, vengeance is not ours. As individuals, it is not ours to punish. Individuals in community should not repay evil with evil. Second, vengeance is God's. That should be clear enough.

But the third answer comes in 13:4. Who is the "avenger for wrath?" Since these are the same words Paul used in 12:19, we might think the answer is God. But here the avenger is "the rulers," "the authority." So does punishment belong to God or to the civil authority? Who has the right? Both. Again, it comes back to secondary causes. The governing authority is God's instrument or "servant" to bring God's wrath (12:19; 13:4). God has the right to punish evildoers; he often does it through the agent of civil government. So if evildoers disobey the civil authority, they suffer the just penalty from God through the means of the humans in charge.

It is on the basis of this passage (combined with some others) that a distinction is often made between, on the one hand, personal revenge or violence and, on the other hand, the punishment enforced by the state or civil authority. God has granted, and we have contracted, to government authorities the responsibility to enforce or uphold what is good and to punish what is evil. This raises further questions.

Can Christians act violently not for personal vengeance but as an agent of the government? Can Christians participate as officers—say, in the police or the military—to punish evil behavior? Some say yes, whereas others say no. Paul does not really say here. He may not envision a Christian being in a military position. He doesn't really specify the Christian role in government. It was still about 250 years until there would be a Christian emperor. So Christians have looked to Romans 13 with a range of opinions on these matters.

3) What should we do? What is our responsibility as Christians toward the civil government? Should we care at all? After all, Jesus (not Caesar) is our Lord. Actually, we are told in several places in the New Testament that we should care. We can sum up Christian responsibility to the civil authorities in three words: pray, pay, obey. All three of these are utterly reasonable when we consider the overall message of Scripture. And we can think about all three actions as our duty, as the debt we owe to the civil authorities.

For the first one—pray—we have to go outside of Romans 13. In 1 Timothy 2:1–2, Paul says that prayers and petitions be made for all people, including "for kings and all those in authority." The context is about the salvation that is offered to all and that God desires for all. Yes, kings and politicians need salvation, too. In addition to their salvation, we need to pray for them to rule wisely and to be guided by godly principles.

Second, citizens should pay (Romans 13:6–7). We hear it also in the text from Matthew 22:15–22, when Jesus was asked about paying taxes.

The principle of paying taxes, especially as Jesus puts it, goes very well with Scripture's predominant attitude toward money. At best, money is neutral. But often, money is a temptation, the acquisition of which can become an obstacle for entrance into God's kingdom. Since the money is Caesar's, give it to Caesar. It is no personal loss. Paul also mentions, more positively, that the authorities deserve to be paid for their efforts.

Third, obey. To be sure, Paul says "submit," not obey. I don't know whether that makes a significant difference. But the command seems fairly clear—among the things we owe are submission and respect. Romans 13:2 implies that there are levels of authority that ultimately ascend to God, for opposing the authority is to oppose the ordinance of God. In an egalitarian society like ours, we often ignore this fact or positively fight against it. But this is why the fifth commandment, to honor father and mother, is about honoring *all* earthly authority, ultimately leading to God. We should be teaching our children to honor all their earthly authorities—parents, elders, teachers, bosses. If someone is never taught to honor parents or to submit to civil authority, then it will be difficult for him to understand the concept of giving honor and obedience to God.

But all this raises another important question that, sadly, Paul does not directly address.

4) What about when the government is bad? Consider the three things we owe government. Pray. Yes, we should still pray for the rulers when they are bad, and perhaps more so. What about paying taxes? Presumably yes. Government leaders and workers still need to be paid. We still need emergency services. Are taxes too high? Is there a lot of money going to waste? Yes. But especially in a republic, we get to have some say in it all. We can exercise our protest and our vote, and then do our best.

What about obedience? Are we obliged to obey evil rulers? Interestingly, when Paul wrote Romans, Nero was emperor (r. 54–68). At the time, he was still a young emperor, about a year into his reign, with much potential for good. When Paul wrote, the government was still God's servant to punish only the evil. The instructions to submit, in Romans 13:3–4, assume a government that upholds the good and punishes the evil. No government does this perfectly, just as no parent does it perfectly. Some are more just than others.

My advice would be the same for the instruction to honor and obey parents. Some parents are better or more just than others. If a parent makes a mistake, has some unfortunate habits, or is not a Christian believer, that doesn't mean that the Christian child has permission to disobey. Likewise, if our president and Congress are bad, it doesn't mean we have the right to run red lights, not pay taxes, or speak evil of everything our leaders do. But no government is perfectly bad, and none is perfectly good. That goes for parents in the home, for small local governments, and even more for the monstrously large state and federal governments of today.

But what about if and when the civil authority is, in some specific and meaningful ways, no longer a servant "for the good" (13:4) but has become a servant for evil? Other voices in Scripture address this circumstance. Later, when the same Roman Empire began to persecute Christians, a situation reflected in the book of Revelation, Rome is referred to as a beast and a harlot—not so much God's servant! We know from Scripture that there are indeed times for civil disobedience.

When the Babylonian rulers told the three Hebrew children to bow down before the idol, they refused (Daniel 3). When the apostles were told to stop preaching in Jesus' name, they said, "We must obey God rather than people" (Acts 5:29). As Augustine and Thomas Aquinas said, and Martin Luther King Jr. repeated, an unjust law is no law at all, and therefore one is not bound to obey it. But like the three Jews and the apostles and Martin Luther King, if we disobey an unjust law, we must be willing to suffer the consequences—a Babylonian furnace, a Jerusalem jail, a Birmingham jail, or whatever the consequence may be.

It is not ours individually to judge the justice of every little law and decide whether or not it should be obeyed. ("I see an unjust stop sign! I must exercise civil disobedience!") If and when there is an actual unjust law, then it is up to the community of God's people, in prayerful study of Scripture and with divine wisdom, to discern together what our corporate and individual responses will be.

When early Christians responded to the persecuting empire in the second and third centuries, they pointed out that the presence of Christians was not a bad thing for the country; they should not be pursued and punished. Far from it! In fact, there were no better citizens of Rome than Christians—a people devoted to loving their neighbors, doing what is good in their local communities, encouraging stable households, and praying for the emperor.

Would that we could say the same thing, that Christians are good for the country. No doubt, Christians are, first and foremost, citizens of Christ's kingdom, the true king who lived and died and rose again. No other king and no other kingdom deserve our full allegiance. As such, there is no better citizen of this country than one whose primary allegiance is to the God of perfect and holy love. Through the strength of the Holy Spirit, as disciples of Christ, let us pray for our leaders. Let us make a difference in this world—first, by making a difference in our homes and in our neighborhoods.

Discussion Questions

1. What are some biblical principles for how Christians should live in and interact with society at large?

2. What does it mean that the civil governing rulers are ordained by God?

3. Does that affect the way you regard the current leaders of this country?

4. How can vengeance or just punishment belong both to God and to governing authorities?

5. As followers of King Jesus, what do we owe to the government?

28

Follow the Law of Love

Romans 13:8–14

IN ROMANS 13:8–14, PAUL returns to the theme that occupied him in chapter 12 and continues to elaborate what it means for believers to be a living, holy, God-pleasing sacrifice. Throughout Romans 12, he emphasized the importance of humility, selflessness in helping others, unhypocritical love, and the refusal to take revenge when wronged. The punishment of evildoers, Paul says, is to come from the Lord, not from you. At the beginning of chapter 13, Paul took a brief aside to say that the civil government is one of those instruments that God can use for punishing wrongdoing. The authorities who seek your good are, in fact, acting as God's servants when they punish wrongdoers, and so they deserve our submission and respect. And now, in 13:8–14, Paul comes back to the theme of love.

In 13:8–10, we have a summary of all the instructions from chapter 12: Follow the law of love. Love, he says, is what we owe to one another. We owe taxes to the government, but we owe love to each other. Paul puts it in terms of debt. As Christians, we will never be debt-free. We will always have a debt that we owe to each other. Specifically, as we remember the immediate situation Paul is addressing, those gentile Christians in Rome owe a debt to their Jewish brothers and sisters in Christ, and vice versa—namely, to love. Not only does he put it in terms of debt, but he also puts it in terms of law.

In verse 9, he quotes from the second table or second half of the Ten Commandments, particularly the ones that directly concern the treatment of others. The Ten Commandments, which are a summary of all the laws of Israel, can be summed up in what Jesus called the two greatest commands: love God and love neighbor (Matthew 22:37–40). In fact, Jesus said that all the 613 commandments of the Torah "hang" on these two laws, these two great love commands. What Paul says here is perfectly consistent with Jesus' teaching. Paul's concern is the tense relationships in the Roman church, and so he focuses on the second table. The second table of the Decalogue is an expression and expansion of the second greatest love command: Love your neighbor as yourself.

This is what it means to keep the law, something Paul clearly saw as still binding. Love was always the central point of the law. For if you truly love your neighbors, then you won't murder, hate, or do any harm. If you truly love others, then you won't steal from them and you won't covet their possessions. Law-keeping, here and any time Paul talks about it, is ethical. The ceremonial requirements and judicial laws of the Old Testament are not for our literal keeping, but the ethical laws, the laws of love, are still in force.

But Paul doesn't stop there. He comes back, as he always does, to give a reason for the commands and for following this law of love. Do this, he insists, "knowing the time" (Romans 13:11). It's not clear what Paul meant by the statements in these verses. It could be that he expected the end of all things to come very soon. Maybe; maybe not. He doesn't say that here. We do know that our personal end, or *the* end, can come at any moment. What he does say is that it's past time to wake up from your sleep.

Do all of this—follow the law of love—"knowing the time." That is, live a certain way because of this age of darkness, the times in which we live. It is as important for us as it was in Paul's day. Now, perhaps more than ever before, is not the time to sit back, take it easy, and watch TV. Imagine, in a time like ours, the church sitting back and saying, "Yep, it looks like our work here is done. Knowledge of God, biblical literacy, devotion to Christ, living a holy life—it is all right where we want it to be."

If we are tempted to think or to act like this, then we need to wake up. It is time to get up and get to work—but doing what? If the church is going to have any impact in our culture today, it's going to be because we know how to show true love. Now is the time to get out of our easy chair, or, as Paul says, to awake from slumber and show our conviction by our lives. As I've heard many times before, "Preach Christ always; if necessary, use words."

Why? Because our salvation is nearer now than ever before. This verse is appropriate any time of year, but it is especially meaningful during Advent. It fits the situation of Israel before the birth of Jesus, and it fits the situation of true Israel today as we await his coming again. Salvation is nearer to us now than when we first believed. The first lights of dawn are breaking through the night, that first thread of light across the horizon. If salvation is nearer, then the deeds of the darkness should be abandoned, stripped off, and the deeds and *weapons* appropriate to the light of day put on. Paul is using military imagery.

The metaphor of stripping off and putting on clothing is also baptism language. Strip off the old in order to make room for the new. Put on the Lord Jesus Christ (13:14). Clothe oneself with Christ. It is the same language Paul used in Galatians 3:26–27. There, to "put on" or "clothe yourself with" Christ is expressly related to a new beginning in baptism.

But it also means to imitate or be like Jesus in this battle. As such, the battle requires a plan of action. And so Romans 13:14 concludes with a very arresting statement: "Make no forethought of the flesh for lusts."

One of the deeds of darkness is the forethought, the planning ahead for evil desires or sin. It is not just committing sin but making plans for sin. How do people plan ahead for evil desires? Instead, God's people should be strategizing about how to avoid lusts and sin. If we have no battle plan to win, it's the same as planning to lose. Winning the battle against sin does not just happen without the power of God, or without our cooperation. Not only must we plan how to resist evil, but we must also plan how to advance the good.

For Paul, the future affects our present. In light of what has already come, and in light of what's soon coming, we ought to live a certain way and follow a certain path—the way of love. Why? Because of the times in which we live, and because our final salvation is nearer now and the glory has broken through already. Light will shine on our deeds. What will that light reveal? What will those deeds reflect about us? Our prayer is that the Holy Spirit would work in us to help us follow the law of love, to love others as God has loved us, and to receive people as they are and help them become what God made them to be. This is what he has done for all of us in Christ.

Discussion Questions

1. How can we plan ahead to avoid sin and evil desires?

2. How might we plan or prioritize our conduct in Christ to accomplish what is good?

29

Prioritize Peace

Romans 14:1—15:13

HAVE YOU HEARD THE story about the man who was shipwrecked and washed up on a deserted island? He survived by himself for years. One day, about ten years into his sojourn, he spotted a ship. He lit a fire and got the sailors' attention. They sent a small boat with a few men to rescue him. The rescuers reached the island. As they were about to get on the boat and take the man to their ship, they noticed that he had built three structures. They asked him about these little huts and how he used them to survive. He explained, "This one is my house. That one is where I go to church. And that one over there is where I used to go to church."

This story points to a phenomenon common in modern, especially North American, Christianity. There are so many churches, one to suit everybody. We can sometimes have trouble going to church even with ourselves, not to mention with others.

Some of you readers have probably been through church splits. Others have found yourselves at a congregation where you did not quite agree with every decision that was made. Perhaps you had a line for yourself personally that, after it was crossed, made it difficult to worship there. Sometimes we find we have done as much good as we can do in a particular group. Or you have done your best to make peace with someone who does not want truth or reconciliation. Maybe there are times when, because of conscience, it is right to go elsewhere. In these cases, we can serve more effectively with another body of Christians.

Church tension can occur in many ways. Personalities are often to blame for the discord. But sometimes there are real issues, doctrines, or practices that can be controversial. What are some issues that you would say are neutral or simply "opinion" but could still cause strife in the church? We can all list matters of preference that people shouldn't get so upset about. You may have an opinion, but you recognize that it's just an opinion. Then there are other issues that we have ideas about, but they seem to be more than *merely* a matter of opinion.

That is fine. But we should realize that there are people who have also felt strongly about the things we regard as mere opinion and that many such issues have been the source of division. We may not have strong feelings about some issues that other people do, and vice versa. That's the rub. We can all agree to grant latitude on matters of opinion, indifferent matters. But it's harder to come to consensus on what those matters of opinion are. My non-essential matter may be for you an essential of the faith. The point here is not to make a list and categorize the items as essential or not essential. I'm simply observing that it depends on whom you ask.

There are other issues that I did not name. We may be aware of other concerns right now, and there are other matters coming down the pike that we may not be aware of yet. And now, here we are. We find ourselves in our respective congregation with specific people. The question for us is, "How do we keep potentially controversial issues from causing division?" The question for the Roman church was the same: "How could they stay unified?"

Church tension did not begin on the deserted island mentioned earlier. It did not begin with American Christianity or even Protestantism. Church tension began when the church began. We see it in Acts 6, between the Grecian and Hebraic Jewish Christians. As long as there are people, there are differences. As the rabbis have often said, "Two Jews, three opinions." Or we might say, wherever two or three are gathered in Jesus' name, there is disagreement among them.

Remember the Jew-gentile tension in the Roman church. So far in Romans, Paul has laid the foundations of what God has done for all of us in Christ and of how we should treat one another in general. The practical instructions of the last two chapters—serve others in humility, follow the law of love, and so on—have been building to address this very specific situation causing tension in the Roman church. Paul lays it out in Romans 14:1—15:4.

The behavior in the church that Paul addresses is that some believers are not accepting those who are "weak" in the faith, and then they are passing judgment on their opinions. The recommended course of action is quite simple: It must stop. "Accept the weak," Paul says (Romans 14:1). Already we have a principle for getting along in the church, and there are several such principles in this section of the letter. I will offer five.

First, there are some matters of belief that are *indifferent* (*adiaphora*). One must recognize that such a category exists. This doesn't mean that those concerns are not important on some level. But they are not matters of the faith per se. They are not what are sometimes called "salvation issues." There is a broad range of things in the middle, between obligatory and impermissible, that may or may not be believed or done. Again, not everything is in this category of the non-essential. And non-essential is not necessarily the same as unimportant; some non-essential matters are more or less important than others. Just because there is a disagreement over a question doesn't mean it is therefore a non-essential matter or that it is not worth discussing. The point here is simply to acknowledge that Paul recognizes such a category. An old saying popularized in the seventeenth century, but expressing a sentiment that is much older, recognizes the same: "In essentials, unity; in non-essentials, liberty; in both, charity." It became a popular slogan in many modern Christian unity movements.

Second, *context matters*. When practices that are (in themselves and as such) non-essential cause believers to doubt or stumble in their faith, or when they come to divide the body of Christ, then they are in some sense no longer non-essential.

The context could make an otherwise unimportant matter important. In and of itself, the position or practice remains indifferent. It is the specific situation that could make an indifferent matter matter. We understand how this can work, even with food. If my friend who struggles with healthy eating has just been diagnosed with Type-2 diabetes and he wants to discuss his new diet with me over at the coffee shop, then it would be bad form for me to order a big brownie covered in ice cream and eat it in front of him while he is talking about his temptation to consume sugar.

Without context, removed from a specific situation, there is nothing wrong per se with me eating this dessert. My eating something that doesn't cause me direct physical harm is not bad, but doing it in front

of him could make him stumble and unnecessarily tempt him to have
something harmful. It would be wrong for him to eat it. And he could
think that it is wrong also for *me* to eat it. He may or may not be right
about that. But in this specific context, my eating becomes wrong. If he
gives me permission and actually has no problem with it, then it is acceptable. As Paul says, don't destroy your brother for whom Christ died,
for something as fleeting as food (14:15).

What is the specific issue in the Roman church? It's not about dessert, but it's close.

Paul says that the weak eat vegetables and no meat (14:2). They
are vegetarians, and perhaps they drink only water and no wine as well
(14:21). They have a very simple, and perhaps healthier, diet. Paul places
himself in the "strong" group (15:1). Who are these groups?

First of all, who are the strong? It is the people who eat meat and
drink wine. Probably mostly gentile Christians, though it includes Jewish
Christians like Paul who have no food scruples. They are more permissive on this question.

Who are the weak? They probably didn't call themselves weak, and
it's unclear how they would have received Paul's characterization of them
in this way. But they are probably mostly Jewish Christians, though it
could include some gentile Christians who have adopted Jewish kosher
laws. But the two groups likely divide along mostly ethnic lines. Thus we
have another manifestation of the Jew-gentile tension.

Why would the weak be vegetarian, especially if they are predominantly Jewish? After all, the Mosaic law allows for some meat. Nothing
prohibits kosher meat. Several things could have contributed to Jewish
Christian vegetarianism, as noted by Witherington and Hyatt: 1) The
meat in the Roman market may not be kosher; even the potentially clean
animals may not have all the blood drained out. There were strict regula-
tions about what the meat could not touch. Preparing kosher meat was
not a concern of pagan butchers. How could kosher Jews know where
the meat that they buy had been? (Today's consumers take for granted
that meat is prepared how they want it and in a healthy way, though they
really don't know! We have no idea where that fast food hamburger meat
came from or where it has been or what it has touched, or even if it's
actual beef!)

2) There was also legitimate concern about market meat being
connected to idolatrous ceremonies. The connection of everything to
idolatry was always a Jewish and Christian concern in a pagan city. Food

sacrificed to idols is not specifically mentioned here, but this was the concern in Corinth (1 Corinthians 8). So it could be an unstated assumption. It was probably the concern when Daniel and his friends abstained from meat and wine but had vegetables and water in Babylon (Daniel 1:8, 12, 16). And it remained a concern for later Jewish Christians. In the second and third centuries AD, Jewish Christians were forced "to eat what was sacrificed to idols" (2 Esdras [6 Ezra] 16:68). 3) Non-Christian Jewish butchers (if there were any), who might be the only ones concerned with kosher and idol-free meat, may have refused to serve Jewish Christians, especially after the Claudian edict that escalated tensions between Jews and Christians. In sum, for a number of reasons, the Roman church had conscientious Jewish Christian vegetarians.

The third principle for church peace: In the case of an otherwise indifferent matter, *don't judge*. It is the main instruction in this section: "Do not judge" (Romans 14:3). It doesn't mean you should never make evaluative judgments, but don't condemn—especially concerning matters of indifference or ambiguity. Don't make a mountain out of a molehill. It's not sinful either to eat or not to eat. But to condemn either practice is sinful. To condemn where the Lord has not condemned is a serious error and one we should keep ourselves from.

In such matters, accept one another and leave the judgment to God (14:4). This is why we should not, and cannot, judge. Just as it is not appropriate to judge someone else's servant, it's not appropriate to judge the Lord's servant. I am not their master; the Lord is. It would be like firing an employee at a store where you are shopping but don't work at. Even if they probably should be dismissed, you have no right. You can complain, you can even recommend discipline, but you can't fire. If, as a shopper, you say to a worker, "You're fired," it carries no real weight.

We are equals. We don't have the power to "fire" each other, not over indifferent matters. What you eat and drink is between you and your master, the Lord. It is not mine to judge. Again, we can teach, we can recommend, we can persuade, but we cannot condemn. God will be our judge (14:10–12). As Isaiah 45 says, and Paul quotes, "Every knee will bow before God," not before us. God is the only one who truly knows a person's heart. We will have to speak before God for our own actions, not someone else's.

Paul gives another illustration of an indifferent matter that probably relates to the Roman church's tension as well. He raises the issue of how different people regard certain days as special (Romans 14:5). Jewish

Christians would probably recommend several days on the religious calendar that were not commanded by Paul for gentile believers to keep.
This falls in the same category as food and drink—non-essential.

The fourth principle is that *an informed conscience matters*. "Be fully
convinced in your own mind" (14:5). After all, this is a matter between
an individual and God. Is that all that is required—personal conviction?
No. It is necessary, but not sufficient. Of course, it has to be about a matter that is truly not essential to the faith. Indifferent matters can become
important when they are so to someone's conscience (14:20). In this case,
the opposite of faith is sin (14:23). It would benefit us to know why we
believe what we believe and why we do what we do. Act on the basis of
informed belief, not with doubt and not with ignorance.

All these principles may raise a whole new set of questions and
issues. For example, could this principle of deferring to the weak be
abused? How does one prevent a minority of "weak" in the church from
taking hostage the church's doctrine and ethics, constantly expecting or
demanding deference to their opinions? That is certainly not Paul's intention here. Why, then, does Paul suggest that, in this case, the gentiles
should defer to the Jews? Why don't the weak just learn and get with the
program? In light of the gentiles' dependence on the Jews, and in light
of the heavy-handedness with which some gentiles have been treating
the Jews, the gentiles owe the Jews some deference in this matter of food
(15:8). Again, the context matters.

Another point raised briefly above is worth mentioning again: Just
because something is not a "salvation issue" doesn't mean it's in every way
unimportant to the faith. There are always better ways to think and believe and behave. As individual Christians, and as the corporate church,
God's people should never be satisfied with going down a worse path and
justify it by saying, "It's not a salvation issue." We are called to spiritual
growth and progress; we should be concerned about individual or congregational stagnation and regression. At times, we may need to take a
stand on or at least advocate some things that are not "salvation issues."

Another question demands attention: Where is the line between essential and non-essential matters? It is always difficult to agree on what
are the essentials and what are the non-essentials of the faith. The fact that
some people wanted to make food—that is, a non-essential issue—into
an essential was part of the problem. But we do have hints in Scripture.

Paul says that he handed on some things that are of "first" importance—the death, burial, and resurrection of Jesus (1 Corinthians

15:3–4)—which implies that there are some things of subordinate importance. They are not unimportant but peripheral in comparison. Clearly some matters are more central to the faith than others. Some commands are "greater" than others, as Jesus said (Matthew 22:37–40; 23:23).

We also have hints in this passage of what should be classified in the essential category. This brings us to the fifth and final principle, which is really the goal: *Peace and unity in worship.* This principle is stated in many ways. God's reign is *not* about food and drink (Romans 14:17). By the way, there is really not much in our culture that's not about food and drink, so this is yet another way in which the kingdom of God is counter-cultural. God's reign or kingdom is not about food and drink or other peripheral matters, but about righteousness, peace, and joy in the Holy Spirit.

This is the overarching principle: Prioritize peace. "Let us pursue the things of peace and the things of building up one another" (14:19). Even when your brother doesn't get it and he wants to make the kingdom about food and drink, prioritize peace. Do not destroy one another; build each other up. Edification, peace, and unity are vital goals of the church's beliefs and practices. Again, we start to see which things are more central than others in the life of the church.

What are the otherwise indifferent matters today that could cause tension among Christians? More frighteningly, what if we don't agree on what those matters are? In our own churches, how have we made sure, or how do we and should we make sure, that our beliefs and practices lead to edification, to building up?

It is often said that one of the secrets of an enduring marriage is to know how to fight (not physically). There is much wisdom in that. Because it's not whether disagreements will happen but, when they happen, how they will be handled. The closer the human relationship, the more negative potential there is for disruption and volatility. But also the more rewarding possibilities for unity and love.

The same is true in a church, which is composed of many complex people, the more who gather together, the greater the potential for disruption and disunity. If there are people, then disagreements and even fights will occur. As in a stable marriage, there is no fight or disagreement that ends in divorce. The same is true for the Lord's church.

In a day of increasing division, now, more than ever, is the time for unity and deepening relationships with one another through Christ, who died and was raised for us. God's people must find unity around the core doctrines and practices of the Christian faith, unity of vision in spiritual growth and outreach, in love and in worship. And when there are differences, as there will be, there must be a willingness to sit down and talk like grown-ups, and above all, a willingness to love one another, no matter what.

What is the purpose of it all? To be at peace with one another is the means that leads to more effective worship. Unity and harmony in worship. Not as a cacophony of voices and sounds, from divided hearts and minds, but the church, by grace, worships as one. If we are truly one and united, then our worship will be unified. This is the goal that Paul expresses. When we are at peace with one another, then we can glorify God together. For when we accept one another in Christ, we are able to praise God together in a more profound, meaningful way (15:5–7).

Discussion Questions

1. What are some doctrinal issues that you would say are "opinion" but could still cause strife in the church?

2. What are some issues you consider to be non-negotiable? How would you handle disagreements about these concerns?

3. Who are the "weak" in today's church? Why would you call them weak? Have you ever considered that you may be weak to someone else?

4. How do you know who should defer to whom in church disagreements?

5. How can we keep non-essential but strongly held beliefs from dividing the church?

30

Godly Plans

Romans 15:14–33

Are you the kind of person who makes New Year's resolutions? How long does the diet work out? How long does working out work out? As a category, New Year's resolutions are a symbol more famous for failure than for success. "The best laid schemes of mice and men go oft awry." Some of these schemes were not very well laid to begin with, so it should not surprise us when they go awry.

But do you have any plans or goals that are important in your personal life? Some people are very goal-oriented, not only at work but also in their personal lives. They have a five-year strategic plan. I know a man who, every year on his wedding anniversary, sits down with his wife and evaluates the previous year of their marriage—what goals were accomplished, where they failed, where they improved, and the like. Then he gets out paper and pen and they set goals and plans for their next year. It may not be very romantic, but it is proactive. This is what is known as a "Type A" personality. On the other extreme are those who do a little more drifting through life, who tend to go wherever the current takes them.

Setting and stating personal goals can be a very good exercise. Think about your goals and plans for service in God's kingdom. What are your plans for kingdom work? What are you going to do? How are you going to step out in faith? Are these questions that you ever consider? Some Christians do think along these lines. Perhaps you have recently stepped

out and tried something new. In most churches, however, 20 percent of
the people do about 80 percent of the work.

If you do not spend time thinking about how you will contribute to
the work of the kingdom and the work of your church, why not? Do we
think that kingdom work is for the professional ministers? Do we think
that the call to discipleship, which Jesus said is to "take up your cross and
follow me" (Mark 8:34), is fulfilled by making an appearance and filling
a spot in a pew one hour a week? We wouldn't say so, but is that how we
behave? Why is that? Or do we think that we have had our day, and we're
too old? Or too young? Or too broken, sad, and depressed? Too sinful?
Or too busy, or have too many kids? Or too poor, too inexperienced, or
too ignorant to step out of our comfort zone and try something new for
the sake of the kingdom?

In ancient Rome, the *ianua* was the door that divides the inside from
the outside world, the outer door of a house. The *ianua* is the threshold.
There's something new when you walk through that *ianua*, across that
threshold, in either direction. You're exiting one world and entering a
new world. There is a looking forward and sometimes, simultaneously, a
looking backward, a leaving behind. We know that something happens
to us physiologically and even psychologically when we walk through a
doorway. Our body and soul experience a change.

All ancient people sensed the importance of this transition. For ancient Romans, the god or spirit who protected the threshold, the door, the
ianua, they called Janus. The god of transitions, the god of beginnings.
When he was not depicted as a gate, he was depicted as a double-faced
head, that is, a head with a face on the front and another face on the back,
thus looking forward and backward. The god of beginnings was invoked
at the beginning of prayers and placed at the head of the list of deities.
The month at the top of the calendar was named for Janus: *Januarius*.

It does not have to be the beginning of a new year for us to find
ourselves in a time of transition. Sometimes we bring about the transition, but at other times the transition is brought to us. Whether or not
the change was sought, it is a time for looking backward and looking
forward. We find ourselves passing through a portal, a threshold. A time
of remembering the good things that have come before and how those
things have shaped who we are, but also a time to leave them behind and
anticipate a fresh start.

As we near the conclusion of Paul's letter to the Romans, we find
out more about his present circumstances. And we find that he is in a

time of great personal transition. He was proceeding through a *ianua*, a door—the end of one phase and the beginning of the next. He is at the threshold. It is the year 55. In the narrative of his life found in the book of Acts, he is writing this letter as he passes through Corinth (Acts 20:1–3). He is on the final leg of what we call his third missionary journey, and he senses the need for a new direction. The last seven years of missionary work around the eastern Mediterranean is now complete. Nothing is left for him in those regions. As we read the final section of the body of this letter (Romans 15:14–33), we overhear Paul's upcoming plans for future ministry and kingdom work.

It is noteworthy, first of all, that when Paul thinks about transitions, when he considers new goals and new plans, he is thinking spiritually. To use Jesus' phrase, he is not thinking about human things, but the things of God (cf. Mark 8:33). What is the difference? When we think about the next phase in our lives, what are the circumstances that precipitate such change, and what are the concerns and considerations?

Often the concerns and questions have to do with physical family and those relationships. From single to married, to having children, to the empty nest. How will we deal with these transitions? Often we think about finances. Which job will lead to better financial security? That is a euphemism for: how can I make more money? How can I pay for college? How can I send my kids to college?

A host of other related questions accompany transitions. Where do I want to live? What kind of house? How much vacation do I get? How much can I spend on vacation? Where will I go on vacation? What kind of car will I buy? It should be a step up from my last one. The same goes for my TV. It's looking small now. How long do I have to keep this old phone, which is now a year old and hopelessly out of date? Where do I want to go to church? A place where I'm comfortable and I get a lot out of it. And so on.

Where is any of that in Paul's five-year strategic plan? Some of those questions I just asked are important. Some of those changes are significant. Part of me wants to say that, even though we don't see it in his letters, Paul probably asked some of those questions sometimes. But after some reflection, there's a more honest part of me that has a very hard time imagining Paul ever asking, "How can I make more money?" It comes in pretty handy, no doubt, and Paul surely was hoping to raise money for his next mission effort. I'm sure he sometimes wondered where his next meal would come from or where he would stay when he entered a new city.

But, "how much vacation will I get? What can my church do for me?" No, these questions were not part of Paul's five-year plan, and I doubt they ever occupied him for long.

What we do find is an assessment of his kingdom work. Looking back, Paul has accomplished quite a bit, in fact, more than any other early Christian missionary. He has preached the gospel and established churches from Jerusalem to Illyricum (Romans 15:19). That means the land around the whole eastern and northeastern Mediterranean basin— in modern terms, Israel and Palestine, and then counter-clockwise on a map to Syria and Turkey, Greece and Macedonia, through the Balkans up to Croatia, and many of the islands in the Mediterranean. It is not a bad record, especially considering that most of that travel was done on foot.

Why hasn't he gone to Rome? There may be several reasons, but he wants to go where the gospel has not been preached before. As he quotes from Isaiah 52:15 (Romans 15:21), Paul saw himself as God's servant, God's instrument, to reach people who have not yet heard. An important principle for Paul seems to be something like: "Everyone deserves the gospel once before anyone hears it twice." Or, as he says, he does not want to build on someone else's foundation (Romans 15:20). The church already existed in Rome and was strong there. It was not without some problems, as we have seen, but if Paul's main purpose is to reach pagans who have not yet heard, then there was no urgent need for him to go to Rome.

But he does plan to see the Roman Christians as he passes through on the way to Spain. If you have your mental map of the Mediterranean turned on, then you see that Paul has spent all his missionary effort in the eastern and northeastern quadrant. Rome, in the center, has been evangelized. Paul has his sights on the western extremity of the Roman Empire and of Europe—the Iberian peninsula, Spain. Presumably, on the way there or on the way back, wherever he may stop, he will also proclaim the gospel and establish Christian communities in those places, too. But Rome is one of the stopping places.

So here is his plan, and it is a tale of three cities or three destinations. First, he is headed to Jerusalem. There he will offer his "service" or "ministry" (15:26–28, 31). This is a reference to the contribution that he has been collecting from predominantly gentile churches for the aid of the churches in Judaea, made up almost exclusively of Jews. What he has said earlier in this letter about the relationship between Jews and gentiles applies again here. The gentile Christians are wild, foreign branches grafted onto the olive tree that is Israel.

Additionally, the evangelists of early Christianity, like Paul, were all Jews, who already knew the Scriptures and the God about whom they spoke. Thus, just as gentile believers in Rome owe deference to their Jewish Christian brothers and sisters, so also, on a larger scale, gentile Christians in general are indebted to the Jews and to the Jerusalem church. The gentile Christians have shared in the Jews' spiritual blessings; the gentiles owe them in material blessings.

For his upcoming journey, Paul requests the prayers of the Roman faithful (15:30–32). As he heads first toward Jerusalem, he asks the church to pray that he may be rescued from unbelievers in Judea, and that his service to Jerusalem may be acceptable to the saints there.

Second, after Paul finishes his work of service in Jerusalem, he will make his way to Rome. It is a perfect stopping point, halfway across the Mediterranean. He asks them to pray that by God's will he may come to them with joy and be refreshed together with them (15:32). In some ways, this whole letter prepares the way for his visit to Rome, so that he will make it to see them, and that, with their help—perhaps including financial help—he will eventually make it to his third destination. Indeed, the epistle to the Romans may also be a mission fund-raising letter.

Third, he plans to go to Spain, a whole, vast, and, as far as he knows, unevangelized territory.

How did these plans go? Were his prayers answered? He made it to his locations, but probably not quite how he expected. Acts tells us about the first two destinations. After Acts 20, he did make it to Jerusalem. He did deliver the contribution. How it was received we are not told. He was rescued from the unbelievers, but not without incident. He was arrested by Roman soldiers in Jerusalem (Acts 21). What that did was save him from certain death at the hands of his Jewish opponents. To rescue him from some forty conspirators, he was taken to prison in Caesarea, where he lingered for two years (Acts 24–26).

In his appeal to the emperor, a right he enjoyed as a Roman citizen, Paul was then transported to Rome, where he remained under house arrest for two more years (Acts 27–28). He was rescued, ironically, by being arrested and incarcerated, and through those means he made it to Rome—presumably at the empire's expense. For those two years in Rome, he did spend time with local believers, probably more time than he wanted, and not under the circumstances he had envisioned.

And that's where the book of Acts ends. We must seek hints in the rest of the New Testament to find that Paul did travel elsewhere after Rome—for example, to places like Crete, which we learn about in the letter to Titus. It is in a letter from Clement, a leader in the church of Rome, who wrote around the year 95, that we learn that Paul did make it to Spain. In his letter, Clement, who was a friend of Paul and is someone who would know, testifies that Paul went "to the extremity of the west" and preached there. To a Roman like Clement, "the extremity of the west" was Spain. Paul eventually made it back to Rome, where he would be martyred under Emperor Nero. Wherever Paul's travels took him, and in whatever order, he did it all through the working of Christ and the power of the Holy Spirit (Romans 15:18–19).

What about God's people today? What are our plans for work in God's kingdom? Because Christ died and was raised for us, we have died to the old ways, to an old set of priorities and human concerns. Our lives are not our own but are hidden with God in Christ. For Paul, traveling to strange and hostile lands—and even martyrdom—is nothing to him. For disciples of Christ, like Paul, to live is Christ and to die is gain (Philippians 1:21). If the Spirit of Christ lives in us, then certain goals and pursuits must take a back seat, while others should not be ignored. In the words of Isaiah 52, like Paul, we, too, are the servants of the Lord, God's instruments.

Based on this text from Romans, Paul provides an example of what a Christ-centered resolution looks like, or what it looks like to set spiritual goals during a time of transition in life. I see nothing in his plans and personal goals for eating healthier and getting in shape. Those are praiseworthy goals for affluent Americans who have never had to worry about their next meal and who can earn money without doing a lick of manual labor. I see nothing in Paul's plans about better financial security or a new chariot. He does want to travel to Spain—Spain sounds lovely—but he has in mind a working vacation.

What are your spiritual goals? In a time of transition, whether it is a new year or new circumstances, what are your plans? Paul wanted to evangelize the world. That's ambitious! Paul was never accused of dreaming too small. Maybe *you* too have preached the gospel from Jerusalem all the way to Illyricum. Great! Whether you've accomplished a little or a lot in God's kingdom, now what? What will you do now? How will you step out in service? How will you grow in grace and knowledge? How will you live more fully and passionately under God's reign? These are the kinds of questions that obviously guided Paul. They are the kinds of questions that should direct us, too, the questions that we lead with. How will you answer those questions? You can figure it out. Do you need suggestions? Choose from the following:

Increase charitable and church giving—round up to the next fifty or hundred, or whatever is affordable. Write a card—one a month or one per week—to encourage someone. Volunteer to help in a food pantry. Volunteer to help or teach in Sunday school. Ask your minister how you can get involved. Volunteer or find out how you can help with other programs in your church or neighborhood. Study. Attend Sunday school. Learn from trusted teachers. Host or help organize a home fellowship group. Practice the lost art of hospitality. Talk to your neighbors. Have people to your house for dinner.

Which area of service will you choose? One of those? Something else? If you don't want to build on someone else's foundation, then start something new. Pick *something*. You know what you can do; you know what you should do. Make a goal. Make a plan. Then pray, as Paul did, and ask others to pray. The plan we set out to pursue may not go exactly as we anticipate. Paul's journey involved suffering, languishing in prison for two years before he ever saw Rome. But he trusted God, and he made it there, protected and transported on the emperor's dime.

May God give us the grace, through the power of Christ and his Spirit, to think about the things of God. May we set godly goals and make godly plans. May God reveal to us ways that we can serve effectively in his vineyard. May he open our eyes to those opportunities. And may he grant us the ability and the will to be faithful servants and to do so joyfully.

Discussion Questions

1. Do you have any plans or goals for service in God's kingdom? What are they? How will you reach those goals?

2. Why do we tend to leave all the church work to the professional ministers?

3. What is your five-year plan? Is it full of human things or godly things?

4. How does your plan stack up to Paul's?

5. How much importance do we give to money in our plans? How much should we give?

31

Greetings and Grace

Romans 16:1–27

THE PREVIOUS REFLECTION OBSERVED how, in a time of transition, we look backward and forward. We have now arrived at the final chapter of Romans, this profound epistle from God's ambassador, Paul. Looking back, what has been revealed in Romans? What have we heard? What have we learned? How have we been encouraged or challenged? Remember I said that if you get Romans, God will get you.

There are so many prominent themes and passages in Romans, it's hard to single out just a few. All are under sin (Romans 3:9). Jews and gentiles alike, without Christ, are morally and spiritually bankrupt. But there is good news. Wherever sin abounds, grace super-abounds (5:20). However, Christ's action on our behalf is not the end of the story but only the beginning. If we have been saved and made right, then let's live like it (8:9–11). We have been given the gift of the Holy Spirit and called to live holy lives that please God. The Spirit lives in us so that we may live for Christ.

And now it's time for Paul to close the letter. He effectively concluded the body of the letter at the end of chapter 15 with his request for prayers. But now it's time for greetings. We are introduced to many names in Romans 16. Chapter 15 shows us that this whole thing was also a letter to the missions committee. He wants some help as he heads to Spain. Now, in chapter 16, we get the names of the people on the committee.

This is the longest greeting in Paul's letters. As we look over this lengthy catalogue of names, we might wonder, if Paul had never been to Rome, then how did he know all these Roman Christians?

Remember that these are people Paul met outside of the city of Rome. People like Priscilla and Aquila (Romans 16:3)—Jewish Christians who, because they were involved in the synagogue debates, were expelled from Rome and even Italy. In the case of Priscilla and Aquila, Paul met them in Corinth (Acts 18:1–2). They have since returned to Rome, so he is sending greetings to people whom he met earlier outside the city. Perhaps others on this list he met in their exile, and maybe in Corinth. Others he knew probably twenty years before when he resided in Jerusalem. He knows many people in the Roman church, though he has never been there himself. The ones he knows from this church are mostly, if not all, Jewish Christians.

That means these are the ones who, upon returning to their home congregation, have been mistreated, looked down on by their gentile brothers and sisters. And so Paul is not only telling his old friends "Hello." He's also telling the gentile Christians there to greet these good people with a holy kiss (Romans 16:16), a kiss of peace, a kiss that testifies, "We are brothers and sisters in Christ, at peace with one another."

Besides simply sending greetings, Paul is accomplishing something more with this long list. He is conveying an important message between the lines: 1) These Jewish Christians are significant and not to be ignored or minimized in the church. 2) If these Jewish brothers and sisters are some of the "weak" (14:1), then they deserve some deference and respect. 3) Their devotion and hard work are emphasized, indicating that the gentiles owe a debt to these devout Jews.

These people must have been important to Paul's ministry over the years. Because Acts 18 tells about Priscilla and Aquila—that they were exiles in Corinth, that they were tentmakers and met Paul, and how they taught Apollos more accurately—we know some of their history with Paul. We don't know the exact stories behind the others. Twenty-six names are mentioned here (about sixteen described or singled out). Eight women are named (and several of them are commended), plus Phoebe and the mother of Rufus.

How many other stories lie behind the many names here, names that we tend to pass over too quickly? Each and every one of these had a history with Paul, whether short or long. They helped make Paul who he was. It is a glimpse at Paul's Facebook page. He is giving some likes and loves here. As you read Romans 16, what stands out? What do you find interesting in these names and brief descriptions? Which stories or people do you wish we knew more about? Here are just a few of the names and possible stories that stand out to me.

Phoebe is described as a "servant" (*diakonos*) from the church in Cenchrea (16:1–2). This is near Corinth. The Greek word *diakonos* often referred to a table waiter and is the source of our word "deacon." It is translated as "deacon" only in reference to a church office (in proximity to "elder" or "bishop"; Philippians 1:1; 1 Timothy 3:12). In this passage, whether it means servant in an official or unofficial capacity may be irrelevant; she is a servant with a specific task. She is the carrier and deliverer of the letter from Paul in Corinth to Rome. This is a great responsibility, and she apparently succeeded, because we have the letter. She has been a benefactor to many, including Paul. That means she supported his ministry, most likely financially. She is probably of high social standing and wealthy, but she is still described as a servant. She prepares the way for Paul, who hopes to visit Rome. She is going ahead of him and will vouch for him to the church.

We have already referred to Priscilla and Aquila (Romans 16:3–4). Six times this couple is mentioned in the New Testament, and four of those times her name comes first. This order may indicate that she was of a higher social standing than her husband. What is new here is that they risked their own lives to save Paul's! This side comment tempts the imagination. What does he mean that they risked their lives? Imagine the story behind that one. Whatever he means, these are people that he could trust his life to.

Paul sends greetings to Andronicus and Junia (16:7). Junia (not Junias) is a female name. Some scholars think that Junia is the Latin equivalent of Joanna (Luke 8:3). That would put her there as an early follower of Jesus himself and one of the benefactors of his ministry. At any rate, this couple, married or not, was among the earliest Christian converts; they were probably in Galilee or Palestine at some point, either from there originally (supporting the Joanna hypothesis) or travelers from Rome to Jerusalem during the feast of Pentecost. They were believers in Christ before Paul was. They also were noted among the "apostles," perhaps witnesses of Jesus entrusted with a special commission from him. Apostles were a special group, but could mean more than just the twelve. An apostle is someone who is sent, so a missionary, someone who did pioneering mission work in the first century. There they are now in the Roman church.

"Greet Rufus" (16:13). He is named in Mark 15:21, which mentioned him probably because he was known to Roman Christians to whom the Gospel of Mark was likely written a little later. His mother served Paul also, probably back in Jerusalem. Her service was so dear to Paul that he says she was a mother to him, too! Imagine the stories behind that remark. It does not take much effort to think of the new convert Saul, during those early days in Jerusalem while he was proclaiming Jesus as God's Messiah, staying in the home of Rufus and his mother. She must have made sure he was well-fed, well-clothed, and well-cared for. She was a mother to Paul, and he loves her like a son.

Just as Luke 8 mentions some of the workers and generous bene-factors who helped make Jesus' ministry possible, these friends and others were some of the people important in Paul's ministry, past as well as future. God placed them in his life at just the right time—God's grace to Paul. They made a difference in his life and ministry. He would not forget them.

Reading Romans 16 and hearing all those names may strike readers on a very personal level. This chapter should get us thinking about the many people who have been in our lives over the years, for whom we should be grateful, lest we forget. I am reminded of lyrics to the Billy Joel song "Say Goodbye to Hollywood": "So many faces in and out of my life / Some will last, some will just be now and then. / Life is a series of hellos and goodbyes, / I'm afraid it's time for goodbye again."

Think of the many people who have come in and out of your life. It's too easy for us to think of those who have mistreated us or betrayed us. That list can be arranged. With a passage of Scripture like this, however, we are invited to think about the saints that God has placed in our lives, how they have made a difference, and how God brought us together.

Are there any Phoebes, real servants who know what it means to be generous? They bailed you out or gave you an interest-free loan when you needed it. Or they just took you out to eat and showed you a good time. God placed them there in your life, evidence of his grace to you.

Are there any Priscillas and Aquilas who worked with you, risking their lives for you? They stepped out on a limb for you. You could trust them with your life. They gave you the benefit of the doubt when no one else would. God placed them there in your life, his grace to you.

Are there any Andronicuses and Junias, people who are outstanding among the apostles? Pillars of the faith who taught you the word of God, models of Christian living who were devout in mission. Perhaps it was a married couple who exemplified discipleship. God placed them in your life, evidence of his grace in your life.

Are there any Christian mothers in your life, whether biological or not? Is there a mom or grandma who would not let you leave the house without breakfast or without a coat on your back? A caring, nurturing mother figure who made you who you are today? Or a Christian father, brother, or sister? God placed them there, his grace to you.

If we have such wonderful, caring people in our lives, tokens of God's love to us, it is by God's super-abundant grace. We all have people whose paths have crossed ours because God placed them there. Like the people Paul mentioned, those people will forever be not only brothers and sisters but also partners in ministry.

Like Paul, we have so many stories of so many people who have come and gone. All these stories and all these people together are woven into the tapestry of our lives. Without them, our own story would be less than full. Even *with* them, their stories and ours are yet incomplete this side of heaven. The best of these relationships on earth leave us wanting more. God has given us a longing, a yearning for completion, that will be filled in eternity—fulfilled when we are embraced together by the God of love, when our destiny is fully realized in union with Christ, who died and was raised for us.

Paul knows all these truths about relationships, and they are reflected in the names and faces of Romans 16. Some of those people he saw again when he finally made it to Rome five years later. Others had probably fallen asleep in the Lord by the time he arrived. But their bond in the fellowship of the Holy Spirit was invincible. And they are a testimony to the love of God, who surely gives us what we need and whom we need when we need it. Whom has God placed in your life? Do we have open eyes and hearts to see and receive the blessings that God gives us through one another? Can we see the others whom God wants to encourage through us? Can we be the Phoebe, the mother, or the father that others need?

> To him who can establish you according to my gospel and the preaching of Jesus Christ—according to the revelation of the mystery kept silent for long ages, but now revealed through the prophetic Scriptures according to the command of the eternal

God for the obedience of faith made known to all the Gentiles—
the only wise God, through Jesus Christ, to him be glory forever.
Amen (16:25–27).

Discussion Questions

1. What have you learned or appreciated most in this study of Romans? Do you see any familiar passages with new eyes?

2. In the greeting section, which names and stories do you find most inspiring?

3. Based on what we know from Scripture, how do you think Priscilla and Aquila might have risked their lives for Paul?

4. Besides your own parents and siblings, do you have a Christian mother, father, sister, or brother who cared for you like a true family member?

5. How can you be that kind of family member, the grace of God, to someone else?

Notes

Just as this book is nothing like an exhaustive commentary on Romans, these notes are not intended to provide references to books that agree or disagree with my interpretation and application. For the curious, however, they provide at times further clarification or background, and at others times a few leads or sources for quotations or notable interpretations that are mentioned in the text.

In general, I have benefited from the commentaries by Ben Witherington III and Darlene Hyatt, *Paul's Letter to the Romans: A Socio-Rhetorical Commentary* (Grand Rapids: Eerdmans, 2004); and Frank J. Matera, *Romans,* Paideia Commentaries on the New Testament (Grand Rapids: Baker Academic, 2010). When I recall specific insights based directly on those studies, I have noted them below.

Translations from Scripture are my own.

1. A Life-Changing Letter (1:1-7)

Augustine (354-430) tells the story of his conversion in *The Confessions* VIII.xii.29-30, trans. Maria Boulding, *The Works of Saint Augustine* I/1 (Hyde Park, NY: New City, 2001), 156-57. Martin Luther (1483-1546) reflects on his reading of Romans 1:17 in *Preface to the Complete Edition of Luther's Latin Writings* (1545), in *Luther's Works,* 34:336-38. John

Wesley (1703–1791) describes his heart-warming experience in his personal journal, for which entry see John Wesley, *A Library of Protestant Thought*, edited by Albert C. Outler (New York: Oxford University Press, 1964), 66. Paul mentions his studies under the famous Rabbi Gamaliel in Acts 22:3.

2. Not Ashamed (1:8–17)

A classic historical study of crucifixion and its scandalous significance is Martin Hengel, *Crucifixion in the Ancient World and the Folly of the Message of the Cross*, trans. John Bowden (Philadelphia: Fortress, 1977). The language of "cultured despisers" is taken from Friedrich D. E. Schleiermacher, *On Religion: Speeches to Its Cultured Despisers* (1799), edited by Richard Crouter, 2nd ed. (Cambridge: Cambridge University Press, 1996), a famous attempt to accommodate Christian faith to post-Enlightenment modernity. In Romans 1:17, every major English translation renders Paul's quotation from Hab 2:4 as the righteous will live "*by* faith." I have retained the more literal "*from* faith" (Greek, *ek pisteos*) to highlight the verbatim connection with the preceding phrase, "*from* faith (*ek pisteos*) to faith."

The story about the Nashville Christmas bombing and the police officers is available at https://www.msn.com/en-us/news/us/nashville-bombing-police-officers-describe-christmas-morning-explosion/ar-BB1cgSzV. The story in *The Atlantic* about the false alarm and its immediate aftermath in Hawaii is available at https://www.theatlantic.com/international/archive/2018/01/pandemonium-and-rage-in-hawaii/550529/.

3. The Economy of Sin (1:18–32)

On the Herschel Walker deal, one of the most lop-sided trades in sports history, see https://www.espn.com/page2/s/list/trades/010716.html. For a very good introduction to natural law ethics from a biblical perspective, engaging ideas in Romans 1 and 2, see J. Budziszewski, *What We Can't Not Know: A Guide*, rev. ed. (San Francisco: Ignatius, 2011). This section of Paul's letter is dependent on or parallel to the thought in Wisdom of Solomon 11–15. See especially Wis 11:15–16; 12:1–2, 10, 23–13:2, 4–6, 8–9; 14:12–13, 22–27; 15:18—16:1. Paul's polemic against the worship of animals and reptiles, and my mention of crocodiles in particular, applies properly to Egyptian religion and the cults influenced by it, which were imported to the Roman world. The idols and gods of other nations were generally anthropomorphic.

For an examination of homosexuality in ancient Jewish and Christian thought, see William Loader, *Making Sense of Sex: Attitudes towards Sexuality in Early Jewish and Christian Literature* (Grand Rapids: Eerdmans, 2013). The best and most comprehensive study of homosexuality in Scripture is Robert A. J. Gagnon, *The Bible and Homosexual Practice: Texts and Hermeneutics* (Nashville: Abingdon, 2001).

5. The Great Advantage (3:1–8)

On the diatribe, see Witherington and Hyatt, *Romans,* 75–76. The reference to our restless hearts finding rest in God is from Augustine, *Confessions* I.i.

6. All Are under Sin (3:9–20)

Suetonius's discussion of the Claudian edict of 49 is reported in his *The Lives of the Caesars* V.xxv.4, translated by J. C. Rolfe, Loeb Classical Library (Cambridge, MA: Harvard University Press, 1959), 2:52–53. New Testament scholars debate the significance of the Claudian edict for Romans. I do not mean to suggest that it was the only factor contributing to Jew-gentile tension in the church in Rome, a situation that was omnipresent in the early church. I am suggesting that the circumstance easily exacerbated the tension. For more on the occasion of Romans, see Karl P. Donfried, ed., *The Romans Debate,* rev. ed. (Peabody, MA: Hendrickson, 1991). Paul was not claiming anything atypical when he declared that all have sinned. Cf. 2 Esdras (4 Ezra) 7:46 (NRSV): "Who among the living is there that has not sinned, or who is there among mortals that has not transgressed your covenant?"

7. Made Right by Grace (3:21–31)

On the issue of faith *in* Jesus and faith *of* Jesus, see Matera, *Romans,* 93–94. Theologians have debated whether the Greek word *hilasterion* (Romans 3:25) should be thought of as propitiation or expiation. That debate, however, is not necessary to the point I am making about the cover over the ark of the covenant. The latest update to the NIV translates *dikaiosyne* in Romans 3:21–22, 25–26 consistently as *righteousness*. This change is an improvement.

8. Made Right through Faith (4:1–25)

The admittedly ambiguous phrases cited in the first paragraph, and others like them, have been controversial in North American fellowships and denominations that tend toward semi- or full-Pelagianism. They are superficially at odds with Jas 2, a problem treated in this chapter. On the relationship between infertility and death in contrast to fertility and resurrection, see Jon D. Levenson, *Resurrection and the Restoration of Israel: The Ultimate Victory of the God of Life* (New Haven, CT: Yale University Press, 2006), especially 108–22, here 119: "Given the construction of personal identity in the Hebrew Bible, infertility and the loss of children serve as the functional equivalent of death."

9. The Foundation of Hope (5:1–11)

The distinction between no hope (despair), misplaced hope (security), and true hope (certainty) is common to the Christian theological tradition. For a discussion, see Keith D. Stanglin, *Arminius on the Assurance of Salvation: The Context, Roots, and Shape of the Leiden Debate*, 1603–1609, Brill's Series in Church History, 27 (Leiden/Boston: Brill, 2007), 149–93.

10. Super-Abundant Grace (5:12–21)

The meme can be seen at https://despair.com/products/dysfunction. On the two different uses of the archetypal Adam, see Matera, *Romans*, 127–29. Augustine coined the phrase "original sin," by which he meant this very strong version of inherited guilt that he also promoted. What's more, Augustine's idea was based in part on a possible but highly unlikely translation of *eph ho* in verse 12—it's not "in whom" or in Adam all sinned, but "because" all sinned. That sin is universal and even affects children was not foreign to Jews. Cf. 2 Esdras (4 Ezra) 7:68 (NRSV): "For all who have been born are entangled in iniquities, and are full of sins and burdened with transgressions." Some modern translations of Gen 2:17 obscure the

word "day," opting instead for something like "*when* you eat of the fruit
.. ." Another possibility for interpreting Adam's death as physical on the
"day" that he ate is that his physical death became certain and imminent.
By anti-Calvinist, here, I mean simply anyone who does not advocate
the full Augustinian version of original guilt. Matera, *Romans*, 138, calls
Romans 5:15–17 "one of the most confusing passages in Scripture." His
discussion is helpful and influences my treatment.

Though not invented by Hart, I take the triad of being, consciousness,
and beauty, as linked with the question of God's existence, more or less
directly from David Bentley Hart, *The Experience of God: Being, Consciousness, Bliss* (New Haven, CT: Yale University Press, 2013). To describe the
effects of the fall (or original sin) as inheriting the penalty but not the guilt
of the first sin, though heterodoxy to a strict Augustinian, is consistent
with the early church and Eastern Orthodoxy, as well as with many strands
within Western Christianity. The Western medieval scholastic theologians
all agreed that an effect of original sin was the loss of the original righteousness with which Adam and Eve were created. They debated whether there
was an additional corruption. The notion of distinguishing the image from
the likeness of God, and that the likeness was lost in the fall, is characteristic of patristic theology from the second century onward.

The most interesting expansion of the Adam-Christ typology in
the early church can be found in various places in Irenaeus of Lyons,
Against Heresies.

11. Dead to Sin, Alive to God (6:1–14)

Weekend at Bernie's (Ted Kotcheff, dir., 20th Century Fox, 1989). My description of baptism includes allusions to the candidate's renunciation of
sin, facing toward the west, and the turn to confession of Christ, facing
toward the east, all features of baptism in the early church. For a comprehensive examination of the topic, see Everett Ferguson, *Baptism in the
Early Church: History, Theology, and Liturgy in the First Five Centuries*
(Grand Rapids: Eerdmans, 2009). The precise quotation, "Dead to the
world, to voices that call me," is from the hymn, "A New Creature," by T.
O. Chisholm and L. O. Sanderson. That song is a wonderful commentary
on Romans 6 and supplement to this meditation. *Dead Man Walking*
(Tim Robbins, dir., Gramercy, 1995). From the patristic era onward, the
Christian tradition has commonly referred to this earthly life as a time of
testing and temptation.

12. License to Live (6:15–23)

The quotation from George MacDonald is in "The Voice of Job," in *Unspoken Sermons*, Second Series (London: Longmans, Green, and Co., 1885), 232. That grace is selective and irresistible to the elect is a main tenet of Reformed or Calvinist theology. My comparison between receiving saving grace and receiving a gift of money is a common one, but my way of putting it is dependent on Jacob Arminius's beggar simile, for which he was unjustly accused by his opponents of (semi-) Pelagianism. See Jacob Arminius, *Apology against 31 Articles*, in *The Works of James Arminius*, 3 vols., translated by James Nichols and William Nichols, London edition (1825–1875; reprint, Grand Rapids: Baker, 1986), 2:52. For further analysis, see Keith D. Stanglin and Thomas H. McCall, *Jacob Arminius: Theologian of Grace* (New York/Oxford: Oxford University Press, 2012), 157–67.

"Once saved, always saved" is a tacit attitude that creeps into the lives even of individual Christians who would not formally espouse the doctrine of irresistible perseverance. *The Force Awakens* (J. J. Abrams, dir., Disney, 2015). The description of eternal progress and growth in knowledge of God and extension toward him is inspired most directly by Gregory of Nyssa, *The Life of Moses*, translated by Abraham J. Malherbe and Everett Ferguson, The Classics of Western Spirituality (New York: Paulist, 1978).

13. Dead to the Law (7:1–6)

The word for slave or servant throughout the latter part of chapter 6 is *doulos*. The verb for serve or be a slave in 7:6 is *douleuo*. In 7:5, the newest edition of the NIV has retained the English word *flesh* (an improvement), but then proceeds thereafter with *sinful nature*. Premodern interpreters were more willing than most modern interpreters to Paul's letter-spirit contrast as a hermeneutical key for biblical interpretation and application. The difference between the (human) spirit—or simply a reality opposed to flesh and letter—and (divine) Spirit is ambiguous in Greek. The ancient manuscripts did not distinguish the latter with an uppercase letter. My transition from lowercase spirit to uppercase Spirit intentionally reflects a bit of the ambiguity.

14. Bearing Fruit for Death (7:7–25)

Quotations of Jekyll's confession throughout this meditation are from Robert Louis Stevenson, *Dr. Jekyll and Mr. Hyde* (New York: Bantam, 1981), 91–92. I have translated the quotation from Epictetus, *Discourses* II.xxvi.4, in *The Discourses as Reported by Arrian, the Manual, and Fragments*, 2 vols., translated by W. A. Oldfather, Loeb Classical Library (Cambridge, MA: Harvard University Press, 1925), 1:432. I have translated the quotation from Euripides, *Medea*, lines 1078–79, in *Euripides in Four Volumes*, translated by Arthur S. Way, Loeb Classical Library (Cambridge, MA: Harvard University Press, 1912), 4:366. I have translated the quotation from Ovid, *Metamorphoses* VII.19–21, translated by Frank Justus Miller, 2 vols., Loeb Classical Library (Cambridge, MA: Harvard University Press, 1971), 1:342. Witherington's discussion of Romans 7 is helpful, in which he also cites Epictetus and Ovid. See Witherington and Hyatt, *Romans*, 193–205. For Augustine's prayer, see *Confessions* VIII. vii.17 (149).

Weakness of the will is a typical translation of the Greek *akrasia* (more literally, "unrestraint"). For an illuminating analysis, see Risto Saarinen, *Weakness of the Will in Renaissance and Reformation Thought* (Oxford: Oxford University Press, 2011), which also includes ancient and medieval background. Augustine describes the problem of *akrasia* well in *Confessions* VIII.ix.21 (151–52). The rhetorical technique of speaking in the person of someone else is prosopopoeia. It was a common interpretive strategy in premodern biblical exegesis. The identification of the "I" is one of the most contested exegetical matters in the history of the church. My interpretation is indebted to the analysis of Jacob Arminius, *A Dissertation on the True and Genuine Sense of the Seventh Chapter of the Epistle to the Romans*, in *Works* 2:488–683. His treatise includes many citations from patristic, medieval, and early modern (including Reformed) commentators who agree that the "I" is not a regenerate Christian. On the specific identification of Adam and those in Adam as the referent of "I," see the helpful analysis in Witherington and Hyatt, *Romans*, 179–205; see also Witherington, *The Problem with Evangelical Theology: Testing the Exegetical Foundations of Calvinism, Dispensationalism, and Wesleyanism* (Waco, TX: Baylor University Press, 2005), 3–37.

For anyone unfamiliar, Blue Bell, from Brenham, Texas, is the best ice cream in the country. It would do you good to become familiar with it.

15. Life in the Spirit (8:1–17)

This is not the place to veer off into a discussion of religious language. In case it is not obvious, by referring to the Spirit with masculine pronouns, I do not mean to imply that the Spirit is a man or even masculine in the sense we associate with a man. I am avoiding *it* for its connotations of the impersonal. Those who are curious for further study may begin with Dionysius the Areopagite, *The Mystical Theology, in Pseudo-Dionysius: The Complete Works,* translated by Colm Luibheid, The Classics of Western Spirituality (New York: Paulist, 1987). It is the Westminster Shorter Catechism that says our chief end is "to glorify God and to enjoy him forever." For the sake of clarity, I am using the words *justification* and *sanctification* as distinct moments in the life of the regenerate believer and as theological shorthand for the beginning and the continuation of the Christian life, respectively. Admittedly, the use of these terms in Scripture (including in Paul's letters) is not always so neat and distinct.

For more on the "already/not yet" dialectic, see George Eldon Ladd, *A Theology of the New Testament,* rev. ed. (Grand Rapids: Eerdmans 1993), 45, 66–67. I capitalize Truth along with Spirit to point to the Trinitarian allusion in John 4:23–24. In the early church, "Truth" was a common description of Jesus Christ, based especially on John 14:6.

16. Groaning for Redemption (8:18–27)

Further descriptions of entropy and the second law of thermodynamics are widely available online. These quotations are taken from the Wikipedia entry on "Entropy," at https://en.wikipedia.org/wiki/Entropy. The song by Kansas is "Dust in the Wind" (*Point of Know Return,* 1978, Kirshner). The Greek translation of the Hebrew and Aramaic Old Testament is the Septuagint (LXX), and it represents the Greek Old Testament text that Paul was familiar with and used. The notion that future redemption involves only disembodied souls was a heresy common both to ancient Gnosticism and to many modern expressions of Christian faith. The ancient heresy was predicated on the belief that material creation is *per se* evil.

The ambiguity of the two translations in Romans 8:26 (between NRSV and NIV) in inherent in the Greek word *katho,* which literally means "according to which." The love that moves the sun and stars is an allusion to the concluding lines of Dante, *Divine Comedy, Paradise,* canto

33, in *The Divine Comedy of Dante Alighieri,* translated by Henry F. Cary, The Harvard Classics (New York: P. F. Collier & Son, 1937), 426.

17. God for Us (8:28–39)

The dominant interpretation of Ps 44, going back to antiquity, is to read the lament in the voice or person of the Jews persecuted before and during the Maccabean revolt in the second century BC. See Keith D. Stanglin, "Adopted in Christ, Appointed to the Slaughter: Calvin's Interpretation of the Maccabean Psalms," in *Biblical Interpretation and Doctrinal Formulation in the Reformed Tradition: Essays in Honor of James De Jong,* edited by Arie C. Leder and Richard A. Muller (Grand Rapids: Reformation Heritage, 2014), 69–93. Kierkegaard's observation is in Søren Kierkegaard, *The Gospel of Sufferings, Christian Discourses,* in *Upbuilding Discourses in Various Spirits,* translated by Howard V. Hong and Edna H. Hong, Kierkegaard's Writings 15 (Princeton: Princeton University Press, 1993), 250. The assumption that the suffering of God's people indicates the impotence or non-existence of God has been around as long as God's people. It is raised in the Old Testament. The early Christian writer Justin Martyr's *Second Apology* addresses this accusation by pagans.

Walter Brueggemann's work has perhaps been the most influential in reinstating lament in Christian thought and worship.

18. God's Promise and Purpose (9:1–33)

Romans 9 is the classic proof text for Augustinian and Reformed accounts of absolute predestination. Many of the thorny theological issues in Romans 9, especially as they relate to the doctrine of predestination, are left untreated here. The literature on such exegetical and dogmatic problems is vast. Let it suffice here to note that my approach is inspired by the interpretation of Jacob Arminius in his *Analysis of Romans 9,* in *Works of Arminius,* 3:485–519, a treatment that still repays careful reading. By the way, the word *predestine/predestination* is not used in Romans 9–11, so the category of unconditional predestination may not be the best lens for reading this large section.

19. The Word Is near You (10:1–21)

Premodern Christian theology took for granted that Christ is the scope of the Old Testament Scriptures. On the issue of early Jewish Christians seeing this more plainly in hindsight, see Keith D. Stanglin, *The Letter and Spirit of Biblical Interpretation: From the Early Church to Modern Practice* (Grand Rapids: Baker Academic, 2018), 21–23. Paul's word for word throughout this section is *rhema*, taken straight from Deut 30 and Ps 19.

20. God Keeps a Remnant (11:1–10)

See Alasdair MacIntyre, *After Virtue: A Study in Moral Theory,* 3rd ed. (Notre Dame: University of Notre Dame Press, 2007), 5. Polycarp's lament is recorded in his pupil Irenaeus's "Letter to Florinus," preserved in Eusebius, *Ecclesiastical History* V.xx.7, 2 vols., translated by Kirsopp Lake, Loeb Classical Library (Cambridge, MA: Harvard University Press, 1926), 1:498.

23. Deep Wisdom (11:33–36)

The conductor of the Oklahoma Christian University Chorale was Dr. Ken Adams. Matera, *Romans,* 275–76, points out the correspondence between the three divine attributes and the three rhetorical questions that follow. The Augustinian statement, *Deus semper maior* (God is always greater), expresses the Christian consensus that our finite conceptions and language can never grasp God. It is also typical of Christian theology to affirm that the language of Scripture is a divine accommodation to imperfect humans.

24. Living Sacrifice (12:1)

The importance of the *why* question is related to the importance of knowing the causes of things—according to Aristotle, the efficient, material, formal, and final causes. *Why* addresses especially the question of final cause. Again I have quoted from the Westminster Shorter Catechism, which says our chief end is "to glorify God and to enjoy him forever." The vertical and horizontal aspects of worship correspond to the two greatest commands, in their proper order: Love God and love neighbor.

25. Transformation by Renovation (12:2)

The Greek word behind "age" is *aion*, distinct from the typical Greek word for "world" (*kosmos*). The often quoted dictum about marrying the spirit of the age is attributed to the early twentieth-century clergyman, William Ralph Inge. Super Bowl LIV was on February 2, 2020. *Kabod* (Hebrew) and *doxa* (Greek) have other meanings as well, but the contexts of these passages clearly imply brightness. "Changed from glory into glory" is quoted from Charles Wesley's hymn, "Love Divine All Loves Excelling," which is quoting from 2 Cor 3:18.

26. A Christian Handbook (12:3–21)

The quotation is from Karl Barth, *The Epistle to the Romans*, 6th ed., translated by Edwyn C. Hoskyns (London: Oxford University Press, 1933), 426–27. The movie scene I describe is from *Idiocracy* (dir. Mike Judge, 20th Century Fox, 2006).

27. God's Servant for Good (13:1–7)

The Greek words used in Romans 12 and 13, *ekdikesis* (vengeance) and *ekdikos* (avenger), refer to the dispensing of justice. The distinction between primary cause and secondary causes is helpful for understanding how both God and creation can be causal factors simultaneously. Although Paul does not address the question here, there is evidence in the New Testament that followers of Christ may hold political and military positions. For King's thoughts on civil disobedience, see Martin Luther King Jr., "Letter from Birmingham City Jail," in *Readings in Christian Ethics: A Historical Sourcebook*, edited by J. Philip Wogaman and Douglas M. Strong (Louisville: Westminster John Knox, 1996), 348–49, citing Augustine and Thomas Aquinas.

That Christians are the best citizens to have in an earthly kingdom was expressed by many early apologists. For example, Origen, *Contra Celsum* VIII.74, translated by Henry Chadwick (Cambridge: Cambridge University Press, 1965), 509–10: "Christians do more good to their countries than the rest of mankind, since they educate the citizens and teach them to be devoted to God, the guardian of their city; and they take those who have lived good lives in the most insignificant cities up to a divine and heavenly city."

29. Prioritize Peace (14:1—15:13)

The popular unity statement has been traced back to Marc Antonio de Dominis (1560–1624). See H. J. M. Nellen, "De zinspreuk 'In necessariis unitas, in non necessariis libertas, in utrisque caritas,'" *Nederlands archief voor kerkgeschiedenis* 79 (1999) 99–106. The reasons why there would be Jewish vegetarians are discussed in Witherington and Hyatt, *Romans*, 334–35.

30. Godly Plans (15:14-33)

The famous quotation about mice and men is from Robert Burns' poem, "To a Mouse" (1785). On Janus, see N. G. L. Hammond and H. H. Scullard, eds., *The Oxford Classical Dictionary*, 2nd ed. (Oxford: Clarendon, 1970), 561. On Paul's travels and martyrdom, see 1 Clem 5:5–7, in Michael W. Holmes, ed., *The Apostolic Fathers: Greek Texts and English Translations*, 3rd ed. (Grand Rapids: Baker Academic, 2007).

31. Greetings and Grace (16:1-27)

It is difficult to meditate for long on Romans 16 and seek to apply it without thinking about one of the best commentaries on the passage: a homily by Fred Craddock. Craddock's main point is that this chapter is much more than merely a list of names, a point that clearly influences my comments here. The three points about the function of the long list of names are adapted from Witherington and Hyatt, *Romans*, 381. The number of names and of those singled out is given in ibid., 380. On Junia's identity as Joanna, see Witherington and Hyatt, *Romans*, 388–89. The Billy Joel quotation comes from his song, "Say Goodbye to Hollywood" (*Turnstiles*, Columbia, 1976).

Index

227